AN INTRODUCTION TO
ECONOMETRICS

AN INTRODUCTION TO ECONOMETRICS

LAWRENCE R. KLEIN

Professor of Economics
Wharton School of Finance and Commerce
University of Pennsylvania

GREENWOOD PRESS, PUBLISHERS
WESTPORT, CONNECTICUT

Library of Congress Cataloging in Publication Data

Klein, Lawrence Robert.
    An introduction to econometrics.

    Reprint of the ed. published by Prentice-Hall, Englewood Cliffs, N.J.
    Includes index.
    1. Econometrics. I. Title.
[HB139.K52 1977]   330'.01'82   77-14612
ISBN 0-8371-9838-0

to S. A. K.

© 1962 by PRENTICE-HALL, Inc., Englewood Cliffs, N.J.

All rights reserved. No part of this book may be reproduced in any form, by mimeograph or any other means, without permission in writing from the publisher.

Reprinted with the permission of Prentice-Hall, Inc.

Reprinted in 1977 by Greenwood Press, Inc.
                          51 Riverside Avenue
                          Westport, CT. 06880

Printed in the United States of America

Preface

The reception given to my *Textbook of Econometrics* (Evanston: Row, Peterson and Co., 1953) convinced me that yet another class of readers were anxious to learn about the rapidly developing subject of econometrics but found that book too advanced in its mathematical treatment. *Textbook of Econometrics* was intended primarily for graduate students with some hope that advanced undergraduates would also be able to use it. A number of students, both graduate and undergraduate, now show an intense interest in finding out what econometrics is all about, but they lack the mathematical equipment to understand most renditions of the subject. The present volume is designed for them.

I wrote *Textbook of Econometrics* with the idea in mind of teaching people "how to do it." I now turn to a different pedagogical problem of giving people an appreciation of modern econometrics without going into the technical details of how to go about doing professional research in the field. For that teaching I can only recommend them to my first book. The present volume is purely an introduction to the *Textbook*. They are to be considered as a complementary pair, and the beginning student should contemplate covering the material in both if he is ultimately to master the subject.

Econometrics is essentially a mathematical subject; therefore I was not able to write a wholly nonmathematical introduction. The goal towards which I have aimed is to write an introduction to the subject without using any mathematics at the collegiate level. There is no use of calculus, advanced analysis, matrix algebra, or other mathematical methods used widely in modern econometrics. I restricted myself to algebraic formulation of models and simple manipulation of relationships by the rules of algebra that any well-prepared high school student would know. Some statistical concepts such as *mean, standard deviation, variance,* and *estimate* are used, but technical inference is not used if mathematical explanations are required.

Arguments are presented in various forms—in words, in simple equations, in numerical examples, and in diagrams. By making arguments from different simplified points of view it is hoped that an appreciative understanding of the subject can be conveyed to all readers. The presentation is not formal or rigorous. I have based the presentation mainly on the work of the great masters. Instead of teaching abstract principles of econometrics, I have taught demand analysis as developed by Henry Schultz, the measurement of production functions as developed by Paul Douglas, the measurement of cost functions as developed by Joel Dean, input-output analysis as developed by Wassily Leontief, income distribution theory as developed by Vilfredo Pareto, and macroeconomic model construction as developed by Jan Tinbergen. Numerous studies building on the work of the masters are also cited and discussed, but the main presentation of the subject is in terms of the concrete studies of these important pioneers. Although their work sometimes appears to be unsophisticated in the most up-to-date terms, they really saw through most of the basic problems and will be a source of inspiration to students for years to come.

Citation of the work of the masters would be incomplete were I to omit the name of Ragnar Frisch, who pioneered in the treatment of multicollinearity, an ever-present problem in econometric analysis. Frisch's work comes into the presentation at several stages.

Numerous examples are presented as a main pedagogical device, but little attention is paid to some fine points of statistical methods involved in these examples. This is in keeping with the spirit of this presentation as an attempt to convey appreciation and understanding without trying to show the steps that must be followed in detail if the reader is to duplicate the efforts involved in the example. There is little here to tell the student what he must do in particular econometric investigations. The principal objective is to give the student a basis for deciding whether or not he wants to do work in econometrics and for evaluating econometric studies that come to his attention.

I have given lecture courses, following closely the organization of this manuscript, at Oxford University and at the University of Pennsylvania. The Oxford students were both graduate and undergraduate. The Pennsylvania students were graduate students. They were first taken through a semester course over the material in this book and then through a second semester using a *Textbook of Econometrics*. At both institutions I was sufficiently encouraged by the reception given to this presentation to write this introductory text. I am indebted to these students for teaching me how to teach them and their successors.

L. R. K.

Contents

1. INTRODUCTION 1

The Subject Matter of Econometrics 1
The Raw Materials of Econometrics 3

2. STATISTICAL DEMAND ANALYSIS 8

The Gross Correlation between Price and Quantity. 8
The Nature of the Random Disturbances 28
A Statistical Demand Function—Postwar United Kingdom Exports to the Dollar Area 33
Statistical Demand Functions—The Demand for Meat and for Fruit in the United States 49
The Use of Cross-section Data in Demand Analysis 52
Pooling of Time-series and Cross-section Samples 61
The Mechanics of Pooling Cross-section and Time-series Samples 70
Problems in Pooling of Cross-section and Time-series Samples 73
Cobweb Models of Demand and Supply 75

3. STATISTICAL PRODUCTION AND COST ANALYSIS 83

The Production Function. 84
The Cost Function 111
The Supply Function 126
Input-output Analysis. 129

4. THE DISTRIBUTION OF INCOME AND WEALTH 140

Relative Frequency, Probability, and Distribution. 140
The Generation of Income Distributions. 160
Systematic Factors in the Distribution of Income 171

5. STATISTICAL MODELS OF ECONOMIC GROWTH AND TRADE CYCLES — 180

Aggregative Economic Systems 180
A Model of Growth—The Great Ratios of Economics 183
A Collection of Models 207
Some Working Models 222

6. APPLICATIONS IN MACROECONOMICS — 236

Forecasting the Trade Cycle 236
Policy Application 251
Simulation of Business Cycles 256
The Use of Sample Surveys and External Information in Applications 261
A Critique of Model Building 266

INDEX — 271

1

Introduction

THE SUBJECT MATTER OF ECONOMETRICS

The main objective of econometrics is to give empirical content to a priori reasoning in economics. The a priori reasoning chiefly consists of what we usually call economic theory. However, general nonquantitative descriptions of economic institutions and their interrelated functioning could serve equally well as a framework for econometric analysis, provided the a priori propositions could be put into a mathematical form. It goes without saying that the great bulk of economic theory can be cast into mathematics, and, once this is done, econometric methods may be considered if the mathematical variables are actually measurable.

In the classroom, lecturers customarily draw, with graceful sweeps of the arm, demand curves, supply curves, production functions, cost functions, consumption functions, cycles of economic fluctuations, and all the similar *relationships* familiar in the analysis of theoretical economics. What is the shape of a typical demand curve for food products? Is the total cost curve for steel linear, or does it eventually come into a range with increasing slope (marginal cost)? Are trade cycles smooth, symmetrical sine curves with four year periods? Questions like these surely must have crossed the minds of many students and teachers. They are typical of the questions tackled by the modern econometric tools. Econometrics is a branch of economics in which measurement of the relationships discussed in a priori economic analysis is studied. In this sense, econometrics plays a service function for economic analysis, but in a more positive rôle it may also lead to the discovery of new relationships or theories hitherto unsuspected from a priori considerations alone.

Econometrics is widely used in policy formation by governments, businesses, and institutions. For this type of work, econometrics serves policy formation rather than pure analysis; but, in fact, to the policy maker, it simply provides an empirically clothed form of analysis. Agricultural price supports, for the maintenance of stable farm incomes, find justification in the extensive estimates of statistical demand equations for food and other agricultural products where it is found that the absolute value of the elasticity coefficients are nearly always less than unity. When a country adjusts its exchange rate, say by devaluation, it is immediately concerned with estimating the price elasticities of exports and imports in order to assess the consequences. Econometric work in this area has been subject to much dispute, and perhaps reliable results are not yet available for use in policy formation. However, the problems involved are typically econometric in nature and the econometric tools are the right ones to apply. Better samples of data and sharper tools should eventually lead to more widely accepted results in international economics.

The effects of changes in taxation and government spending on the level of over-all demand and employment can be analyzed in terms of an econometric system of the aggregative economy. In these systems consumer and business reactions to tax rates and expenditure multipliers are relevant magnitudes estimated by econometric methods. In several countries aggregative systems have been constructed which have usefully shown the results of alternative fiscal policies.

In estimating the relationships of economic theory, or in testing theory, we generally think of relationships in which one or more economic variables affect some other economic variable. In demand relationships the quantity demanded is pictured as a mathematical function of price and income, or in cost functions the total cost is viewed as a function of total output. Quite a different type of relationship is considered in the theories of income and wealth distribution. These too are econometric problems, namely, to describe the

Introduction 3

statistical properties of the income and wealth distributions and similar phenomena. The treatment of such problems has important application in the econometrics of demand analysis, yet they are significant econometric problems in their own right.

The fine structure of the economy is described in terms of individual consumers and producers, separate commodities and their prices, and so on. In principle such atomistic units could be used directly in the whole of economic analysis, but in practice, econometric as well as other, we must cut through the fine detail and summarize through aggregation. We conduct our analysis eventually in terms of composite commodities (durables, all food, exports from the United Kingdom to the Dollar Area, and so on) and groups of people (all nonfarm consumers, steel producers, all corporations, skilled workers, farmers, and so on). The index number or aggregation problem is, therefore, an integral part of econometric analysis and is a technical problem that must be carefully considered at the initial stages of an investigation. It is a measurement problem in economics of the purest sort.

THE RAW MATERIALS OF ECONOMETRICS

The life blood of econometrics is statistical series giving measures of variables. Although econometricians may, as well as anyone else, take nonstatistical aspects of life into account, only the quantifiable aspects of economic life form part of econometrics proper.

The statistics of prices, production, employment, purchases, exports, weather conditions, and many other variables relevant to economic behavior or decision-making provide the raw materials for econometric research. These data may emanate from official government sources, official international agencies, business firms, trade associations, trade unions, sampling organizations, or any other office which gathers economic information. Of course, any person engaged in econometric research is completely free to gather his own data from primary sources. In reality the great bulk of econometric studies are based on official statistics published by governments, international agencies, or well-established markets. Such organizations release a vast quantity of statistical data every week, month, quarter, or year on the results of economic activities falling within their terms of reference. The typical releases provide what is commonly called a sample of *time-series data.* Thus a regularly released monthly index of industrial production gives a monthly time-series of an important quantity variable in economic analysis. It is on the basis of the month-to-month variation in a series of this type, in relation to associated monthly variations in other series, that the econometrician attempts to estimate economic relationships.

The econometric approach is intimately based on the mathematical theory of statistics, a theory which tells us how to make inferences about a population on the basis of a sample. The samples of statistical theory are reasonably well-behaved and well-constructed. The neatest and most elegant theorems, in fact the ones the econometrician draws upon, assume that the sample is randomly selected.

When we are looking for fundamental laws of behavior that satisfy a wide variety of life situations, we want a time-series sample that has a wide representation of experiences. Usually we are glad to take whatever data are available and consequently have little scope to select a random sample of observations among those available to us. On occasion we discard a small number of observations that clearly belong to a different universe. If our universe consists of peacetime patterns of behavior, we are justified in excluding the abnormal experience of wartime years when the universe is distorted. If one were interested in some well-defined universe of behavior under conditions of full employment and prosperity, sample values pertaining to depression periods could be excluded. In practice we usually take whatever time-series data are available, with the exclusion of some odd periods such as wartime years and hope that these data cover a wide enough variety of external circumstances so that they would be a random and representative sample of the universe, which is assumed to be described by a relationship that holds for an infinite number of external circumstances. We may look upon our universe as an infinite number of all possible economic decisions that could have been made on some subject and our sample as a particular set of such decisions that were actually made.

Another type of sample commonly used in econometrics is obtained from cross-section data. These data refer to the activities of individual economic units at some common period of time. A family expenditure survey is a common example. During a given month or quarter, data are collected from a group of families on their individual outlays for various items of expenditure, their income, and other

Introduction

pertinent data on their demographic and financial characteristics. From family-to-family variation in expenditures, income, and other variables, estimates of income elasticity of demand and similar parameters are calculated in such data collections. A group of business accounting statements, covering a given period of operations, would also form a cross-section sample from which to estimate business patterns of behavior on the basis of inter-firm variations. Some people have even tried to estimate behavior patterns from a cross-section sample of international variations. In the case of a sample of families principles of random selection are not difficult to envisage. In nationwide samples one is frequently dealing with millions of families in the universe. From lists of persons (electoral rolls) or lists of dwelling units (tax rating lists) it is possible to draw a representative sample. In practice a purely random sample is seldom drawn, but the departures from this norm are well-defined and can be accounted for in subsequent econometric computations.

Samples drawn for surveys of family activities fall under the heading *samples of human populations*. The universe is the totality of all families or individuals being considered. If we associate typical decisions with particular people, our universe consists of economic decisions and can therefore be regarded as the same universe being considered in the case of time-series samples.

Frequently, firms in an industry are not numerous. In some cases 100 or 200 units exhaust the population, and we do not find it useful to select a representative sample of firms in a cross-section study of a small industry. We would, in fact, select the whole universe and study the inter-firm variation of all 100 or 200 units. In this situation it is vital to come back to the concept of a universe of an infinite number of decisions from which a particular cross-section collection in some period represents a sample. Here we are on about the same ground as in the usual time-series sample.

The statistical methods used in econometrics would be like those developed for many other branches of study for use with the samples of the type we usually have were it not for one distinguishing feature. The statistical data of econometrics are drawn from samples of *nonexperimental observations*. It is sometimes said that nature provides the econometrician with experiments; that is, we use data drawn from the actual outcome of the economic process and not from an experiment designed to portray some particular relationship.

When an agricultural scientist is studying the relationship between application of fertilizer and crop yield, he designs controlled experiments on trial plots. He fixes and controls dosages of fertilizer and measures the result in crop yield. A physical scientist concerned with some aspect of Boyle's laws could control temperature in a laboratory setting, vary volume at different preassigned levels, and record the resulting amounts of pressure. A relationship, subject to experimental error, can be studied in this way and statistical tools are designed to estimate the relationship in the face of just this type of error.

In economics we are not as fortunate with our raw materials. We are not able to hold external conditions constant, assign varying prices to a consumer (or group of consumers), and simply record the resulting purchase decisions. We are merely able to observe an associated set of prices and purchases in a setting in which many other consumers in different circumstances are making similar decisions. Econometrics, in trying to reconstruct the actual decision process, must take account of all the simultaneous events and relationships closely tied to the one occupying central interest at the moment.

In most fields of natural science the methods of controlled experiment, with applications of the appropriate and conventional tools of statistical analysis, are familiar. To cite an example of a scientific field which faces statistical problems similar to those of econometrics, we mention meteorology. This example may help to clarify and demonstrate the statistical problem of econometrics as it will be unfolded in subsequent chapters.

QUESTIONS AND PROBLEMS

1. Is the measurement of national income an *econometric* problem?

2. Name and describe three relationships studied in economic theory which can be estimated as subject matter of econometrics. What are the *parameters* of these relationships?

3. What bodies of statistical data would you collect in order to carry out the econometric investigation of the relationships cited in Question 2?

Introduction 7

4. Name and describe three relationships studied in economic theory that have not been, or cannot in principle be, studied by econometric methods. Give reasons why the econometric approach is not suited to the measurement of these relationships.

5. Suppose that you had ample resources for constructing an experiment to test the economist's theory of the individual firm or individual household behavior. What statistical data would you collect and how would you use them to estimate particular economic relationships?

2

Statistical Demand Analysis

It is often easier to teach a subject by way of illustration. A continual pouring out of abstract and formal results in econometric theory may leave the reader cold and uninformed; therefore, one of the central problems of application in the subject is selected for primary treatment. All the main techniques and problems of econometrics can be treated in connection with the statistical estimation of demand relationships. Other problem areas could equally well have been selected (production functions, cost curves, business-cycle models) but they will be developed in less detail in later chapters. From the framework of demand analysis, the main parts of econometrics will be studied. A great diversity of econometric methods and problems come clearly to light in the course of demand analysis alone.

THE GROSS CORRELATION BETWEEN PRICE AND QUANTITY

At the very beginning of a course in economic analysis, the student is introduced to the idea of a demand curve. It is a downward sloping curve in a two-dimensional diagram, with price on one axis and quantity demanded on the other. Practice varies on the choice of variable to be measured along the vertical and horizontal axes. The analysis is in no way affected by our decision to measure price vertically.

Statistical Demand Analysis

How would one go about estimating an actual demand curve for shoes, tea, stationery, motor cars, sugar, or any other familiar product? It may be thought that a curve fitted to a collection of market statistics on transactions (quantity exchanged and price paid) in some particular

Fig. 2.1. Demand curve

commodity at different points of time would be a reasonable approximation to the demand curve for that commodity. Suppose that the transactions data are plotted in pairs as points on a two-dimensional diagram. Statisticians call this a *scatter diagram*. A technical method of estimation will be described in some detail below. At this point we are more concerned with basic concepts. Let us assume that by some method, say the technique of linear correlation, a line

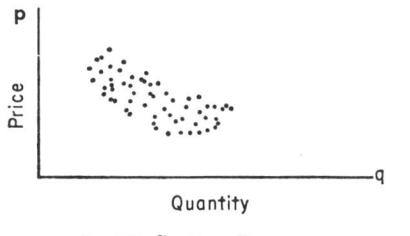

Fig. 2.2. Scatter diagram

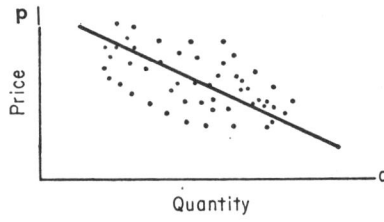

Fig. 2.3. Line fitted to scatter

of best fit can be passed through a scatter of price-quantity points. Our first task will be to criticize such a construction as a possible approximation to a demand curve. In view of the following critical questions, this crude procedure is usually inadequate for determining a statistical demand curve:

(1) Is the relation actually *identified* as a demand curve and not some other relationship?

(2) Has attention been paid to the important *ceteris paribus* proviso that lies behind the two-dimensional demand curve?

(3) What does economic theory tell us about the mathematical form of the demand relationship?

(4) What is the relation between individual and market demand?

The identification problem

Simply having a scatter of points with a downward tilt in the price-quantity plane does not insure that we have an actual demand pattern. The supply function relates price and quantity as well, but

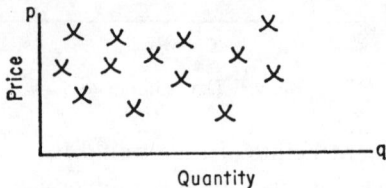

Fig. 2.4. A supply-demand scatter

this relationship has an upward slope. We should not identify the estimated pattern as the supply function for the good in question, but we cannot rule out the possibility that we, in fact, have a "mongrel" relation which is some mixture between the supply and demand functions. A graphical analysis of this situation, going back to an early discussion on the first attempts at statistical determination of demand relationships, brings out this point clearly.

The model underlying Fig. 2.4 is as follows:

a. demand function   price = function of quantity demanded + error,

b. supply function   price = function of quantity supplied + error,

c. market clearing   supply = demand + error.

Each cross in Fig. 2.4 represents a point of simultaneous solution of the system of three equations (a, b, c). At each point of time, there must be an error term in at least one of the three equations, and there may be one in each; otherwise there would be no scatter of intersection points. The equilibrium system (a, b, c) would remain

Statistical Demand Analysis

fixed. A full understanding of the role of error is essential, but this point will not be pursued until later, when it will be more fully elaborated.

The mathematical system of equations (a, b, c) is often called a *model*, an abstract and simplified picture of a realistic economic process given in the form of mathematical equations. All models are not mathematical, but those on which econometric analysis is based are of the mathematical type. Actually, supply-demand interactions and price formation, in any particular market consisting of many

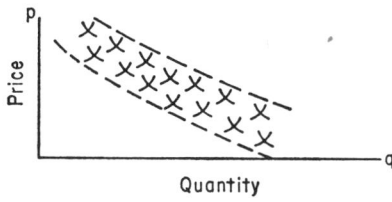

Fig. 2.5. Scatter of stable demand and variable supply

atomistic units, would require an elaborate explanation if full treatment were given to each transaction. Our model gives a simplified explanation of what is taking place in this market, by focusing attention on the most essential aspects. Models are not unique, and in some cases compromise must be made on "simplicity" in order to gain an adequate representation of reality.

The supply-demand model (a, b, c) is written with price as a function of quantity supplied or demanded. Frequently, economic textbooks reverse this procedure and express quantity as a function of price. As long as we consistently follow good econometric practice it should not matter which way we write the system at this stage, but when we come to statistical estimation of coefficients some definite decisions must be made about which variables are explanatory and which are to be explained.

If the demand function remains very stable, possibly as a result of small fluctuations in its error, and if the supply function is subject to great variability, the scatter of crosses will look very different from that in Fig. 2.4. A curve fitted to the crosses of Fig. 2.4 is not likely to trace out either the supply or demand function closely. It may trace out a "mongrel" function. In Fig. 2.5, we have a picture of a scatter of crosses in which demand is stable and supply is variable.

This is the best possible situation for estimating a price-quantity relation which can be *identified* as a demand function. If demand were highly variable and supply were stable we would tend to get a picture of the supply function in the price-quantity scatter.

The econometrician, in dealing with linear relationships, sets out to estimate a demand function:[1]

$$q_t^d = \alpha + \beta p_t + u_t,$$

q_t^d = quantity demanded at time t,

p_t = price at time t,

u_t = error at time t,

α, β = constant parameters.

The issue may be confused by the fact that two other equations are included in the model of this market.

$$q_t^s = \gamma + \delta p_t + v_t,$$
$$q_t^d = q_t^s + w_t,$$

q_t^s = quantity supplied at time t,

v_t = error at time t,

w_t = error at time t.

These two may be combined, by substitution, to get

$$q_t^d = \gamma + \delta p_t + (v_t + w_t).$$

We do not, in any way, alter the validity of our two equations for q^d if we multiply one by λ and the other by μ to get

$$\lambda q_t^d = \lambda \alpha + \lambda \beta p_t + \lambda u_t,$$
$$\mu q_t^d = \mu \gamma + \mu \delta p_t + \mu(v_t + w_t).$$

That is to say, if the original version of the equations held good, then these two new versions also hold good. We may combine these two equations into one by adding both sides. The result is

$$q_t^d(\lambda + \mu) = \lambda\alpha + \mu\gamma + (\lambda\beta + \mu\delta)p_t + \lambda u_t + \mu(v_t + w_t),$$
$$q_t^d = \frac{\lambda\alpha + \mu\gamma}{\lambda + \mu} + \frac{\lambda\beta + \mu\delta}{\lambda + \mu} p_t + \frac{\lambda u_t + \mu(v_t + w_t)}{\lambda + \mu}.$$

[1] In this example we shall write quantity as a function of price. The student should become familiar with different ways of looking at the same thing.

The econometrician has no way of distinguishing between this "mongrel" result and the true demand curve. They are both linear relationships between q_t^d and p_t with unknown constant coefficients and additive errors, which are not directly observable. The "mongrel" equation can even have negative slope like that of a true demand curve since the multipliers λ and μ are completely arbitrary; that is,

$$\frac{\lambda\beta + \mu\delta}{\lambda + \mu}$$

can be either negative or positive through a suitable selection of λ and μ.

Let us recapitulate what we have just done. We set out to estimate a linear demand function. We observed, at the same time, that a supply function and market clearing equation were also part of the model. With very simple algebraic principles, we combined these latter two equations into one, associating q^d with p linearly. We next performed legitimate algebraic operations on this equation and the original demand equation to derive a new linear expression associating q^d with p. If the original model formed a valid system, then the equation derived by this algebraic operation also expressed a valid relationship. It is possible, however, that the derived equation has little economic relationship with the original demand function that we were trying to estimate. This is the problem of identification.

Within the framework of linear relationships, the criteria for identification in supply-demand systems are definite and easy to formulate. In the preceding demonstrations we multiplied both sides of equations by common factors and added equations. We may say that we derived *linear combinations* of equations. If in a system of linear equations we are concerned with the identification of some particular equation, we say that the equation in question is identified provided it is not possible to derive, by linear combinations of some or all the equations of the system, another equation that contains exactly the same variables as the equation being considered. In the preceding example we did derive a "mongrel" equation from linear combinations of supply and demand equations that contained the same quantity and price variables as the demand function, plus an unknown random error. The error was, in fact, a linear function of the original errors.

In Fig. 2.5, we see a case in which it is possible to identify a linear demand relation, even though both the supply and demand functions are linear equations in exactly the same variables. The key to identification in this case is the fact that one function is decidedly more variable than the other. The variance of u_t, the random disturbance to demand, is small relative to the variance of v_t, the random disturbance to supply.[2] In effect, this is an a priori restriction on the specification of the model. If we have reason to believe that one disturbance is more variable than another

variance (u_t) is less than some fraction of variance (v_t),

or
$$\text{var}(u_t) < k \text{ var}(v_t), \quad 0 < k < 1,$$

then we have an identifying restriction on the system. In the "mongrel" equation the disturbance is a linear composite, and its variance is a linear function of the separate variances of u_t and v_t. The composite variance cannot be small, as is the variance of u_t, since it depends on the variance of v_t, which is relatively large. Of course if the multiplier μ is very small, the contribution of var (v_t) to the over-all variance will be small. However, it will also ensure that the parameters of the "mongrel" equation differ by only small amounts from the parameters of the *demand* function.

Specification of the nature of the random disturbances may therefore be a method of achieving identification. In fact, the great pioneering work of Henry Schultz was on sound footing when he claimed to be estimating *demand* functions for agricultural products.[3] The supply of domestically produced agricultural products in America depends, to a large extent, on the vagaries of the weather. Supply as a function of prices, or even other conventional economic variables, is a highly variable function from season to season, depending on complex meteorological phenomena. Demand for primary agricultural products, however, is very stable over time. It will have a small disturbance variance compared with the supply equation; therefore, we have good reason to believe that Schultz estimated demand and not

---

[2] The random errors associated with the different equations of a model are sometimes called *disturbances, shocks,* or *perturbations.* We use these terms synonymously. Some writers draw a distinction between "shock" and "error," but this is not a necessary practice.

[3] H. Schultz, *Theory and Measurement of Demand* (Chicago: University of Chicago Press, 1938).

supply equations. His demand equations were identified by restrictions on the relative sizes of disturbance variances.

Other identifying restrictions have been used in linear demand analysis. They nearly always take the form of specifying which variables enter the equations. The demand and supply model is written above as though quantity and price are the only relevant measureable variables for the problem. Let us suppose that climatic variables can be objectively measured and fitted, with their appropriate causative roles, into the supply-demand model. Instead of assuming purely random shifts in the conditions of supply, we assume a new model in which a part of the shift can be explicitly measured by something like number of inches of rainfall, number of hours of sunshine, or number of degrees of heat during the growing season of an agricultural product. In reality the influence of weather may be very complicated. Storms and extreme conditions may destroy a crop; too much rainfall during a harvest season may hamper productive operations; and so on. We extract some systematic and visible measures of weather influence, but others may remain in the random disturbance.[4] The error term is assumed to be composed of the agglomerate effect of numerous independent minutiae. We measure as many of these disturbing factors as possible, include them in our equations of the model as separate variables, and dispose of all the remaining under the heading "random disturbance," relying on the laws of probability to tell us what to expect from these neglected factors.

An alternative model is, therefore,

$$q_t^d = \alpha + \beta p_t + u_t,$$
$$q_t^s = \gamma + \delta p_t + \epsilon r_t + v_t,$$
$$q_t^d = q_t^s + w_t.$$

This is the same as the preceding model, except for the fact that r_t, a measure of rainfall, is included in the supply equation as a separate variable. We still have three equations, but now there are four variables: q_t^d, q_t^s, p_t, and r_t. The economic mechanism shows how to

[4] Some investigators have proposed the use of yields at geographically dispersed experimental plots, farmed under control conditions, to measure the composite effect of weather influences.

determine the three economic variables q_t^d, q_t^s, and p_t when *given* the random disturbances u_t, v_t, and w_t and the external variable r_t. We shall call the economic variables *endogenous* variables and the external variables *exogenous* variables. The laws of nature (meteorology in this instance) determine the values taken on at each point of time by r_t, independent of economic decisions or behavior in the supply-demand market. Rainfall affects the economy but is not affected by the economy. We cannot say the same of the endogenous variables.[5]

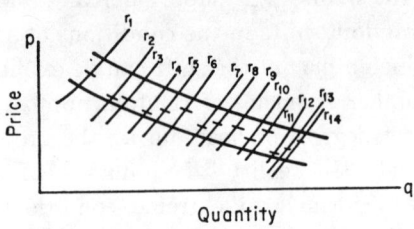

Fig. 2.6. Scatter of supply with rainfall induced shifts and stable demand

Regardless of the relative variabilities of u_t and v_t, the supply function drawn with respect to quantity and price axes will shift according to the different values assumed by r_t. This will help us to identify the demand function. If the major reason for shifting supply is rainfall variation, with both demand and supply functions remaining otherwise quite stable, we shall have the graphical situation depicted in Fig. 2.6. At each point of time, the rainfall variable and the supply disturbance v_t take on new values calling forth a different supply function. The shifts need not be parallel or monotonic, but they serve to trace out points on the demand curve within the limits imposed by its random shifts.

From the graphical picture, one can see that it makes little difference whether the supply curve shifts widely as a result of purely random forces or measurable objective forces; either type of shift produced a set of points following the general path of demand. In the algebraic analysis of the problem, though, the result may appear somewhat differently.

It is no longer possible to multiply through linear demand and

[5] Instead of *endogenous* and *exogenous* variables, we sometimes use the classification *dependent* and *predetermined*. The former coincides with *endogenous* variables. The latter may include prior or lagged values of *endogenous* as well as *exogenous* variables.

supply functions by separate constants and combine them, by addition, into a new equation containing exactly the same variables as the original demand function, linearly related and subject to an unknown, nonobserved, random disturbance. The linear combination of supply and demand functions, the "mongrel" equation, will, in the present model, be

$$q_t^d = \frac{\lambda\alpha + \mu\gamma}{\lambda + \mu} + \frac{\lambda\beta + \mu\delta}{\lambda + \mu} p_t + \frac{\mu\epsilon}{\lambda + \mu} r_t + \frac{\lambda u_t + \mu(v_t + w_t)}{\lambda + \mu}.$$

Here we have a linear relation among quantity, price, and rainfall subject to a random disturbance. This cannot represent the demand equation since there is no ground for assuming that rainfall has a direct effect on demand behavior. It could, however, be confused with the true structural equation of supply, as far as the statistician is concerned. For these reasons, demand is identified, but supply is not, in the present model. The absence or presence of variables in the separate equations of a model is a means of identification, as well as specification of the nature of the random disturbance. The identifying features are more generally viewed as *restrictions*. On the one hand, we may restrict the relative sizes of disturbance variability in the equations of demand and supply; on the other hand we say that the coefficient of r_t in the demand equation is restricted to be zero. These restrictions are not exhaustive. Coefficients need not be made equal to zero in order to gain identifying information. If they are made equal to any a priori values, the process of identification is helped. If coefficients of different variables must be kept in certain known fixed proportions, we gain identifying information. These are all types of *linear restrictions* appropriate to identification in linear systems of equations. Specific nonlinearities for different equations may be helpful in obtaining identification, but we shall not go beyond linear systems at this point.

It is obvious from Fig. 2.5, that the more variable is the supply function and the less variable the demand function, the closer the scatter of points approximates the demand function and discriminates between the two relationships. Identification can be weak or strong depending on the magnitude of the ratio between the two measures of variability. Similarly, the explicit treatment of the rainfall variable in the second model is not going to identify the demand curve as sharply if this variable has a smaller, as compared with a larger, degree of variation. Identification cannot be cheaply achieved in any particular investigation by simply adding some weak or marginal variable to one of the relationships of a system. One must add something substantial and significant which had been previously neglected.

The *ceteris paribus* clause

The treatment of the rainfall variable in the supply-demand model illustrates a second problem in interpreting the gross scatter of price-quantity points as the drift of a demand function. A demand curve, as the concept is used in theoretical economics, is supposed to be drawn under very strict conditions, that is, for given tastes, incomes, prices of related goods, and a generally fixed environment. It is important to distinguish, in economic analysis, between movements along the curve and shifts of the curve itself. When the given conditions stated above are not met, we have shifts of the curve. In the identification problem, shifts of the curve, especially in relation to concurrent shifts of the supply curve, were crucial. Shifts of the supply curve were also analyzed by introduction of an explicit shift variable, namely, r_t, a measure of rainfall. In the same way, shifts in the demand curve can, in part, be explicitly measured by such variables as consumer income and prices of related goods.

When we collect a set of price-quantity statistics from market transactions over a period of time we rarely find that the *ceteris paribus* assumptions of theoretical economics are met. Other variables related to demand behavior are changing over the sample period. For this reason, the gross relationship between price and quantity is not likely to trace out the demand relationship that we seek to estimate. However, the situation can frequently be remedied if we extend our relationship from one between two variables, quantity and price, to one associating many variables simultaneously. Instead of a simple relationship such as

$$q_t^d = \alpha + \beta p_t + u_t,$$

we should start out by assuming, for example, a relationship of the form

$$q_t^d = \alpha_0 + \alpha_1 p_t + \alpha_2 y_t + \alpha_3 p'_t + \alpha_4 z_t + u_t.$$

In the latter formulation quantity demanded is assumed to depend

Statistical Demand Analysis

(linearly) on price p_t, consumer income y_t, price of a related good p'_t, a trend to measure changes in consumer tastes z_t, and the disturbance u_t. The prices of several related goods could be introduced, and other measures of financial position besides income may be used. Tastes might be represented by an automatic linear trend

$$z_t = t, \qquad t = 0, 1, 2, 3, 4, \ldots$$

In general, a demand relationship can be extended to great length for the appropriate treatment of any particular problem and, because other things usually do not remain equal over periods of time, it will be necessary in empirical demand work to proceed from the outset with a multivariate relationship. As was shown in the preceding section, restrictions on the coefficients of some of these new variables in the different equations of the system will serve to identify the relationships involved. The extra variables referred to in this section, such as y_t and p'_t, are specific to demand behavior.[6] A different set of extra variables would be suggested for a description of supply behavior.

Economic theory and the form of the demand relationship

Under the *ceteris paribus* clause, economic theory tells us that the demand function has a negative slope. With price measured along the vertical axis, a priori analysis may suggest broadly that necessities are represented by a very steep curve (demand insensitive to price fluctuations) and that luxuries are represented by a more gently sloped curve (demand sensitive to price fluctuations). There is no a priori basis for saying that the function is curved or linear. The classical theory of consumer behavior can, however, tell us a few things of interest that restrict the form of the function used in practical work. The static theory starts out from a utility function, of unknown form, which makes an individual's psychic level of satisfaction depend on the goods he consumes.

Utility = function of quantities of goods in a consumer's budget,

or

$$u = f(x_1, x_2, \ldots, x_n).$$

[6] Prices of related commodities are important in supply as well as demand behavior, but the commodities related on the supply side may well be different from those related on the demand side.

The economic problem for the consumer is to maximize u subject to the budget constraint

expenditure aggregated over all goods = income

or

$$\sum_{i=1}^{n} p_i x_i = y.$$

For a given set of prices $(p_1, p_2, \ldots, p_n)$, this implies

$$\frac{\text{marginal utility of } i\text{-th good}}{\text{marginal utility of } j\text{-th good}} = \frac{p_i}{p_j}.$$

There are $n - 1$ such independent marginal utility ratios. Marginal utility, like total utility, depends on the quantities of goods consumed. Therefore the left hand ratios depend on the quantities of goods consumed. The marginal utility equations provide $n - 1$ relationships between quantities and *relative* prices or price ratios. Together with the budget equation, we have n equations which enable us, under ordinary conditions, to solve for each of the quantities as a function of all the prices and income. These are the demand functions of classical economic theory. There is, however, an important property of these functions. They are homogeneous of degree zero in prices and income. By this expression we mean that if all the prices in the marginal utility equations are multiplied by the factor λ, the equations are unaffected since this factor cancels in the numerator and the denominator of the price ratios. Similarly, in the budget equation, this multiplying factor cancels from the left and right sides as follows:

$$\sum_{i=1}^{n} \lambda p_i x_i = \lambda \sum_{i=1}^{n} p_i x_i = \lambda y,$$

or

$$\sum_{i=1}^{n} p_i x_i = y.$$

Thus, we write the theoretical demand functions as

$$x_1 = g_1\left(\frac{p_2}{p_1}, \frac{p_3}{p_1}, \ldots, \frac{p_n}{p_1}, \frac{y}{p_1}\right),$$

$$x_2 = g_2\left(\frac{p_1}{p_2}, \frac{p_3}{p_2}, \ldots, \frac{p_n}{p_2}, \frac{y}{p_2}\right),$$

$$\ldots$$

$$x_n = g_n\left(\frac{p_1}{p_n}, \frac{p_2}{p_n}, \ldots, \frac{p_{n-1}}{p_n}, \frac{y}{p_n}\right),$$

and say that the quantity demanded depends on all the relative prices of the system and on real income. These general demand curves have been written in a particular way to bring out the property of zero order homogeneity, namely, by placing the i-th price in the denominator of all ratios for the i-th demand equation. The homogeneity property could be expressed in other ways as well. One such way which is of interest is the following.

Define

$$p = \sum_{i=1}^{n} w_i p_i = \text{weighted average of all prices}$$
$$\text{with } w_i \text{ as fixed weights } (\sum_{i=1}^{n} w_i = 1),$$

$$x_i = h_i\left(\frac{p_1}{p}, \frac{p_2}{p}, \ldots, \frac{p_n}{p}, \frac{y}{p}\right).$$

In this form, the variable y/p is a more conventional measure of real income since it is, in effect, a "deflation" of money income y by a weighted average of all prices of consumer goods.

The marginal utility equations, which are derived from the total utility functions, are used, together with the budget equation, to yield the demand functions. Hence, the parameters of the utility function will determine the parametric structure of the demand functions. Tastes and other subjective characteristics of consumers are reflected in these parameters and thereby in the demand functions. Since the utility functions are not measureable in practice, we begin statistical analysis directly with the demand functions. However, the latter depend on the utility functions and will change when the utility functions change. If changes in tastes are gradual and can be represented by smooth trends, they can be accounted for by the explicit introduction of such variables into the demand functions.

Other models of consumer behavior have been constructed in which there is planning and utility maximization over a time horizon subject to budget constraints involving borrowing and lending. This brings expectations, debts, assets, and similar variables into the demand functions. We shall not go into these more complicated formulations in this volume, but it should be pointed out that analogous principles of homogeneity can be extended to the demand function implied by such analysis. Also, the theory of utility maximization can be pushed further to derive interesting restrictions on demand functions, particularly on "cross-elasticities" of demand. We shall not touch upon these matters.[7]

For reasons of identification and meeting the *ceteris paribus* conditions for demand functions, we have seen that the function must be multivariate. However, in the present section we see that these several variables should be combined in a particular way. Economic theory gives no suggestion as to whether the functions are linear or curved in some specific way, but for any practical choice in a given problem, theory does suggest homogeneity restrictions. Thus, if the functions are to be linear, we may write[8]

$$x_{it} = \alpha_{1i}\frac{p_{1t}}{p_{it}} + \alpha_{2i}\frac{p_{2t}}{p_{it}} + \ldots + \alpha_{ni}\frac{p_{nt}}{p_{it}} + \beta_i\frac{y_t}{p_{it}} + u_{it}.$$

An alternative would be

$$x_{it} = \alpha'_{0i} + \alpha'_{1i}\frac{p_{1t}}{p_t} + \alpha'_{2i}\frac{p_{2t}}{p_t} + \ldots + \alpha'_{ni}\frac{p_{nt}}{p_t} + \beta'_1\frac{y_t}{p_t} + u_{it}.$$

Linearity may be considered from two points of view. To the economist who wants to make use of a demand function with numerical parameters, linearity in quantity demanded, relative price, and real income give a simplified form of the equation that facilitates analysis. Linearity is, however, only a convenience and must at times be sacrificed in favor of reality. However the statistician who wants to estimate the unknown parameters on the basis of observed values of the economic variables is principally interested in having a function that is linear in the parameters. It is possible to have a demand function that is nonlinear in the variables, thereby achieving a higher degree of economic realism, but linear in the parameters. A simple example is the parabolic form

$$x_{it} = \alpha_{0i} + \alpha_{1i}\frac{p_{1t}}{p_t} + \alpha_{2i}\frac{p_{2t}}{p_t} + \ldots + \alpha_{ni}\frac{p_{nt}}{p_t} + \beta_{1i}\frac{y_t}{p_t} + \beta_{2i}\left(\frac{y_t}{p_t}\right)^2 + u_{it}.$$

The marginal real income effect in this equation varies, making the equation nonlinear in real income, yet the unknown parameters all enter in the first degree. The statistician's task, as we shall develop later, is made simpler by use of this device. The computational

---

[7] See H. Wold and L. Juréen, *Demand Analysis* (New York: John Wiley and Sons, Inc., 1951).

[8] The constant term in the linear function is α_{ii}.

problems for the statistician in nonlinear systems are quite formidable, and the underlying statistical theory is developed primarily for linear systems. Therefore, we usually go to great lengths to keep the formulations of demand functions linear in the parameters, whereas we frequently drop the linearity assumption for the variables.

In some cases the inherent curvature of an economic relationship can be displayed in a nonlinear function which can be transformed into a linear function. Exponential or logarithmic functions in econometrics are widely used because they lend themselves so readily to transformation into linear functions. Demand functions of the constant elasticity type, a form used frequently by Marshall in his exposition of theory, can be written as[9]

$$x_{it} = A_i \left(\frac{p_{1t}}{p_t}\right)^{\alpha_{1i}} \left(\frac{p_{2t}}{p_t}\right)^{\alpha_{2i}} \cdots \left(\frac{p_{nt}}{p_t}\right)^{\alpha_{ni}} \left(\frac{y_t}{p_t}\right)^{\beta_i} u_{it}.$$

If logarithms are formed on both sides, the equation is transformed into

$$\log x_{it} = \log A_i + \alpha_{1i} \log \frac{p_{1t}}{p_t} + \alpha_{2i} \log \frac{p_{2t}}{p_t} + \cdots + \alpha_{ni} \log \frac{p_{nt}}{p_t}$$
$$+ \beta_i \log \frac{y_t}{p_t} + \log u_{it}.$$

Writing logarithms as primed quantities, we could express this as

$$x'_{it} = A'_i + \alpha_{1i} \left(\frac{p_{1t}}{p_t}\right)' + \alpha_{2i} \left(\frac{p_{2t}}{p_t}\right)' + \cdots + \alpha_{ni} \left(\frac{p_{nt}}{p_t}\right)'$$
$$+ \beta_i \left(\frac{y_t}{p_t}\right)' + u'_{it},$$

which is, in effect, a linear equation. It is linear in parameters. This is the most common nonlinear function that is transformed into a linear function in demand analysis, or in all of econometrics, but other forms also have this convenient property.

Theory tells us that the demand for a good is a function of relative

---

[9] If this equation were expressed in absolute instead of relative prices and money instead of real income, the homogeneity property could be brought out by requiring that all the exponential parameters add to zero.

$$x_{it} = A p_{1t}^{\alpha_{1i}} p_{2t}^{\alpha_{2i}} \cdots p_{nt}^{\alpha_{ni}} p_t^{\alpha_i} y_t^{\beta_i} u_{it},$$

where

$$\sum_{j=1}^{n} \alpha_{ji} + \beta_i + \alpha_i = 0.$$

prices of all commodities in a consumer's budget and of real income. In econometric practice this formulation is condensed into a more manageable equation relating demand to price of the good being studied, the general price level, prices of one, two, or three closely related goods (substitutes or complements), and income. Although prices of all other goods in the system may be included, for the sake of completeness, in a theoretical model they are not individually significant enough to be given explicit treatment in empirical studies. In some investigations other variables may also be considered. From the dynamic theory of consumer planning over time we may be led to introduce such variables as past values of income (lags), stocks of net financial assets, or stocks of physical assets.

The aggregation of individual demands

The economic theory of consumer behavior described in the preceding section yields a formulation of an individual's demand function but market data, such as those plotted in Fig. 2.3, do not depict the result of a single individual's behavior. They show the result of a whole community's behavior. We must justify the use of a concept of an aggregate demand function for individual commodities in order to identify our statistical estimates with theoretical demand curves.

A second problem of aggregation arises in the selection of commodities for which demand functions are to be estimated. The demand for sugar or other individual primary products, studied in the earliest works on statistical demand analysis, involved few problems of aggregation. However, the demand for food, motor cars, all durables, and other major heterogeneous groupings in the consumer's budget raise important index number problems.

For general forms of demand functions, two precise results of a very restrictive nature are known in the theory of consumer behavior. First, if the incomes of a group of people all change in the same proportion, and if each member of the group is assumed to have the same elasticity, then this common individual income elasticity is estimated by market elasticity. Second, different goods whose prices all change in the same proportion may effectively be treated as a single good as far as the central propositions in the theory of consumer behavior are concerned. It is well known, however, that income change and price

Statistical Demand Analysis

change are highly dispersed. These propositions are more theoretical niceties than practical results for empirical work.

For strictly linear systems, some more usable results can be established. Suppose that the j-th individual's demand for the i-th product can be expressed as

$$x_{it}^{(j)} = \alpha_{0i} + \alpha_{1i}\frac{p_{1t}}{p_t} + \alpha_{2i}\frac{p_{2t}}{p_t} + \ldots + \alpha_{ni}\frac{p_{nt}}{p_t} + \beta_i\frac{y_t^{(j)}}{p_t} + u_{it}^{(j)}.$$

The prices are assumed to be uniform in the market to all buyers. The quantities demanded, incomes, and disturbances are assumed to vary among individuals. The parameters are assumed to be constant among individuals. If these individual functions are added over all persons in the market we have

$$\sum_{j=1}^{N} x_{it}^{(j)} = N\alpha_{0i} + N\alpha_{1i}\frac{p_{1t}}{p_t} + N\alpha_{2i}\frac{p_{2t}}{p_t} + \ldots + N\alpha_{ni}\frac{p_{nt}}{p_t} + \beta_i \sum_{j=1}^{N}\frac{y_t^{(j)}}{p_t} + \sum_{j=1}^{N} u_{it}^{(j)}.$$

Dividing both sides of the equation by N, we get

$$\bar{x}_{it} = \alpha_{0i} + \alpha_{1i}\frac{p_{1t}}{p_t} + \alpha_{2i}\frac{p_{2t}}{p_t} + \ldots + \alpha_{ni}\frac{p_{nt}}{p_t} + \beta_i\frac{\bar{y}_t}{p_t} + \bar{u}_{it},$$

where

$$\bar{x}_{it} = \frac{\sum_{j=1}^{N} x_{it}^{(j)}}{N} = \text{per capita demand for the } i\text{-th good},$$

$$\bar{y}_t = \frac{\sum_{j=1}^{N} y_t^{(j)}}{N} = \text{per capita income},$$

$$\bar{u}_{it} = \frac{\sum_{j=1}^{N} u_{it}^{(j)}}{N} = \text{per capita disturbance for the } i\text{-th good}.$$

If the individual demand function were nonlinear, say parabolic in income as in a previous example, aggregation is not as easy. The sum of first powers of a variable is the first power of the sum. For this reason linear equations are easily aggregated. However, the sum of second powers of a variable is not the second power of the sum; therefore aggregation of a parabola involves new problems. The identity, taken from elementary statistics,

$$\frac{\sum_{j=1}^{N} (y_t^j)^2}{N} = \frac{\sum_{j=1}^{N} (y_t^j - \bar{y}_t)^2}{N} + \bar{y}_t^2$$

tells us that the aggregation of the parabola gives a market equation in which per capita demand depends on, in addition to per capita income, the square of per capita income and the average squared deviation about per capita income.[10] The latter term is the *variance* of the income distribution. Thus we must take account of two characteristics of the income distribution, its average level and its dispersion. A new element is in the market demand relation.

The problem of aggregating over commodities to obtain expressions for demand functions of major categories of demand is more complicated. It can be simplified if we start out with the other formulation of the general linear demand function

$$x_{it} = \alpha_{1i} \frac{p_{1t}}{p_{it}} + \alpha_{2i} \frac{p_{2t}}{p_{it}} + \ldots + \alpha_{ni} \frac{p_{nt}}{p_{it}} + \beta_i \frac{y_t}{p_{it}} + u_{it}.$$

We shall omit superscript j here since we are not concerned with aggregation over individuals at this stage. Multiplying both sides by p_{it} and adding over a subgroup $1, 2, \ldots, n_1$ gives

$$\sum_{i=1}^{n_1} p_{it} x_{it} = p_{1t} \sum_{i=1}^{n_1} \alpha_{1i} + p_{2t} \sum_{i=1}^{n_1} \alpha_{2i} + \ldots$$
$$+ p_{nt} \sum_{i=1}^{n_1} \alpha_{ni} + y_t \sum_{i=1}^{n_1} \beta_i + \sum_{i=1}^{n_1} p_{it} u_{it}.$$

We define a price index of all the goods in the subgroup as

$$p_t^{(1)} = \sum_{i=1}^{n_1} w_i p_{it},$$

where

w_i = weight of the i-th good in the subgroup price index.

---

[10] This identity is used in statistics to show how the variance of a frequency distribution can be computed by a short cut.

Statistical Demand Analysis

Dividing both sides of the aggregated equation by this price index gives

$$\frac{\sum_{i=1}^{n_1} p_{it}x_{it}}{p_t^{(1)}} = \frac{p_{1t}\sum_{i=1}^{n_1}\alpha_{1i} + p_{2t}\sum_{i=1}^{n_1}\alpha_{2i} + \ldots + p_{n_1 t}\sum_{i=1}^{n_1}\alpha_{n_1 i}}{p_t^{(1)}}$$

$$+ \frac{p_{n_1+1,\,t}}{p_t^{(1)}} \sum_{i=1}^{n_1} \alpha_{n_1+1,\,t} + \ldots + \frac{p_{n,\,t}}{p_t^{(1)}} \sum_{i=1}^{n_1} \alpha_{ni}$$

$$+ \frac{y_t}{p_t^{(1)}} \sum_{i=1}^{n_1} \beta_i + \frac{\sum_{i=1}^{n_1} p_{it}u_{it}}{p_t^{(1)}}.$$

The left hand term is interpreted as the value spent on the subgroup deflated by a price index of the subgroup. It is an index of the subgroup quantity. We shall call it $x_t^{(1)}$. The first fraction on the right hand side is a ratio between two different weighted combinations of the n_1 prices in the subgroup. In the numerator the weights are the sums of the coefficients in the demand equation. In the denominator the weights are w_i. As an approximation, we may take this ratio to be a constant. The next terms are successive relative prices, that is, ratios between each of the prices outside the subgroup and the subgroup index. Then we have the income term deflated by the subgroup index. The disturbance term can be interpreted as a ratio between two weighted averages of prices in the subgroup. In the numerator, the weighted average has random weights and in the denominator fixed weights. We call the composite a new random variable $u_t^{(1)}$. The equation can be rewritten as

$$x_t^{(1)} = \alpha_0^{(1)} + \alpha_1^{(1)} \frac{p_{n_1+1,\,t}}{p_t^{(1)}} + \ldots + \alpha_n^{(1)} \frac{p_{nt}}{p_t^{(1)}} + \beta^{(1)} \frac{y_t}{p_t^{(1)}} + u_t^{(1)}.$$

From this point, aggregation over individuals can proceed as above.

All these procedures of aggregation involve strong assumptions and approximations. The results would be even more approximate if the parameters were assumed to vary among individuals. For this more complicated case, as well as for various types of nonlinearity, particular results can be obtained. From time to time, in the context of specific problems, some of these findings will be brought out in the exposition to follow.

It can readily be seen how the assumption of linearity simplifies the results for aggregation into market behavior. If the nonlinearity is of the constant elasticity type, the model can be transformed, as shown above, into a linear model in logarithms. The present propositions stated in terms of means of ordinary (arithmetic) magnitudes can be translated into means of logarithms, which in turn are logarithms of *geometric* means. Market data in the form of arithmetic totals usually do not permit the calculation of geometric averages. Since a sum of logarithms is not the logarithm of a sum, we cannot make a direct translation into logarithms of market totals where individual functions are logarithmic. In some circumstances there are, fortunately, fixed relations between arithmetic and geometric means. These will be explained for particular problems below.

Demand analysis, in the first statistical applications, was formulated in terms of market totals as though such units were natural. We find, however, that if a careful correspondence is made between traditional theory, which is couched in terms of individual demand for particular commodities, and statistical calculations of market data, an aggregation bridge must be constructed. If attention is paid to this bridge, the choice of different index numbers and the role of income distribution become much clearer. The econometrician should always analyze the aggregation implications of his calculations with market data.

We have seen, in this section, that linear functions present few problems, especially if it can be assumed that the parameters in the linear functions are the same for all individuals. Nonlinear functions usually bring phenomena of income distributions into aggregate demand functions.

THE NATURE OF THE RANDOM DISTURBANCES

In econometrics, as distinct from mathematical economics, one cannot neglect the random variables in the relationships being considered. Econometrics does not deal with exact relationships; probabilistic considerations are fundamental throughout.

The pure theory of consumer demand shows how a relationship may be derived, via the route of utility maximization, expressing quantity demanded as a function of relative prices and real income. Apart

Statistical Demand Analysis

from the additional factors that must be brought into the demand equations to represent consumer planning over time, can the research worker honestly say relative prices and real incomes exhaust the list of factors that might influence demand? There may be an epidemic, a disturbance in international relations, a sudden and temporary change of fashion and, in fact, a veritable multitude of factors that may have a direct effect on demand, but which are not accounted for explicitly in the theoretical derivation of the relationship. These extra factors are not permanent, regular, or measurable, yet they are definitely present and not necessarily negligible. If there is found to be a major systematic factor which strongly influences demand and is not included in the theory, then theory must be altered to encompass this variable.

Let us write the typical demand function as

$$x_{it} = \alpha_{1i}\frac{p_{1t}}{p_{it}} + \ldots + \alpha_{ni}\frac{p_{nt}}{p_{it}} + \beta_i\frac{y_t}{p_{it}} + \gamma_1 z_{1t} + \ldots + \gamma_m z_{mt},$$

where $z_{1t}, \ldots, z_{mt}$ are a large number of minor disturbing variables which influence demand. Individually, each z_{it} is said to be minor in the sense that it is not always significant, that it influences some persons and not others, and that it fluctuates out of rhythm with the general economic situation. However, the cumulative effect of all the z_{it} together need not be minor. We hope our theory is powerful enough so that p_{jt}/p_{it} and y_t/p_{it} account for most of the variation in x_{it}, but this need not be so.

There is a basic theorem in the mathematical theory of probability that says, in a very general way, that averages of random variables tend to follow the *normal distribution*, as the number of items making up the average increases without limit, regardless of the original distributions of the components of the average. A proviso might be made that the components of the average be mutually independent. The normal distribution has a symmetrical, bell-shaped pattern. It is not the only distribution that has this appearance, but it is the most important among all such distributions. In fact, it is safe to say that it is the most important single distribution of statistical theory.[11] The linear function

$$\gamma_1 z_{1t} + \ldots + \gamma_m z_{mt}$$

[11] In Chapter 4 a number of nonsymmetrical distributions are discussed.

is in fact, nearly like an average. It is proportional to a weighted average

$$(\gamma_1 + \ldots + \gamma_m) \frac{\gamma_1 z_{1t} + \ldots + \gamma_m z_{mt}}{\gamma_1 + \ldots + \gamma_m} = (\gamma_1 + \ldots + \gamma_m)\bar{z}_t,$$

where $\bar{z}_t$ is a weighted average of the z_{it} with weights

$$\frac{\gamma_i}{\gamma_1 + \ldots + \gamma_m}.$$

If this is a market relation, there has been a prior averaging of the z_{it} for individual people. There are many such neglected variables, and they are averaged again as noted above. Therefore, we have grounds for appealing to the *central limit theorem* of probability and assuming that the equation can be written as

$$x_{it} = \alpha_{1i} \frac{p_{1t}}{p_{it}} + \ldots + \alpha_{ni} \frac{p_{nt}}{p_{it}} + \beta_i \frac{y_t}{p_{it}} + u_{it},$$

where u_{it} is a normally distributed random variable. In some applications, we shall simply want to say that u_{it} is a random variable following some unspecified distribution law. We shall be on firmer ground, however, if we can specify the precise distribution function, and the best choice is the normal function. This is the "best" choice in the sense that there is the above-noted tendency of averages of random variables to be normal and that statistical theory is worked out in full for the normal case.

There is a presumption among some investigators that u_{it}, the random disturbance, must be small. We are pleased if it is small, but smallness is not an objective to the econometrician. He is interested in getting the best possible statistical estimate of the model, and it may be inherent in the nature of the economic process that the random disturbance is not small. As we remarked above, the function describing agricultural supply is subject to wide variability, compared with demand, and, even if we are able to identify explicitly such additional factors as weather variables, there still may be a wide random fluctuation in the function. The objective for the econometrician is to use a sample of real-life data to get the best estimate of all the parameters of the problem. These parameters are α_{ji}, β_i, and the

Statistical Demand Analysis

parameters of the probability distribution of u_{it}. If the disturbance is normally distributed, we are primarily interested in the measure of dispersion of the distribution (its standard deviation) which may be large or small. Whatever it is, the econometrician must try to estimate it. He is not primarily seeking high correlation but rather, basic explanation up to a random error. The laws of probability are called upon to take over from that stage. It may be more important to have purely random errors, in any sample of data, rather than purely small errors. If the econometrician provides an explanation apart from a random factor, no more can be asked of him.

In the early days of the development of econometrics, the emphasis was on a random element entering through imperfect measurement. It was assumed that the formal relationships, the demand functions depending on a limited number of traditional variables, were exact but that each variable was subject to measurement error. Even assuming the most refined techniques of collection and measurement of basic economic information, it seems unlikely that market equations can be exactly defined in terms of two, three, or even ten variables. The justification above for the random errors in terms of neglected factors cannot be avoided. Nevertheless, errors of observation and measurement do occur. Index numbers are approximate. Samples are used for many components of our collection of statistical economic information. The aggregation of individual to market relationships involves errors. Difficult statistical problems arise if we try to combine measurement error with the error of missing variables in our model. We shall, therefore, neglect error of measurement at this stage and develop our statistical tools on the basis of the other type of error.

QUESTIONS AND PROBLEMS

1. Monthly statistics of U.S. coffee imports and prices for 1954 are given in Table 2.1. Plot the price-quantity values in the form of a scatter diagram. Does a free hand curve fitted to these points trace out a demand curve? Should any other statistical variables be taken into account in the estimation of the demand function for coffee? An attempt is made to eliminate seasonal influences on imports by presenting the quantity data in terms of deviation from the corre-

TABLE 2.1
Monthly Coffee Imports and Prices, U.S.A.

Quantity (change from corresponding month of 1953, thousand bags)			Price (Santos #4 N.Y. $/lb.)		
1954	Jan.	435	1953	Nov.	.585
	Feb.	103		Dec.	.613
	March	−304	1954	Jan.	.725
	April	−229		Feb.	.760
	May	−156		Mar.	.858
	June	−28		Apr.	.870
	July	−494		May	.855
	August	−442		June	.870
	Sept.	−1470		July	.883
	Oct.	−390		Aug.	.755
	Nov.	−607		Sept.	.718
	Dec.	−405		Oct.	.700

sponding month of the preceding year. Criticize the technique. Is it reasonable to lag imports two months behind prices?

2. In Table 2.2, annual price and quantity values for U.S. coffee imports are given for the period 1929-58, with the war years, 1942-45, excepted. Plot these points and contrast the scatter diagram with that for the monthly values in Question 1.

Can you account for the differences in appearance of the two scatter plots? What other variables are relevant for the estimation of the demand relationship from these annual data?

3. The Keynesian consumption function may be regarded as an aggregate demand function. Can you show any formal relationship between the consumption function and demand functions of microeconomic theory? You may use linear relationships to simplify your answer.

4. Suppose that the distribution of income is made more equal, *cet. par.* How would this affect the demand for luxuries and for necessities? How would you take the income distribution factor into account in the formulation of a demand function?

5. Life insurance is purchased by many consumers. Outline a demand theory for life insurance. What variables are included in this demand function? Is the function homogeneous of degree zero in prices and income?

TABLE 2.2
Annual Coffee Imports and Prices, U.S.A., 1929-58

	Quantity (mo. av., thous. bags)	Prices (mo. av., Santos, #4, N.Y., $/lb.)
1929	934	.221
30	1008	.132
31	1097	.087
32	946	.107
33	993	.093
34	960	.112
35	1105	.089
36	1096	.095
37	1069	.111
38	1252	.078
39	1269	.075
40	1295	.072
41	1420	.114
46	1719	.187
47	1571	.264
48	1746	.268
49	1838	.318
50	1536	.509
51	1693	.543
52	1689	.541
53	1752	.585
54	1423	.783
55	1637	.570
56	1771	.583
57	1733	.573
58	1682	.489

A STATISTICAL DEMAND FUNCTION—
POSTWAR UNITED KINGDOM EXPORTS TO THE DOLLAR AREA

We now have the groundwork for embarking on a study of demand in a particular market and showing the development of the appropriate statistical methods as we work our way systematically to results on a typical problem. The market selected for initial study is that for exports from the United Kingdom to the dollar area (United States, Canada, and dollar Latin America). A demand function covering this entire market involves a high degree of aggregation. It is not the demand for a single product, yet it is not as aggregative as a demand function for total United Kingdom exports. We have singled out a particular currency area.

From the traditional theory of demand in foreign trade, we start with the hypothesis that British exports to the dollar area ($x_\$$) are a function of relative prices ($p_\$/p_£$) and the level of production in the dollar area ($P_\$$)

$$x_{\$t} = \alpha_0 + \alpha_1 \left(\frac{p_\$}{p_£}\right)_t + \alpha_2 P_{\$t} + u_t.$$

If we measure $x_\$$ by a quantity index of exports and $P_\$$ by an index of physical production, the basic homogeneity property is satisfied by this linear equation.

Foreign trade statistics are collected and published on an elaborate basis. In this particular problem, exports by currency area are reported in value terms. To get an index of quantities, we deflate (divide) the monetary values by an index of export prices. All these data are available monthly, and we combine months into quarters of a year to obtain a quarterly series for the period since 1948, the base year for our index values.

Relative prices enter the equation to show the alternative costs to dollar area purchasers of buying either a home produced or an imported, British good. The United Kingdom principally exports manufactured goods to the dollar area. Therefore the relevant dollar price indicator is the index of wholesale prices of nonfarm, nonfood products. Such an index is readily available for the United States. An index chiefly consisting of manufactured goods was used for Canada, and a general price index of Venezuelan imports was used for dollar Latin America. The three indexes were averaged together in weighted proportions according to the countries' comparative shares of United Kingdom exports in a base period. This gave the numerator $p_\$$. The denominator was measured by the price index of British exports. Since the time period of sample observations covered the devaluations of 1949, $p_£$ had to be reduced by the fraction 2.8/4.0 in order to reflect the actual cost of sterling commodity transactions to a dollar area purchaser. No adjustment need be made for tariff charges during the period covered.

The level of production is introduced to show either the income effects as analyzed in the theory of demand in international trade or

Statistical Demand Analysis

the production needs for unfinished materials and capital goods. The American and Canadian industrial production indexes are readily available. Production and real income in dollar Latin America are indicated by the level of Venezuelan export volume. The three production measures are averaged over the countries as was done with the components of the dollar-price index, $p_\$$.

Since the data are on a quarterly basis, there may be seasonal forces at work influencing their inter-relationships. It would be feasible to use seasonally adjusted series, that is, data adjusted by the usual methods applied for seasonal variation. Instead of using series that have already had systematic computations built into them, it may be preferable to add some explicit seasonal variables to the equation and use purely unadjusted data. Assuming that the seasonal factors are linear and additive, we rewrite our equation as

$$x_{\$t} = \alpha_0 + \alpha_1 \left(\frac{p_\$}{p_£}\right)_t + \alpha_2 P_{\$t} + \beta_1 Q_{1t} + \beta_2 Q_{2t} + \beta_3 Q_{3t} + u_t,$$

where

$Q_{1t} = 1$ in first quarter periods
$= 0$ in all other periods,

$Q_{2t} = 1$ in second quarter periods
$= 0$ in all other periods,

$Q_{3t} = 1$ in third quarter periods
$= 0$ in all other periods.

In each of the first three quarters of any year only one of the Q_{it} variables is nonzero. The associated coefficient β_i shows how the level of the whole equation must be adjusted for that quarter's seasonal influence. In the fourth quarter, all the Q_{it} are zero, and the level of the equation is given by α_0.

Because of time lags involved in ordering goods at great distances and required periods of production for many goods, exports of a given period are likely to be associated with prices and production of an earlier period. We finally proceed with an equation of the form

$$x_{\$t} = \alpha_0 + \alpha_1 \left(\frac{p_\$}{p_£}\right)_{t-1} + \alpha_2 P_{\$, t-1} + \beta_1 Q_{1t} + \beta_2 Q_{2t} + \beta_3 Q_{3t} + u_t.$$

Given a sample of market observations on the variables in this demand function during the period 1948-56, how do we estimate the α's, β's, and the properties of the random variable u_t? This is the usual problem of statistical inference: how to infer the characteristics of a population on the basis of an observed sample.

The variable u_t is assumed to be made up of numerous small neglected factors, that is, factors that are unrelated to those explicitly considered on the right hand side of the equation. Since these are factors operative during time period t, they should not be related to prices and production of an earlier time period. Having a constant term in a linear equation α_0 enables us to assume that u_t is, on the average, zero. Let us, therefore, sum the equation over all sample values and adopt the assumption that u_t averages to nought over all the sample time periods $t = 1, 2, \ldots, T$.

$$(1) \quad \sum_{t=1}^{T} x_{\$t} = T\alpha_0 + \alpha_1 \sum_{t=1}^{T} \left(\frac{p_\$}{p_\pounds}\right)_{t-1} + \alpha_2 \sum_{t=1}^{T} (P_\$)_{t-1} + \beta_1 \sum_{t=1}^{T} Q_{1t} + \beta_2 \sum_{t=1}^{T} Q_{2t} + \beta_3 \sum_{t=1}^{T} Q_{3t}.$$

This relation carries the reasonable implication that averages of the sample values must satisfy the estimated equation when numerical values are finally assigned to the unknown parameters.

Next let us multiply both sides of the equation being estimated by $(p_\$/p_\pounds)_{t-1}$ and add all the products. The result will be

$$(2) \quad \sum_{t=1}^{T} x_{\$t} \left(\frac{p_\$}{p_\pounds}\right)_{t-1} = \alpha_0 \sum_{t=1}^{T} \left(\frac{p_\$}{p_\pounds}\right)_{t-1} + \alpha_1 \sum_{t=1}^{T} \left(\frac{p_\$}{p_\pounds}\right)_{t-1}^{2}$$
$$+ \alpha_2 \sum_{t=1}^{T} (P_\$)_{t-1} \left(\frac{p_\$}{p_\pounds}\right)_{t-1} + \beta_1 \sum_{t=1}^{T} Q_{1t} \left(\frac{p_\$}{p_\pounds}\right)_{t-1}$$
$$+ \beta_2 \sum_{t=1}^{T} Q_{2t} \left(\frac{p_\$}{p_\pounds}\right)_{t-1} + \beta_3 \sum_{t=1}^{T} Q_{3t} \left(\frac{p_\$}{p_\pounds}\right)_{t-1}$$

We have omitted, in (2), the summed product

$$\sum_{t=1}^{T} u_t \left(\frac{p_\$}{p_\pounds}\right)_{t-1}$$

because this term is set equal to zero. In the previous step, for deriving (1), we assumed that the average value of u_t is zero. We now assume that u_t is, in a statistical sense, independent of $(p_\$/p_\pounds)_{t-1}$, in fact, independent of all the explanatory factors in the equation.

A measure of association between any two variables x and y is the

Statistical Demand Analysis

coefficient of correlation. It may be defined as

$$r_{xy} = \frac{\sum\limits_{i=1}^{n}(x_i-\bar{x})(y_i-\bar{y})}{\sqrt{\sum\limits_{i=1}^{n}(x_i-\bar{x})^2 \sum\limits_{i=1}^{n}(y_i-\bar{y})^2}}.$$

In the numerator we have the sum of products of deviations of the two variables from their mean values. If one or both have zero means, we need not use mean deviations and can simply write the numerator as $\sum\limits_{i=1}^{n} x_i y_i$. In the denominator, we have the product of sums of squared deviations of each variable about its mean. If divided by the number of observations in the sample n, these sums of squared deviations would become *variances*. The whole denominator expression is introduced in order to make the coefficient of correlation independent of units of measurement, that is, a pure number.

If we were to have no association between the two variables x_i and y_i, the numerator would have to vanish. Now returning to our problem of estimating the export demand function, we say that the assumed vanishing of

$$\sum_{t=1}^{T} u_t \left(\frac{p_\$}{p_£}\right)_{t-1}$$

is justified on the grounds that there is no association between u_t and any of the explanatory variables in the equation. The original equation can be multiplied through on both sides by $(P_\$)_{t-1}$ and summed, by Q_{1t} and summed, by Q_{2t} and summed, and by Q_{3t} and summed. By the same arguments we obtain

(3) $\sum x_{\$t}(P_\$)_{t-1} = \alpha_0 \sum (P_\$)_{t-1} + \alpha_1 \sum \left(\frac{p_\$}{p_£}\right)_{t-1} (P_\$)_{t-1} + \alpha_2 \sum (P_\$)_{t-1}^2$
$\qquad + \beta_1 \sum Q_{1t}(P_\$)_{t-1} + \beta_2 \sum Q_{2t}(P_\$)_{t-1} + \beta_3 \sum Q_{3t}(P_\$)_{t-1},$

(4) $\sum x_{\$t} Q_{1t} = \alpha_0 \sum Q_{1t} + \alpha_1 \sum \left(\frac{p_\$}{p_£}\right)_{t-1} Q_{1t} + \alpha_2 \sum (P_\$)_{t-1} Q_{1t}$
$\qquad + \beta_1 \sum Q_{1t}^2 + \beta_2 \sum Q_{1t}Q_{2t} + \beta_3 \sum Q_{1t}Q_{3t},$

(5) $\sum x_{\$t} Q_{2t} = \alpha_0 \sum Q_{2t} + \alpha_1 \sum \left(\frac{p_\$}{p_£}\right)_{t-1} Q_{2t} + \alpha_2 \sum (P_\$)_{t-1} Q_{2t}$
$\qquad + \beta_1 \sum Q_{2t}Q_{1t} + \beta_2 \sum Q_{2t}^2 + \beta_3 \sum Q_{2t}Q_{3t},$

(6) $\quad \Sigma\, x_{\$t} Q_{3t} = \alpha_0 \Sigma\, Q_{3t} + \alpha_1 \Sigma \left(\dfrac{p_\$}{p_\pounds}\right)_{t-1} Q_{3t} + \alpha_2 \Sigma\, (P_\$)_{t-1} Q_{3t}$
$\quad\quad\quad\quad\quad + \beta_1 \Sigma\, Q_{3t} Q_{1t} + \beta_2 \Sigma\, Q_{3t} Q_{2t} + \beta_3 \Sigma\, Q_{3t}^2.$

Equations (1) through (6) provide a means of estimating the unknown coefficients. As economists, we are primarily interested in analyzing relative movements in $x_\$$, $(p_\$/p_\pounds)$, and $P_\$$ for given numerical values of the coefficients α_i and β_i. As statisticians, we are primarily interested in estimating the unknown values of α_i and β_i for known sample observations on $x_{\$t}$, $(p_\$/p_\pounds)_{t-1}$, $(P_\$)_{t-1}$, and Q_{it}. Equations (1) through (6) are a set of six linear equations in the six unknowns α_0, α_1, α_2, β_1, β_2, and β_3. The sums of products and simple sums of observed variables are known numerical quantities determined by the values of the sample observations.

The task of solving six equations in six variables, even though they are linear, may seem formidable, but systematic methods which greatly simplify the work are explained elsewhere in statistics and advanced econometrics texts.[12] The present problem looks more complicated than is actually the case because of the use of the three seasonal variables. The terms $\Sigma\, Q_{1t} Q_{2t}$, $\Sigma\, Q_{1t} Q_{3t}$, and $\Sigma\, Q_{2t} Q_{3t}$ are all zero by nature of the definition of Q_{it}. Since these variables can assume only the values zero or unity, all sums and products involving them are comparatively easy to form. Moreover, the whole set of linear equations has a symmetrical pattern, and this greatly simplifies the computations for a solution. In this chapter it is sufficient to say that values of the unknown coefficients can be estimated by calculating a solution set from the six equations. The final result is

$$x_{\$t} = -211.63 + 0.91 \left(\dfrac{p_\$}{p_\pounds}\right)_{t-1} + 2.27(P_\$)_{t-1}$$
$$- 14.86 Q_{1t} + 0.53 Q_{2t} + 1.00 Q_{3t}.$$

Except for the Q_{it}, the variables are all measured as index numbers with base values of 100 in the year 1948. The equation states that, other things held constant, a one point change in the index of relative prices is associated, on the average, with a change of about .9 point in the index of export quantity. If dollar area prices rise relative to sterling prices, British exports rise, but if sterling prices rise relative

---

[12] Details are given in Chapter IV of L. R. Klein, *A Textbook of Econometrics* (Evanston: Row Peterson & Co., 1953).

Statistical Demand Analysis

to dollar area prices, British exports fall. This is the usual case of the downward sloping demand function with substitution effects. For given values of $p_\$$, $P_\$$, and Q_i, the net relation between $x_\$$ and $p_£$ yields the curve plotted in Fig. 2.7.[13] This is the *ceteris paribus*

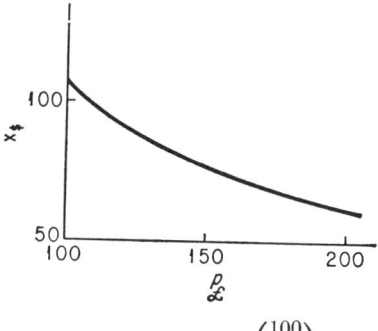

Fig. 2.7. $x_{\$t} = 15 + 91 \left(\dfrac{100}{p_£}\right)_{t-1}$

type of demand function, but it was statistically estimated by dropping the *ceteris paribus* assumption and explicitly taking other factors into account. The coefficient of production $P_\$$ implies that we can expect, other things equal, that a one point change in the index of output will call forth a change in the same direction of 2.27 points in the index of exports. As is generally suspected, demand in this market is more sensitive to income or production effects than to relative price effects.

In the first quarter of any year, the constant term in the linear function is put at -226.49 ($= -211.63 - 14.86$). In the second quarter it is higher at -211.10 ($= -211.63 + 0.53$) and in the third quarter at the highest level for the year at -210.63 ($= -211.63 + 1.00$). In the fourth quarter each Q_{it} vanishes, and the constant term is estimated at -211.63. Thus the normal seasonal pattern, after taking into account the seasonal movements of prices and production, is for a low point in the first quarter following Christmas sales, and a high point in the third quarter just preceding Christmas sales. The other two quarters are quite close together between the extremes.

Had our linear function been expressed directly in terms of logarithms, the coefficients would have been *elasticities*. To derive

---

[13] The variables other than $p_£$ are set at base values (100) and the fourth quarter season is selected. Since $(p_\$/p_£)$ is on an index base of 100, the coefficient .91 has to be multiplied by 100 in order to treat both $p_\$$ and $p_£$ as indexes on a base of 100. Otherwise the ratio would be 1.0 instead of 100 in the base period.

elasticity coefficients from those in a linear arithmetic equation, we must multiply the estimated coefficient parameters by

$$\frac{\left(\frac{p_\$}{p_\pounds}\right)_{t-1}}{x_{\$t}} \quad \text{and} \quad \frac{(P_\$)_{t-1}}{x_{\$t}}$$

for relative price and production elasticities respectively. At each variable point on the relation, the elasticity will differ. At the base period values, all variables are simultaneously 100. Therefore, the ratios by which we multiply the coefficients to get elasticities are unity, and the linear coefficients themselves are elasticities. At the point of sample averages we have

$$\text{average} \left(\frac{p_\$}{p_\pounds}\right)_{t-1} = 114.2,$$

$$\text{average } (P_\$)_{t-1} = 117.2,$$

$$\text{average } x_{\$t} = 153.3.$$

At the point of means, the relative price elasticity is 0.67, and the production elasticity is 1.73.

The numerical equation was written without an error term because the best single numerical value that can be assigned to this term, in the absence of special knowledge, is its average, zero. The coefficients, too, in a sense, are average values. Therefore the equation is written entirely as an average estimate.

Although the errors are assumed to average to zero, we expect individual values to be distributed about zero. We require a measure of their dispersion about zero, namely, their standard deviation or variance. The errors are not observables for the sample, but the differences between actual exports and those estimated by the numerical equation, the *residuals*, give a distribution of values from which the properties of the distribution of errors can be estimated. The dispersion or variance of residuals provides an estimate of the variance of error. We write

$$S_u^2 = \frac{1}{37 - 6} \sum_{t=1}^{37} \left[x_{\$t} + 211.63 - 0.91 \left(\frac{p_\$}{p_\pounds}\right)_{t-1} - 2.27(P_\$)_{t-1} \right.$$
$$\left. + 14.86 Q_{1t} - 0.53 Q_{2t} - 1.00 Q_{3t} \right]^2 = 215.81.$$

Statistical Demand Analysis

In the brackets we have numerical residuals. Instead of dividing their sum of squares by the number of sample observations, we divide by a smaller number, the number of observations minus the number of constants used in estimating the residuals. The resulting divisor represents the number of "degrees of freedom" in the problem. By including more variables and using more constants, we can achieve nearly an automatic reduction in the size of residuals. Therefore we need to adopt a penalty measure in order to restrain one from going too far in this direction.

We have formed the estimate of this export demand equation by imposing the conditions that each of the explanatory factors is uncorrelated with the residual variation. These conditions are derived from the underlying probability assumptions that the disturbances are independent of the particular explanatory variables used. The equations used to solve for the estimates of the coefficients could have been reached by another route. They are *least squares* equations; that is, they yield values of the coefficients that make the sum of squares of residuals

$$\sum_{t=1}^{37} \left[x_{\$t} - \alpha_0 - \alpha_1 \left(\frac{p_\$}{p_\pounds}\right)_{t-1} - \alpha_2 (P_\$)_{t-1} - \beta_1 Q_{1t} - \beta_2 Q_{2t} - \beta_3 Q_{3t} \right]^2$$

as small as possible. Our derivation above is more elementary, but the theory of least squares would serve equally well. In either case the rule for forming the estimation equations, called *normal equations* in least squares correlation theory, is simply to multiply both sides of the equation to be estimated by each of the explanatory variables, in turn, and then to sum over all sample observations. We also use the fact that the equation is satisfied by the sample mean values.

The principle of least squares leads to estimates of the coefficients that give a smaller value for S_u^2 than that obtained from any other set of numerical values. It also gives the maximum degree of correlation. A general definition of the squared value of the coefficient of correlation, to cover multivariate relationships as well as the bivariate formula presented above, is

$$R_{y \cdot zz \ldots}^2 = 1 - \frac{S_u^2}{S_y^2} \frac{T-1}{T},$$

where

S_u^2 = estimated variance of residuals, computed as above, taking the number of degrees of freedom into account,

and

$$S_y^2 = \frac{1}{T} \sum_{t=1}^{T} (y_t - \bar{y})^2 = \text{sample variance of } y_t.$$

In this formula, we have the multiplier $(T - 1)/T$ to take account of the fact that one degree of freedom is used up in estimating S_y^2 from the sample data. The mean value $\bar{y}$ must be used in order to compute S_y^2. The formula for R^2 given above is thus adjusted for degrees of freedom. It is usually written as $\bar{R}^2$ to distinguish it from the ordinary case in which no account is taken of the degrees of freedom used up. In the above formula, y is assumed to be a linear function of x, z, and other variables. In the example being treated in this section, the coefficient of correlation works out to be $R^2 = 0.868$.

Still another interpretation of the estimates in this problem is possible. If the error term u_t consists of a set of mutually independent variables drawn from the same normal distribution, we can say that the estimates of the type found above are *maximum likelihood* estimates. By this expression we mean that the estimated values of the coefficients and variance of u are such that they maximize the probability of obtaining the observed sample.

The normal distribution (density form) for some variable u having a zero mean is

$$\frac{1}{\sqrt{2\pi}\,\sigma_u} e^{-\frac{u^2}{2\sigma_u^2}}.$$

Suppose, now, that we have a whole sample of values of u_t: u_1, u_2, ... , u_{37}. If each of these is mutually independent of each other, the joint probability of the whole set is obtained by multiplying their individual probabilities,

$$\left(\frac{1}{\sqrt{2\pi}\,\sigma_u}\right)^{37} e^{-\frac{1}{2\sigma_u^2} \sum_{t=1}^{37} u_t^2}.$$

In the exponent we find the sum of squared errors because exponential functions are multiplied by the adding of exponents. To maximize the above expression for probability (density) functions, we minimize

Statistical Demand Analysis

the sum of squares

$$\sum_{t=1}^{37} u_t^2$$

because it comes into the exponent with a negative sign. Thus we are back to the previous version of the problem; namely, a choice of estimated coefficients that minimize the residual variation.

The maximum likelihood interpretation requires both normality and mutual independence of u_t. The other two interpretations made no such assumptions, but the statistical properties of the estimates, as will be explained below, are better if the independence assumption is valid. The normality assumption, if it can be made, is useful in carrying out statistical tests of estimates, but is not essential.

There could be a lack of mutual independence among u_t in a wide variety of ways, but one of the most common forms of dependence in economic time-series is *serial correlation*. In this form of dependence we have u_t a linear function of $u_{t-\theta}$, the value of u_t, θ periods earlier. Trends and cycles, which are common among economic variables, tend to produce positive serial correlation. If our hypothesized demand equation is not sufficiently well stated so that large systematic variables are left in u_t without being explicitly taken into account in the equation, we may find that the actual residuals of a sample are serially correlated. It is advisable in a problem dealing with economic time series to compute all the residual values and plot them on a chart for visual inspection for randomness. A statistical test safeguarding against the presence of serial correlation is provided by the statistic (ratio of the *mean square successive difference to the variance*)

$$\frac{\delta^2}{S^2} = \frac{\sum_{t=2}^{37} (r_t - r_{t-1})^2}{\sum_{t=1}^{37} r_t^2} \frac{37}{36} = 1.866.$$

In the numerator we have the sum of squares of first differences of the residuals r_t, and in the denominator we have the sum of squares of the residuals. Probability tables are available from which we can see, for a given sample size, the chance of getting a value at least as large as that actually obtained provided there is no serial correlation in the true values. In a sample of 40 observations, we find that the value of δ^2/S^2 must be between 1.45 and 2.65 if we are to accept the independence hypothesis at a probability level of five per cent, that is, a level such that the probability of getting a sample value as large as the one obtained as a result of chance forces is five per cent. If we chose the level of one per cent, we would have to have values between 1.25 and 2.85 in order to accept the hypothesis of independence.[14]

This aspect of the econometric problem is important because we are primarily interested in having random residual variation, and not necessarily small residual variation. In any case, the method of estimation makes the residual variation minimal, in the square, for the assumed form of the equation. If a sample is sufficiently large, say of 100 or more observations, we may go even further and test the residual variation for its conformity to the normal distribution, or indeed, to any other well known law of probability.

This discussion leads into another important part of the statistical problem in econometrics, which is sampling error and efficiency. To write an estimated demand equation in terms of apparently precise numerical coefficients, often with several decimal points, may be deceptive. The particular values computed for the coefficients depend on the sample observations. If the sample had been different, by chance, as it may well have been, the numerical estimates would have been different. We need a measure of uncertainty to be attached to each of our estimates to show that they depend on a mere sample of observational data.

Conceptually, the idea of sampling error can be explained in the following way. Suppose that the explanatory variables are fixed. Think of another set of purchase decisions (for British exports to America) which differ from the original set because of the presence of a fresh and independent set of disturbing factors. This is purely conceptual because we cannot alter the sample situation at will; economics is a nonexperimental discipline, and we accept actual market outcomes for our sample observations. Nevertheless, we can imagine a hypothetical sampling experiment, and we can, equally well, imagine it to be repeated over and over again. With each

[14] The critical limits of test values spread wider as the probability level is reduced since, under the hypothesis of no serial correlation, the probability varies inversely with the degree of serial correlation, which, in turn, varies inversely for positive correlation with the statistic δ^2/S^2. In this problem we are usually seeking to accept the underlying hypothesis of no serial correlation. In another test, to be given below, we are often seeking to reject the underlying hypothesis (zero coefficients).

Statistical Demand Analysis

sample drawing, even though the explanatory variables are fixed, purchase decisions will vary because disturbances vary. We shall have different estimates of the coefficients associated with each sample. There will be a whole distribution of values of each coefficient, and the dispersion of that distribution will be a measure of sampling error.

For a truly controlled experiment of the type used in natural sciences, such a repeated sampling scheme with fixed explanatory variables can be readily carried out. In sample surveys, to be discussed later in this chapter, repeated sampling is a realistic possibility. For the usual time-series investigation, it is a hypothetical model. Mathematical reasoning beyond the limits of this text would be required to derive the formulas for computing sampling errors in the multivariate equation being estimated. By intuition and analogy, however, it is possible to explain the rationale of the measures.

The sampling error of the estimated coefficient of z_t in the two-variable equation

$$y_t = \alpha + \beta z_t + u_t,$$

depends on three things: (1) the size of the sample; (2) the variability of z_t within the sample; and (3) the variability of u_t. If the sample included the whole population of possible observations, which may be an infinite population, we would have no sampling error. It seems reasonable to say that the sampling error should vary inversely with the sample size.

The reliability with which we estimate β from a sample ought to depend on how much z varies. It is difficult to see how much of the fluctuation in y is accounted for by fluctuation in z unless z varies enough to give us a good picture of its influence. Sampling error should vary inversely with the variability of z. In the scheme of repeated sampling with fixed values of z_t, the only reason we get different samples and different estimates is because of the variability of u_t. If u_t is drawn from a probability distribution with wide dispersion, we shall tend to get a wide dispersion of estimates, from sample to sample, of β.

Call b the estimate of β. Then we have for the sampling error formula

$$\text{variance } (b) = \frac{\text{variance }(u)}{\frac{\sum (z_t - \bar{z})^2}{T}}.$$

In this formula the numerator is estimated, as explained above, by the mean sum of squares of residuals from the computed equation. The denominator is simply the sum of squares of sample observations of z_t about its mean. The larger the sample size T, the larger is the sum of squares in the denominator, assuming that additional values of z_t are not precisely equal to the sample mean. Similarly, the larger the variance of z, the larger is the denominator. Thus increasing sample size and increasing variance of z contribute to a reduction in sampling error. It is quite evident that the larger the variance (u) is, the larger the sampling error will be.

In our problem of the dollar area demand for British exports, there are several explanatory variables, therefore the denominator must be altered to take this fact into account. A mathematical generalization of a single magnitude into an array of several is known as *matrix algebra*. The square array of coefficients of the α's and β's in equations (1) through (6) is the particular matrix relevant to the present problem. Instead of using the reciprocal or inverse of a single magnitude such as

$$\frac{1}{\sum_{t=1}^{T} (z_t - \bar{z})^2},$$

we use the more advanced concept of the reciprocal or inverse of a whole array or matrix. The diagonal elements of such an inverse, which can be evaluated by elementary arithmetic operations, when multiplied by variance (u), give the variances of the associated coefficient in the multivariate equation. We write our numerical equation as

$$x_{\$t} = -211.63 + 0.91 \left(\frac{p_\$}{p_\pounds}\right)_{t-1} + 2.27(P_\$)_{t-1} - 14.86 Q_{1t}$$
$$(29.6) \quad (0.24) \qquad \qquad (0.17) \qquad \quad (6.78)$$
$$+ 0.53 Q_{2t} + 1.00 Q_{3t},$$
$$(7.01) \quad \ (6.99)$$

with the parentheses enclosing the estimated standard deviations of each of the coefficients. These are the square roots of the variances.

In large samples, the sampling distributions of the estimated coefficients tend toward the normal distribution. If the disturbances are normal variables, this would be true of any size sample. It is known from tables of the normal distribution, that a range made up of 1.96

Statistical Demand Analysis 47

standard deviations on either side of the mean cuts off 95 per cent of the area under the curve. We, therefore, say that the estimated coefficient, plus or minus approximately two standard deviations, forms a 95 per cent confidence interval for the estimate. We mean that in repeated samples, if such an interval were constructed about the estimated value of the coefficient, there would be a tendency to include the true value of the coefficient in the interval 95 per cent of the time. These intervals show bands of uncertainty for the parameter estimates. In small samples, instead of using 1.96 from the normal distribution, we use a multiplier $t_{.05}$ from the table of the t-distribution. For each sample size, adjusted for degrees of freedom, this table gives a value of t for the five per cent level of probability. In samples of size 40, the $t_{.05}$ value is 2.021, whereas in samples of size 20, it is 2.086. The choice of a 95 per cent level of confidence (five per cent level of error) is arbitrary but fairly conventional. For smaller levels of confidence, the multiplier is smaller and for higher levels, the multiplier is higher.

It is frequently of interest to ask whether a confidence interval for a parameter estimate includes zero as a possible value for the unknown true value. The zero value is critical since a variable with a zero coefficient in a linear equation carries no weight in the equation; it may as well have been omitted. Indeed, the problem of statistical inference can be turned about and changed from a problem of interval estimation into a test of a hypothesis. The interval can be viewed as consisting of all the acceptable hypotheses for a given probability level.

Starting out with an a priori hypothesis (the null hypothesis) about the size of the coefficient to be estimated, let us say a zero value, we calculate the probability of getting a t-value, or normal curve deviate, as large or larger than that actually found in the sample. The smaller is the value of this probability, that is, the larger is the t-ratio or normal deviate, the less inclined is the statistician to accept the null hypothesis. If the probability is less than some critical value, usually put at five per cent, we say that the underlying hypothesis of the zero coefficient is in conflict with sample facts and accept the role of the variable in the linear equation as significant.

In the numerical example, the t-ratios of the coefficients of relative prices and of production are both much larger than two. Therefore the probabilities associated with these estimated values are less than five per cent, and we judge zero values as being unlikely. We claim that the variables are significant. The constant term in the equation and the seasonal indicator for the first quarter are both significant. We cannot, on the other hand, reject the hypothesis that the coefficient of Q_{2t} or of Q_{3t} is zero. These seasonal indicators are not significant.

Other tests are possible, but the t-test is one of the most common in econometrics. This test need not be confined to a zero critical value. In many economic problems we are interested in the divergence of parameters or simple functions of them from unity or some other figure. The appropriate ratio is

$$t = \frac{a - \alpha}{S_a},$$

where

a = parameter estimate,

α = assumed or hypothetical value,

S_a = sampling error of the estimate.

If α is zero, the ratio is simply

$$t = \frac{a}{S_a}.$$

QUESTIONS AND PROBLEMS

1. Let the market demand for good i be represented as

$$x_i = 10 - .45 \frac{p_i}{p} + .07 \frac{y}{p},$$

where

x_i = quantity demanded of good i,

p_i = price of good i,

p = general price level,

y = money income.

Find the elasticity of demand with respect to p_i/p for values

(i) $x_i = 5,$ $\frac{p_i}{p} = 15,$ (ii) $x_i = 10,$ $\frac{p_i}{p} = 12.$

Statistical Demand Analysis

Is the elasticity with respect to p_i/p different from that with respect to p_i? In answering this question, does it matter whether p_i is a negligible or significant component of p?

2. Linear arithmetic and linear logarithmic demand functions have been suggested as possible parametric forms to be used in statistical demand analysis. Can you suggest other possible forms of statistical demand functions? For what commodities would you use such functions? Do they satisfy the homogeneity conditions?

3. In simple (bivariate) correlation theory there are two possible least squares regressions. In demand analysis, we might view these as the regression of price on quantity or the regression of quantity on price. For typical samples of economic data, which regression do you think would give the higher estimate of price elasticity?

4. In comparing the goodness-of-fit of a linear arithmetic versus a linear logarithmic demand function to the same sample of data, are the respective correlation coefficients, when one is in arithmetic and the other in logarithmic units, good statistics to use?

5. In Problem (1) p. 32, series are given on monthly (change in) coffee imports and price. Form the least squares regression of quantity on price (two months earlier). Compute regression coefficients, correlation coefficient, residuals, variance of residuals, and sampling error of the regression slope. Analyze the significance of your results.

STATISTICAL DEMAND FUNCTIONS—THE DEMAND FOR MEAT AND FOR FRUIT IN THE UNITED STATES

Because of the time lag involved and the dominance of the dollar area economies over the rest of the world, it makes sense to assume a one-way direction of causation in the example above of the United Kingdom exports to the dollar area. For smaller and less influential countries than the United Kingdom, it would be even more legitimate to assume one-way directions of causation with or without benefit of time lags. In studying American demand vis-à-vis the rest of the world, this type of assumption would not be justified.

The nature of the economic process, whether it is due to theoretical or institutional factors, should be brought to bear intimately on the statistical procedures used. This is an important lesson to be derived from modern econometric thought. We now turn to an example in which the causal chain direction is reversed, and examine the consequent shift in statistical approach to the problem. Consider the demand for a perishable agricultural product in a self-sufficient country. This is the type of market with which Henry Schultz was primarily concerned. Thus we are brought into contact with the substance of early econometric work.

The line of causation is not from market prices to demand. Supply is partly related to price, but with a definite time delay as a result of the necessary period to sow and to reap. It is also, as was mentioned earlier in connection with identification, very much affected by rainfall, temperature, hours of sunshine, wind, pestilence, and numerous other natural causes. We might justifiably assume that supply is predetermined at point in time t. Since the product is assumed to be perishable, supply is virtually the same as demand.[15] Current price is influenced by the clearing of the market, therefore we assume a one-way causation from quantity to current price. If income is included as another demand variable we might assume, with much less justification and only as a first approximation, that the industrial economy influences agriculture but not vice versa.

Statisticians at the United States Department of Agriculture have for many years made statistical estimates of demand elasticities for farm products. In one of these studies K. Fox estimated demand functions for a large number of detailed food products. He chose the form

$$\log p_t = \alpha_0 + \alpha_1 \log X_t + \alpha_2 \log Y_t + u_t,$$

p_t = price during time period t,

X_t = per capita production during time period t,

Y_t = per capita disposable real income during time period t,

u_t = random disturbance during time period t.

In some cases he introduced supplies or prices of related commodities and other special variables, but the essence of his general approach is contained in the equation connecting the three variables above.

For purposes of statistical estimation he made a further specifica-

---

[15] In some cases, production may be unharvested, thus causing supply in our sense of a predetermined variable to be different from demand.

tion about the random error. He assumed that u_t was highly serially correlated from period-to-period (year-to-year) in his sample. He, in fact, assumed

$$u_t = u_{t-1} + v_t,$$

where v_t is a random variable without serial correlation. This implies a serial correlation coefficient of *unity* in the original disturbances.

If the basic demand equation holds for the t-th period it also holds for the $t - $ 1st period.

$$\log p_{t-1} = \alpha_0 + \alpha_1 \log X_{t-1} + \alpha_2 \log Y_{t-1} + u_{t-1}.$$

On subtracting the equation for period $t - 1$ from that for period t, we get

$$\log p_t - \log p_{t-1} = \alpha_1(\log X_t - \log X_{t-1}) + \alpha_2(\log Y_t - \log Y_{t-1}) + u_t - u_{t-1},$$

or

$$\Delta \log p_t = \alpha_1 \Delta \log X_t + \alpha_2 \Delta \log Y_t + \Delta u_t.$$

From the condition imposed on u_t and u_{t-1}, we can write this as

$$\Delta \log p_t = \alpha_1 \Delta \log X_t + \alpha_2 \Delta \log Y_t + v_t,$$

in which the disturbance term is now a random variable without serial correlation. Transformations to first differences are often used in econometrics to avoid serial correlation in residual variation and is a valid procedure so long as the true disturbances can be assumed to have a serial correlation of unity.

For a sample of annual data covering the interwar period 1922-1941, Fox has estimated the demand for meat as[16]

$$\Delta \log p_{mt} = -1.07 \Delta \log X_{mt} + 0.86 \Delta \log Y_t.$$
$$\phantom{\Delta \log p_{mt} = -1.}(.07)\phantom{\Delta \log X_{mt} + 0.}(.07)$$

A similar equation has been estimated for fruit.[17]

$$\Delta \log p_{ft} = -0.94 \Delta \log X_{ft} + 1.06 \Delta \log Y_t.$$
$$\phantom{\Delta \log p_{ft} = -0.}(.12)\phantom{\Delta \log X_{ft} + 1.}(.21)$$

Both of these equations are estimated by the method of least squares as developed above. They are regressions (or multiple correlations)

---

[16] See K. Fox, *Econometric Analysis for Public Policy* (Ames: Iowa State University Press, 1958) p. 75 and 105.
[17] *Ibid.*

of prices on production and income, all variables being first differences of logarithms.[18] By reversing the transformation from first differences back to levels, the constant term α_0 can be estimated by assuming that the mean value of u_t is zero.

$$\text{mean log } p_t = \alpha_0 + \alpha_1 \text{ mean log } X_t + \alpha_2 \text{ mean log } Y_t.$$

The two normal equations for estimating α_1 and α_2 are

$$\sum_{t=1}^{19} \Delta \log p_t \Delta \log X_t = \alpha_1 \sum_{t=1}^{19} (\Delta \log X_t)^2$$
$$+ \alpha_2 \sum_{t=1}^{19} \Delta \log Y_t \Delta \log X_t,$$

$$\sum_{t=1}^{19} \Delta \log p_t \Delta \log Y_t = \alpha_1 \sum_{t=1}^{19} \Delta \log Y_t \Delta \log X_t$$
$$+ \alpha_2 \sum_{t=1}^{19} (\Delta \log Y_t)^2.$$

Since the equations are written in logarithmic variables, elasticity coefficients are easily obtained. The numerical value for $-\alpha_1$ provides an estimate of *price flexibility*. Its reciprocal is an estimate of price elasticity.[19] The price elasticity of demand for meat is 0.93 (subject to sampling error), and for fruit it is 1.06 (subject to sampling error). The respective income elasticities are 0.80 (subject to sampling error), and 1.13 (subject to sampling error). Both products have nearly unit price or income elasticity, a rather high coefficient for agricultural products, in general, but both these goods tend to have more of a "luxury" character than do the great majority of agricultural products. There is no a priori reason to believe that these elasticity coefficients are unreasonable.

THE USE OF CROSS-SECTION DATA IN DEMAND ANALYSIS

Econometricians are poor in their ownership of revealing bodies of statistical information. We take whatever samples we can get and

---

[18] In first-difference form, the constant term is excluded from the regressions, as we have written them. Therefore standard methods of multiple correlation applied to this problem must take this fact into account.

[19] Meat can be stored for limited periods of time. Therefore the use of a production variable in the demand function for meat includes demand for storage as well as for export. The estimated parameters do not reflect, directly, domestic consumer demand elasticity.

try to do the best possible job with them. There is no reason to stop with the gathering of samples based on time-series aggregates of the types used in the preceding examples. In such samples we estimate fundamental parameters on the basis of time variation, from period to period, of economic quantities for an individual economic unit or an aggregate of units and for an individual good or an aggregate of goods. We could equally well base our estimates on a different type of variation, namely, spatial, instead of time, variation arising from inter-individual differences at a given point of time. A sample of inter-individual differences will be called a *cross-section* sample. In general it provides us with new and independent information which should not be neglected by econometricians. In the present context of demand analysis a cross-section sample will be a sample of family budgets showing expenditures on main items of family consumption, together with information on family income, family composition, and other demographic, social, or financial characteristics.

Henry Schultz, in his great pioneering study on statistical laws of demand, chose to confine his empirical work to aggregative time-series samples. In two recent contributions on statistical demand analysis, Stone and Wold rely on both time-series and cross-section data.[20] The use of cross-section data has a long history certainly dating back as far as Le Play and Engel.[21] Engel's laws are crude approximations to some of the patterns of regularity that we seek to establish in modern econometrics, and, in fact, the term "Engel curve" is still widely used to show the variation in family expenditure associated with variations in family income. To a large extent, the collection of family-budget data for econometric purposes comes about as a by-product of the construction of cost-of-living or consumer-price indexes. Now they are widely used in statistical demand analysis.

A family-budget sample is usually collected by personal interview surveys with individual families during a short interval of time. The sample is frequently based on probability calculations and designed to be representative of some universe of consumers, say a whole nation.

[20] R. Stone, et al., *Consumers' Expenditure and Behaviour in the United Kingdom, 1920-1938* (Cambridge: Cambridge University Press), 1954. H. Wold, and L. Juréen, *Demand Analysis* (New York: John Wiley and Sons, Inc.), 1951.

[21] An excellent collection of Engel curve estimates from family-budget data in a great many different countries is given in H. S. Houthakker, "An International Comparison of Household Expenditure Patterns, Commemorating the Centenary of Engel's Law," *Econometrica*, Vol. 25 (1957), pp. 532-51.

Let us consider food expenditures as a concrete example. This is the item dealt with in Engel's law. **"The percentage of income spent on food declines as income increases."**

If we were to subject a proposition like this to scientific statistical test, ideally we ought to single out a particular sample of families and allow their incomes to vary, *keeping all other relevant factors constant,* and observe the variations in the percentages of their incomes spent on food. In an ordinary time-series sample we observe an average of this percentage over successive periods when other

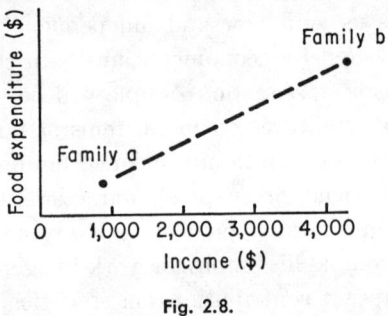

Fig. 2.8.

variables as well as income are changing. These observations are recorded as the actual outcomes of purchase decisions and not as controlled experimental readings for the ideal case. A family-budget survey generally provides information for several hundreds or thousands of families on expenditures and incomes during some fixed interval of time. The data may be for a week, a month, or possibly a year preceding the inquiry date. If two families with different incomes are selected from the sample, they will usually have different expenditures as in Fig. 2.8.

Family *b* has larger income and expenditure than does family *a*. The basic assumption in cross-section analysis is that family *a* would spend as much on food as family *b* does if its income were as large as *b*'s. There may be a time delay in the adoption of new habits of spending, and if *b* has been in its income position long enough to acquire fully the spending habits of people at that level, it is only in the long run that we can expect *a*'s spending to be patterned after that of *b*'s when its income changes to *b*'s level. Thus we generally expect to estimate long run relationships from this type of data. A picture with two families is, of course, extreme and simply shows

Statistical Demand Analysis

the sorts of variations being discussed. The typical sample will appear as in Fig. 2.9. The average drift in this scatter of points is the estimate of the expenditure-income relationship. In econometric time-series analysis, we assume that *differential periods of time are homogeneous*, except for differences in the explicit variables of the system that we measure, and for differences in random effects. Over long historical sweeps of time, this assumption may become very tenuous. In the analysis of cross-section data, we assume that *different people are homogeneous*, except for the differences in the measurable

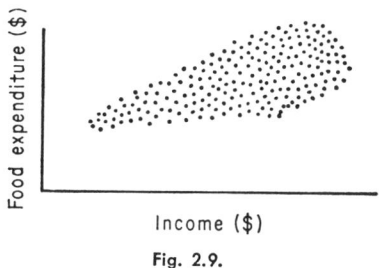

Fig. 2.9.

variables of the problem and a random error. Are people alike in their food expenditures, except for differences accounted for by income variations? This is a basic question confronting the user of a family-budget survey sample.

The theory of demand would suggest that individual expenditure depends on the whole set of prices of goods in the consumer's budget and on income. In Fig. 2.9 we have considered income alone as an explanatory factor, but if the sample is asked about expenditures during a specific time period in the past, all individuals were faced by the same market conditions except for possible geographical differentials of a low order of importance. A significant fact about cross-section samples for a single period is that price variables, and indeed other market variables such as interest rates and wage rates, are effectively held constant. This is not to say, however, that everyone in a sample pays the same prices for all food items. Actual prices paid as a result of quality and product differentiation within the broad groupings, in fact, vary from family to family and are probably systematically related to income levels, but all families in the sample are faced with the same market possibilities over a given period of time.

The *ceteris paribus* assumptions applied to the gross scatter of

Fig. 2.9 involve us with considerations similar to those in the application of the assumptions to the gross time-series scatter of Fig. 2.2, but with different variables being relevant. The number of persons in the family, their age, the strenuousness of their work, their social tastes, and similar personal factors may well have independent effects on food consumption apart from income differences. In family-budget surveys dealing with individual family units there are many

TABLE 2.3
Food Expenditure by Income Class and Family Size
Survey of Consumer Expenditures, 1950, U.S.A.
White Families Living in Large Cities in the North

	Average Food and Beverage Expenditures ($)					
Income class ($)	Single consumer	Two person family	Three person family	Four person family	Five person family	Six or more person family
Under 1,000	349	614	1,578	1,027	360	
1,000-1,999	577	730	898	867	1,082	
2,000-2,999	809	944	1,077	1,240	1,413	1,356
3,000-3,999	820	1,098	1,261	1,315	1,475	1,661
4,000-4,999	1,400	1,287	1,450	1,533	1,691	1,851
5,000-5,999	1,276	1,511	1,602	1,668	2,047	2,127
6,000-7,499	1,668	1,487	1,790	1,910	1,981	2,110
7,500-9,999	2,125	1,810	1,994	2,353	2,276	2,740
10,000 and over	2,075	2,685	2,745	2,501	3,613	3,342

such "nuisance" variables that must be taken into account in the statistical estimation of demand parameters. Average age, average family size, regional distribution of families, and similar variables may change only gradually over time. Therefore economic applications of estimated demand functions, which are also averages in their final form, may attach little significance to these factors. That is why we call them "nuisance" variables. They can, however, be quite important in obscuring the underlying relation between expenditure and income because such demographic and other personal characteristics do vary widely among individuals in a single cross-section sample.

In the case of food consumption, the most important "nuisance" variable is family size. In simulating a controlled experiment, we can classify a sample into different groups according to the family size and examine the expenditure-income relation in each group. In Table 2.3 the data for such a tabulation, together with a control

Statistical Demand Analysis

on two other "nuisance" variables, race and city type, are given for the United States in 1950. These data come from the 1950 Survey of Consumer Expenditures in which almost 12,500 consumer units were interviewed throughout urban areas of the country on their expenditures, incomes, assets, debts, and other economic, social, or financial characteristics. They show the average expenditure among all consumer units within a given income class when the selected units are restricted to being of a given size (one, two, three, four, five, or six or more persons), white, and living in a large northern city. Such averages would be obtained as in Fig. 2.10. The large crosses are

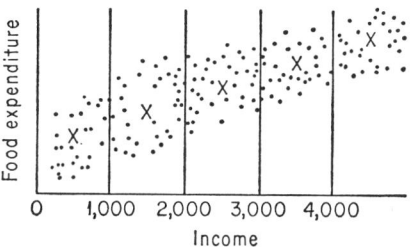

Fig. 2.10. The relation between food expenditures and income for a given family size

simple arithmetic averages of the expenditure values associated with the dots in each of the income columns. Instead of considering the highly dispersed pattern of the individual dots we look at the smoother pattern depicted by the arrangement of crosses which will fit an average line or curve of relationship between expenditure and income. For each family size, a new graph will be given by the sample data.

Broadly speaking, the figures in Table 2.3 show a regular growth of expenditures as income increases (growth within a column of the table), and as size increases (growth within a row of the table). Sampling fluctuations will cause occasional reversals in the table.[22] There are many different ways of dealing with the nuisance effect of family size. One can compile tabulations, as we have done, and fit a numerical relationship for each size class. The expenditure and income data can be expressed on a per capita basis by dividing each

---

[22] The two cases of relatively high expenditure in the lowest income class (income under $1,000 and family size of three or four persons) are probably explained by the presence of some families with temporarily low income for the survey year who are living on past savings or credit at a higher level than is customary for people who are permanently at such low income levels. The lowest income class may also include some old people with small incomes who are living on capital.

family's variables by the number of persons in the family. This procedure is sometimes refined by expressing all variables *per equivalent adult* instead of per person. The equivalent adult scales give different scores to people depending on their stage in the typical life cycle. Another alternative would be to introduce a separate numerical variable into a trivariate relationship (food expenditure, income, and family size).

Without classifying by race, Houthakker in his international study of Engel's law estimated a trivariate relation for this particular American sample. He expressed expenditure and income as logarithms and computed, by the method of least squares, the equation

$$\log E_f = \alpha + \beta \log Y + \gamma \log N + u,$$

E_f = expenditure on food,

Y = total expenditure,

N = number of persons in family,

u = error.[23]

His calculations give

est β = 0.693 (sampling error 0.017),

est γ = 0.224 (sampling error 0.016).

This computation is for large cities in the North and was repeated for different city size classifications over the country. For all classes of American cities pooled together he estimates

est β = 0.692 (sampling error 0.002),

est γ = 0.221 (sampling error 0.002).

The coefficients are nearly the same, but as a result of the enlargement of the sample from about 3,300 to about 12,500 the sampling errors have fallen drastically. A large part of the decrease in sampling error is also accounted for by the increased spread of the explanatory variables as the geographical coverage is widened.

[23] Houthakker uses total expenditure instead of income as an explanatory variable in his Engel functions. This is done partly to achieve homogeneity throughout his international collection of samples since income variables are not always available in past family-budget surveys. In recent years, some research workers have argued that total expenditure is a better classifying factor and explanatory variable in Engel functions because it is more closely related to the permanent economic status of individuals than income. Income is more likely to include transitory and unexpected elements.

Statistical Demand Analysis 59

The logarithmic relationship has the property of constant elasticity. The coefficient of log Y is the income (or total expenditure) elasticity estimate. In this sample, as in all the international samples investigated by Houthakker, the income elasticity of demand for food is less than unity, as should be the case with necessities, in support of Engel's law about the decline in percentage spent as income rises. It is this type of equation, based on interfamily differences, that is used as supporting evidence for a law which, ideally, represents the way a given family would behave under differing income situations with other variables held constant.

The coefficient of family size in Houthakker's numerical equations shows the influence of economies of scale. As a family grows in size, the percentage increase in outlay needed to feed the expanded family is much less than the percentage growth in family size.

If the total family-budget is split into four main groups, food, clothing, housing, and all other items combined, food and housing are generally estimated, by Houthakker, to have income elasticities of less than unity, whereas the clothing and miscellaneous groups have elasticities of more than unity. The former two may be called necessities and the latter two luxuries by this criterion.

The use of cross-section samples in this way to estimate income elasticities is certainly a net contribution to our fund of econometric knowledge, but some critical remarks are in order to help students appraise the validity of this approach. Individual family differences are very large, and a large number of "nuisance" variables must be taken into account in order to be sure that we measure the relevant income elasticity which is not covered up or confounded by other effects. In Table 2.3 we have taken account of race, city size and location, family size, and income. Age, other characteristics of family type, wealth, recent income change, and education are examples of plausible variables that can be obtained from sample survey inquiries that should be considered for explaining at least some components of expenditure. Elaborate cross-classifications, or the ultimate disaggregation into the original family units (12,500 joint observations in the 1950 Survey of Consumer Expenditures), exhibit much more variability than do the averages in the grossest of classifications. Hence, it may be more difficult for the statistician to isolate the underlying pattern of regularity. In Fig. 2.10 the heavy crosses follow a regular path with little dispersion, but the multitude of individual dots are widely dispersed. In several dimensions wider dispersion is more difficult to comprehend, yet it is of the utmost importance that one is not misled by seeming regularities that are not basic, and that one goes far in making different families homogeneous, except in respect of the explicit variables of the problem.

In many family-budget surveys the finest detail may give figures on pounds of meat, flour, bread, and so on. Items of clothing, fuel, and other components of a budget may be in physical units. In broader groupings, such as the four mentioned above, monetary units are used. In these cases we may be concealing the fact that people in higher income classes buy higher priced items of superior quality in the same general line of merchandise than do poorer people. There is an element of trading-up in most Engel curve estimates. Elasticities computed in physical terms may be lower than those computed in value terms. Unless one has an explicit measure of trading-up to be used as a separate variable or as a correction factor for monetary expenditure, the results may be misleading. This is especially important when we come to the question of combining estimates from cross-section with those from time-series samples.

QUESTIONS AND PROBLEMS

1. Some typical classes of goods and services in consumers' budgets are:

- a) food
- b) shelter
- c) clothing
- d) fuel
- e) durables
- f) recreation
- g) personal services.

Rank these by degree of price elasticity, degree of income elasticity, and goodness-of-fit for estimated demand functions.

2. Do logarithmic demand functions of the form

$$\log E_{ij} = \alpha + \beta \log y_j + u_{ij}$$

provide good graduations to all components of family expenditures and savings in the estimation of Engel curves from family-budget data?

E_{ij} = expenditure on the i-th commodity by the j-th family unit.

y_j = income of the j-th family unit.

u_{ij} = random disturbance.

Statistical Demand Analysis

Hint: Consider extreme cases of very low or very high income units. Do values of E_{ij} computed from the logarithmic function for extremes of y_j correspond to a priori notions of consumption of necessaries or luxuries by people in the extremes of the income range?

3. Why are single cross-section samples not suitable for the estimation of price elasticities of demand? Would a time-series of cross-section samples be more suitable for this purpose?

4. Expenditures by urban consumer units from a cross-section sample in Japan, April 1960, show the mean expenditures by income class in Table 2.4.

TABLE 2.4

Income class (yen per month)	Average income	Average expenditures	No. of households
Under 5,000	1,414	17,653	39
5,000- 9,999	7,279	11,958	55
10,000-14,999	12,456	14,108	129
15,000-19,999	17,725	18,529	242
20,000-24,999	22,295	22,618	381
25,000-29,999	27,316	25,786	397
30,000-34,999	32,219	30,992	336
35,000-39,999	37,279	34,590	285
40,000-44,999	42,268	39,816	192
45,000-49,999	47,226	42,046	136
50,000-59,999	54,274	49,585	193
60,000-69,999	64,251	57,022	83
70,000-79,999	73,887	68,117	52
80,000-89,999	83,823	66,500	19
90,000-99,999	93,381	90,130	21
100,000 *and over*	131,884	113,714	27

What is the average expenditure in the whole sample? In the last column, we have the frequency distribution of income in the sample. Suppose that all incomes were to increase by five per cent, what would be the expected level of mean expenditure? Suppose that the income distribution in a later year for these same class intervals were to be 30, 49, 130, 220, 375, 410, 346, 300, 190, 135, 211, 85, 50, 25, 20, and 33. What would be the expected level of mean expenditure?

POOLING OF TIME-SERIES AND CROSS-SECTION SAMPLES

If prices or other market variables are effectively held constant in a single cross-section sample, the net relationship of demand to income can possibly be estimated from data of this type. Given this independent estimate of demand parameters associated with income, one can use time-series aggregates of market data to estimate the demand parameters associated with prices. The price parameters cannot be easily estimated from cross-section data, but possibly both sets of parameters can be estimated jointly from time-series data, as was discussed previously and as many investigators have done.[24] Why then, it may be asked, should one want to combine the two samples? Why not do the job at a single stroke from the time-series data?

To these questions there is the obvious answer, given already, that econometric information is scarce and that any fresh samples providing an independent insight should not be overlooked. There are, however, cogent reasons dealing with specific technical problems that suggest the pooling of the two types of samples. These are (1) multicollinearity, (2) the effects of income distribution, (3) identification, and (4) least-squares bias.

Multicollinearity

Multicollinearity was recognized, especially by R. Frisch, at a very early stage of development of econometrics to be a phenomenon typical of many economic time-series. It is, in broad terms, the tendency of many economic series to move together in the same trend and business-cycle patterns over time. It is an expression of common cause running through many economic variables. Relative price and income are suggested, by theory, as the two major explanatory variables in a demand function. However, the statistician will not be able to isolate their separate contributions if they move together in a time-series sample. In a three-dimensional problem associating demand with relative price and real income, the sample of time-series observations should form an egg-shaped cluster of points in space. A linear demand function is represented by the best fitting plane in this three-dimensional cluster. If relative price and real income move together, the egg-shaped cluster tends to degenerate towards a vertical plane in space. In the limiting case, where there

---

[24] Some authors have tried to estimate price elasticities from cross-section data on the basis of inter-regional price differentials, but the results obtained are generally unsatisfactory. A sequence of cross-section samples over time may perhaps be used to estimate price parameters, but such procedures have not been widely used, if at all.

Statistical Demand Analysis

is perfect correlation between relative price and real income as a result of common cause, the cluster does become a vertical plane suspended in space. There are an infinite number of best-fitting

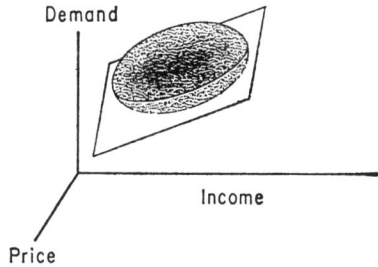

Fig. 2.11.

planes all passing through this vertical scatter of points. The goodness-of-fit is measured vertically (parallel to the demand axis), and any plane passing through the line of best-fit to the vertical scatter in two dimensions is also a plane of best-fit in three dimensions. If we carry the argument a step further and consider the case in which

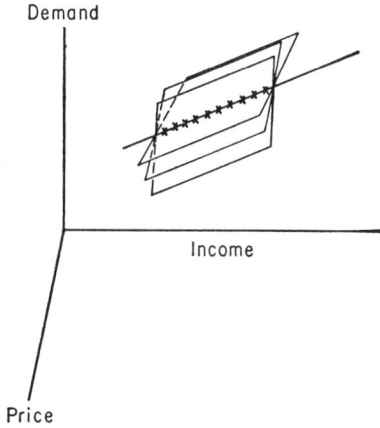

Fig. 2.12.

price and income are perfectly correlated with demand, as well as with each other, the vertical scatter of points shrinks to a line suspended in space. In Fig. 2.12, we have an unlimited number of planes passing through this line. All these planes fit the observed data equally well, for all the points along the line lie in each plane. Although we have a case of perfect multiple correlation, there is an indeterminacy as to which equation (plane) to choose as the best.

When the explanatory variables are not perfectly correlated, but merely have a high correlation, there is a tendency towards indeterminacy, but not absolute indeterminacy, of the best-fitting plane. The warning light to the statistician that multicollinearity is serious, is that sampling errors in individual coefficients become large. The separate influences of each variable are shown by their respective coefficients in a linear equation, and these coefficients will not be very precisely estimated even though the over-all correlation for the entire equation is high. Inter-correlation of the explanatory variables is a relative matter. It is not possible to say whether separate influences can be singled out if the inter-correlation is at least .6, .7, .8, .9, or even higher. The sampling error of an individual coefficient depends on both the inter-correlation with other explanatory factors and on the over-all correlation of the whole equation. If the former is high relative to the latter, indeterminacy appears.

The preceding discussion could be adjusted, *mutatis mutandis*, if price were to be explained in terms of production and income. Many demand studies, however, have been conducted by estimating a least squares correlation equation with quantity as the dependent variable and relative price and real income as the independent or explanatory variables. Often evidence of high inter-correlation between relative price and real income has been found. This has been the case in many studies of import demand for the period between the two great wars. The relative price (or terms of trade) and income effects cannot be easily separated. Hence, it was argued that the price elasticity findings from these equations would not be useful in analyzing the effects of currency devaluations such as those we had in 1949.[25]

If a prior estimate of the income elasticity is made from cross-section data and the price elasticity alone is estimated from time-series data, it is assumed that the complications of multicollinearity have been skirted. This is one of the forceful reasons in favor of combining the two sample types.

Income distribution

Income distribution is obscured in time-series aggregates, although one could conceivably prepare a time-series of dispersion, skewness, or

---

[25] See the critical analysis by G. H. Orcutt, "Measurement of Price Elasticities in International Trade," *Review of Economics and Statistics* XXXII (1950), pp. 117-32.

Statistical Demand Analysis

some other characteristics of the income distribution besides its average, and use these directly in estimates of a demand function from a time-series sample without prior analysis from family-budget data. However, the straightforward and the soundest way to examine the effects of income distribution on demand, is to examine the expenditure-income relation at the individual level where the relative position of different people in the income distribution can be readily observed and correlated with actual expenditure decisions. Indeed, a general advantage of cross-section sample data is that they bring us in close contact with the decision-making units at the microeconomic level.

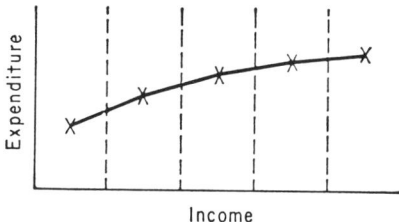

Fig. 2.13.

A simple linear relationship between expenditure and income for each individual in a sample will aggregate into the same form of linear relationship for time-series aggregates, provided the basic behavior pattern does not change. This point of aggregation has already been demonstrated above (p. 25). If, however, the expenditure-income relationship is nonlinear, aggregation is not as simple. It was shown above that a parabolic relationship aggregates so that the variance of the income distribution, as a time-series variable, must be included in the aggregative equation. For different types of nonlinearity and different types of income distribution the aggregation results may work out in varied ways.

A general method of aggregating a nonlinear expenditure equation can be illustrated graphically. Within each class of income from a family-budget survey, the average expenditure is computed as shown by the crosses in Fig. 2.13. The relationship is curved. Average expenditure, for any time period in a sample, can be computed, as an estimate, from this graph by weighting the average amounts in each income class by the fraction of the population estimated to be in that class. Let us call w_{jt} the fraction of families in the j-th income class in the t-th time period, and $\bar{E}_j$ the average expenditure in the

j-th income class in the survey. Average expenditure for the t-th period is estimated as

$$\bar{E}_t = \sum_{j=1}^{n} w_{jt}\bar{E}_j,$$

where there are n income classes.

From reports of tax authorities or sample surveys, it is possible to construct an annual series of fractions in each of several income classes. Thus the w_{jt} may be available for each yearly time period to show the effects of a changing income distribution. If the distribution of income were to remain fixed, there would be no necessity for taking this factor into account in combining cross-section with time-series data. In the absence of frequently repetitive data on income distribution, it is common to make some highly simplifying assumption such as that every family's income changes by periods in the same direction and by the same proportion as does the total social income. On this assumption, one can obtain estimates of the income distribution for a whole series of time periods starting from a given distribution for the fixed period of the family-budget survey.

Computed expenditure, $\bar{E}_t$ in the preceding formula, is a value that depends on the level and distribution of income. When it is subtracted from the actual expenditure of each period, we obtain the residual expenditure that is not already accounted for by fluctuations over time in the level and distribution of income.

The expenditure averages by income classes are valued in the price system of the period during which the sample survey occurred. The weights from income distributions of periods different from the base period should be based on income values suitably adjusted for changes in the general level of prices. Alternatively, it would be possible to revalue the average expenditure figures, instead of the income figures, to the system of current prices. However, this would take us away from the basic assumption that demand depends on real, instead of money, income and relative, instead of absolute, prices. The computed residual variable, with appropriate adjustments for changes in the general level of prices, is then correlated with a time-series of relative prices to estimate price elasticity or some other price parameter. This is the essence of the technique of pooling the two bodies of statistical information. The formal mechanics of this will be set out below. At this stage we continue our discussion of reasons for using cross-section samples.

Statistical Demand Analysis

Identification

Identification has already been discussed from a conceptual point of view. It is a definite problem in the interpretation of equations computed from observations which are themselves the outcome of the mutual interplay of such equations in the market process. Without going into the specification of the supply side of the market and the forces of price and income determination, one cannot be sure that a computed equation can, in fact, be identified as a demand function. The income parameters estimated from Engel curves in a cross-section sample of family budgets are not, in the same way, confounded with supply parameters. Family-budget statistics, to be sure, are parts of a more detailed solution of a very large system of microeconomic equations, but they are displayed in patterns that are clearly based on demand behavior. We introduce curvature to show how expenditure functions ought to appear on the basis of consumer demand behavior alone, quite independent of supply or other economic behavior. Specific nonlinearities may give identifying information. Moreover, a single body of economic agents is associated with family-budget observations; namely, the household units. Aggregative market data may, on the other hand, be attributed to bodies of either producing or consuming units.

The fundamental assumptions that are called into play in order to interpret the drift of the scatter of interindividual differences as part of a structural demand function imply, as was explained above, that parameters or elasticities are *long-run* and not *short-run* in character. Therefore, as far as the identification problem is concerned, the Engel curve estimates must be identified as long-run parameters. This point must be kept in mind when combining them with time-series data for the estimation of parameters that may be of a short-run nature. This is a difficulty of pooling the two bodies of data. It is not to say that pooling cannot usefully be done, but it must be done properly and carefully. It can then actually assist in identification.

Bias

Bias inherent in the use of the principle of least squares correlation theory for curve fitting has, for the most part, been avoided in the examples dealt with thus far. We have carefully selected cases in which the causation pattern is likely to be one-way from the explanatory or independent variables to the dependent variables. In cases of this sort, the ordinary theory of correlation, which deals with one single equation at a time is appropriate in the sense that it avoids statistical bias. If the causal pattern is not uni-directional, the fitting or estimating procedure should be generalized from single equation methods to equation systems methods and the latter are much more complicated and intricate.

The principle of least squares for estimation of parameters in a single equation implies the assumption that the explanatory variables are statistically independent of the random error term. This is the approach to the methods of estimation presented earlier. It is not difficult to show that the independence assumption, in turn, is the same thing as one-way causation. Let us suppose that we want to estimate an equation of the form

$$x_t = \alpha + \beta y_t + u_t,$$

in which there is not one-way causation. This would mean that in addition to the equation above, there must be at least one other equation in the system associating these two variables

$$y_t = \gamma + \delta x_t + v_t.$$

From the second equation we find that $\sum_{t=1}^{T} u_t y_t$ cannot generally be assumed to vanish, as we require in the least squares estimation of the first, since

$$\sum_{t=1}^{T} u_t y_t = \gamma \sum_{t=1}^{T} u_t + \delta \sum_{t=1}^{T} u_t x_t + \sum_{t=1}^{T} u_t v_t$$

$$= \delta \sum_{t=1}^{T} u_t x_t + \sum_{t=1}^{T} u_t v_t.$$

In this expression, we have made use of the fact that $\sum_{t=1}^{T} u_t$ vanishes because u_t has a zero average. The left-hand side of our derived expression cannot vanish because $\sum_{t=1}^{T} u_t x_t$ does not vanish, and there is no reason to expect it to be the negative of $\frac{1}{\delta} \sum_{t=1}^{T} u_t v_t$. This situation would not occur if y_t were in a one-way relationship with x_t and had its own independent causal mechanism.

In the estimation of the demand for perishable agricultural commodities, it was found plausible to assume a one-way causation from production (or quantity) to price. The other explanatory variable, income in the whole economy, is less obviously assumed to be in a one-way causation relationship with either price or quantity, and this is where the cross-section sample makes its contribution. Even if the demand function being estimated concerns a single commodity that is comparatively minor in the whole economy, it is not justifiable to assume a one-way causal effect from national income to either price or quantity. One might argue that spinach price or quantity has no effect on national income while national income has a significant effect on spinach price or quantity. Neglect of the former line of causation, when it is present, cannot be said to be negligible because the bias so introduced, even though small in absolute value, is not necessarily small in relation to the size of the parameter being estimated. If demand for all consumer goods or demand for a large bloc, such as the food bloc, affects national income as well as being affected by national income the same may be true of each component of food demand, and the percentage bias introduced by carrying out statistical estimation under a patently wrong set of assumptions is not negligible.

The assumptions appropriate for cross-section data relating to individual families are quite different. If we argue that there is largely a one-way causation between family income and each component of family expenditure, we are not basing the case on the largeness of one item and the smallness of another. We are basing it on the institutional structure of society. For the most part, industrial workers and other employees take whatever income they can get for socially accepted working hours and allocate their expenditures accordingly. To some extent, people can choose leisure or consumption and can influence their investment income by not spending (saving) or spending. However, the former choice is largely restricted by contractual bargaining processes for a whole group of people, and the latter is a very long-run matter open to a select few. The least squares correlation of expenditure and income at the microeconomic level in a cross-section survey is a great simplification in statistical procedure that helps to avoid the problems of estimation bias that would be present if time-series aggregates alone were used.

THE MECHANICS OF POOLING CROSS-SECTION AND TIME-SERIES SAMPLES

We have presented arguments in favor of enlarging our sample of information to include cross-section as well as time-series data. We now give the formal presentation of how this is done in a linear equation. In order to make the correspondence between the two samples of data as great as possible we shall choose a particular way of writing the demand function. Let us assume that the demand for a particular commodity x takes the form

$$x_{it} = \alpha + \beta \frac{y_{it}}{p_{xt}} + \gamma \frac{p_t}{p_{xt}} + u_{it},$$

$$i = 1, 2, \ldots, N,$$

$$t = 1, 2, \ldots, T.$$

There are N families in the society at the time of a cross-section sampling, and there are T periods in a time-series sample. This linear equation meets the usual homogeneity requirements of economic theory; it depends on relative price and deflated income.

The cross-section sample is taken at some particular time point. Let us call it t_0. The observations in this sample are on monetary expenditure and monetary income during period t_0. We estimate, from the Engel function,

$$p_{xt_0} x_{it_0} = a + b y_{it_0},$$

$$i = 1, 2, \ldots, N.$$

The coefficient b is an estimate of β in the original demand function, while a is an estimate of $(\alpha p_{xt_0} + \gamma p_{t_0})$. This can be seen by multiplying through the original equation by p_{xt_0} and letting $t = t_0$ throughout.

$$p_{xt_0} x_{it_0} = \alpha p_{xt_0} + \beta y_{it_0} + \gamma p_{t_0} + p_{xt_0} u_{it_0}$$
$$= (\alpha p_{xt_0} + \gamma p_{t_0}) + \beta y_{it_0} + p_{xt_0} u_{it_0}.$$

In this equation the prices are fixed as of t_0, and the error term is scaled by the price multiplier. The only variable quantities are those that depend on subscript i; namely, expenditure, income, and error.

$$Z_t = \frac{1}{N} \left(\sum_{i=1}^{N} x_{it} - b \sum_{i=1}^{N} \frac{y_{it}}{p_{xt}} \right).$$

Statistical Demand Analysis

This will be per family consumption of x in time period t after having removed the effect of income variations. We now are reduced to the problem of estimating the relation

$$Z_t = \alpha + \gamma \frac{p_t}{p_{xt}} + u_t.$$

In practice, one usually forms a customary least squares regression of Z_t on p_t/p_{xt}, but in view of the discussion above on bias, this may not always be the best procedure. In the case of perishable food crops, we form the regression of price on quantity, but the synthetic variable Z_t does not have the desired statistical properties that are found in the total supply of such products. Z_t is a constructed variable that combines both quantity and real income. Since there is an income component in Z_t, it may not be satisfactory to assume that Z_t and u_t are independent, because u_t and $\Sigma\, y_{it}$ are not independent. A possible simple method of estimation in such an event would be from the two following equations.

$$\bar{Z}_t = \alpha + \gamma \left(\frac{\bar{p}_t}{p_{xt}}\right),$$

$$\sum_{t=1}^{T} Z_t x_t = \alpha \sum_{t=1}^{T} x_t + \gamma \sum_{t=1}^{T} \left(\frac{p_t}{p_{xt}}\right) x_t.$$

The first equation is merely the familiar condition that the equation pass through the point of sample means. The second is derived by multiplying both sides of the equation to be estimated by x_t, the per family consumption during period t, and summing over sample observations. We assume x_t to be independent of u_t in the case of demand for perishable agricultural commodities, or for total food consumption. This is the assumption that we have been making throughout this chapter for demand analysis in American agriculture. Thus, the summed product of u_t and x_t becomes zero, and we have the second of the two estimation equations. For other products, pooling techniques may be desirable, but they will not necessarily be used with single equation methods of estimation.

In estimating the demand for a wide variety of food products in the United Kingdom, Stone made use of the pooling technique. He estimated demand functions for items of food of the form

$$\log x_{rt} = \alpha + \beta \log y_t + \gamma \log \frac{p_{rt}}{p_t} + \delta \log \frac{p_{st}}{p_t} + u_{rt},$$

x_{rt} = consumption of the r-th food product per equivalent adult in period t,

y_t = real income per equivalent adult in period t,

p_{rt} = price index of the r-th food product in period t,

p_{st} = price index of the related s-th food product in period t,

p_t = price index of all other consumer goods in period t.

The equivalent adult scale was constructed from a priori weights assigned to different family members. In some equations, the price of more than one related good was introduced. The constant elasticity form of demand functions was used throughout.

From family-budget data of the period 1937-38 and 1938-39, Stone estimated β from Engel curves. The family-budget data on equivalent adult scales were formed into logarithms, and a simple least squares estimate was found for β. In practice, total expenditure was used instead of total income so that the computed elasticity was scaled down by a constant factor. Also, a measure of social class and an extra effect of family size were allowed for in the Engel curve correlations. The income elasticity estimated from the Engel curves was then substituted directly into the above equation with no adjustments for aggregation or any other complications in pooling procedures. With an estimate of β, call it b, he formed the synthetic variable from aggregative time-series data

$$Z_t = \log x_{rt} - b \log y_t$$

and estimated the multiple correlation equations for that variable and the relative prices. To allow for the fact that the errors u_{rt} may be correlated in time, he transformed all his aggregative variables into year-to-year differences. He formed the least squares regression of

Statistical Demand Analysis

synthetic quantity on price as though the causal pattern ran from the latter to the former. His findings for the United Kingdom in the interwar period are, for food as a whole,

estimated income elasticity = 0.53 (sampling error 0.04),

estimated relative price elasticity = 0.58 (sampling error 0.21).

A regression of quantity on price is more suitable for food consumption in the United Kingdom than in the United States because Britain is not self sufficient in agriculture. Supply is not a predetermined variable, but even in this case the world price of food imports are hardly independent of British expenditure decisions as Britain is so large in the world market. Hence, the causal pattern is two-way. Single equation methods used by Stone are subject to question.

PROBLEMS IN THE POOLING OF CROSS-SECTION AND TIME-SERIES SAMPLES

It is not necessarily advantageous to pool cross-section and time-series samples. Do estimates from the two samples have the same meaning? To answer this question we must look at various problems that we have mentioned already, that is, the problems of long-run versus short-run adjustment parameters, appropriate accounting for "nuisance" variables, and aggregation.

It need not be true that cross-section samples give estimates of parameters in purely long-run functions, whereas time-series samples give estimates of parameters in purely short-run functions. Families can be classified according to recency of income change or grouped into occupational or age classes of differing degrees of income variability in order to estimate both short- and long-run income parameters. Similarly, in time-series samples, lags and rates of change of price variables can be introduced so that both long- and short-run parameters can be estimated. In the simplest and the crudest approach, there is probably a tendency to estimate long-run parameters from cross-section samples and short-run parameters from time-series samples, but in a carefully designed study this problem can be overcome.

When Stone combined family-budget with time-series data, he looked into the effects of two important "nuisance" variables in making cross-section estimates of income elasticity. He took family size (equivalent adult scales) and social class into account as separate variables. Region, occupation on a more refined basis than social status, income change, price expectations, and other "nuisance" variables may have been important. In other countries and in estimating equations for other commodities, different "nuisance" variables have been found to be important. These can be appropriately taken into account, but it is only worth stating that the investigator must take on a heavy burden of extra computation and analysis if he is to combine the two types of samples properly.

As we noted above in connection with Houthakker's Engel curve estimates, quality differences emerge in the use of expenditure instead of physical quantity data. The variation of price by income class is, in a sense, a problem of "nuisance" variables. In pooling cross-section and time-series estimates for computing Swedish demand elasticities, Wold found some large discrepancies between income elasticities for expenditure and for quantity. Expenditure elasticities tend to be much greater than quantity elasticities. Time-series samples, however, are usually adjusted for movements in the general price level, and they tend to provide estimates of quantity elasticities.

In linear models, the aggregation problem is simple and straightforward as was shown earlier. In a logarithmic model, even though all equations are transformed to appear linear in logarithms, there is a problem of aggregation because market data for time-series aggregates are ordinary arithmetic sums, and the logarithms of these sums are not the same as the sums of logarithms. It is necessary in all but the purely linear arithmetic case to make a definite assumption about the distribution of income. In some cases it may be possible to find reasonable assumptions so that characteristics of the income distribution need not be introduced as specific variables in the time-series part of the pooling process. However, as a rule, it is necessary to introduce specific distributional measures in order to combine the microeconomic cross-section data with the macroeconomic time-series data.

In all of our treatment of cross-section data, we have introduced an enormous simplification by assuming that the unknown parameters are constant among all individual families. If this is not so, we attempt to estimate average parameters, and this leads to a much more complex theory of aggregation.

COBWEB MODELS OF DEMAND AND SUPPLY

Agricultural supply is often a predetermined variable at time point t, as we discussed above, due to the influence of weather and other growing conditions on yields. Part of the influence of factors affecting supply can be attributed to economic conditions, however, and in agricultural markets this influence is transmitted with a definite time lag. The lag is inherent in the nature of the problem because of the time required for plantings to mature. Acreage decisions are often based on the previous season's price adjusted for whatever last minute developments are known or suspected. Yield on the planted acreage determines production, and it is at this stage that growing conditions have their effect.

If we relegate, for the moment, growing conditions to the random error, a supply-demand model for an agricultural market may take the linear form

$$x_t^d = \alpha + \beta p_t + u_t,$$
$$x_t^s = \gamma + \delta p_{t-1} + v_t,$$
$$x_t^s = x_t^d + w_t.$$

Quantity demanded depends on current prices, quantity supplied depends on last season's price, and the market is cleared except for random error. The price-supply relationship with a definite lag involved is not reversible in time. Therefore the parameters of the supply equation should be estimated by forming the least squares regression of x_t^s on p_{t-1}. The causal pattern is one-way.

The estimation of the demand equation is less obvious as both x_t^d and p_t are endogenous variables in this model, and it would not seem logical to assume that either one is independent of u_t. It was pointed out earlier that the minimization of a sum of squared errors for finding parameter estimates in a linear equation is equivalent to following the implications of the assumption that the error is independent of the explanatory (independent) variable of the regression. Although it is not obvious that either endogenous variable, x_t^d or p_t, can be assumed to be independent of u_t, is there some obscure relation in the system suggesting that the assumption of one case of independence is more reasonable than the other?

Let us begin with a new assumption, namely, that u_t and $(v_t - w_t)$

are independent. The implication of this assumption is that the disturbances to demand behavior are independent of those affecting supply and market clearing behavior. If we believe that supply disturbances are strongly dominated by natural causes, whereas demand disturbances are individualistic and subjective, this independence assumption might be reasonable. Nevertheless, against this argument, we must recognize that events of a socioeconomic nature can simultaneously affect both demanders and suppliers even though these are distinct groups of people. If we are able to assume, however, that u_t and $(v_t - w_t)$ are independent, then it follows that x_t^d is independent of u_t, whereas p_t is not independent of u_t.

The supply equation may be written as

$$(x_t^d + w_t) = \gamma + \delta p_{t-1} + v_t,$$

by substitution from the equation of market clearing. We shall next transpose w_t, multiply both sides by u_t, and sum over values of t. The result is

$$\sum_{t=1}^{T} x_t^d u_t = \gamma \sum_{t=1}^{T} u_t + \delta \sum_{t=1}^{T} p_{t-1} u_t + \sum_{t=1}^{T} u_t (v_t - w_t).$$

By assumption, we know that the average of u_t is zero and that u_t is independent of $v_t - w_t$. Therefore, we set the first and last terms on the right-hand side equal to zero and have

$$\sum_{t=1}^{T} x_t^d u_t = \delta \sum_{t=1}^{T} p_{t-1} u_t.$$

The right hand side of this equation also vanishes because the random disturbances occurring at time t are independent of price at time $t - 1$. In fact, we have already used this type of assumption in estimating the supply equation from the least squares regression of x_t^s on p_{t-1}.

Thus, we are led to the conclusion that

$$\sum_{t=1}^{T} x_t^d u_t = 0.$$

However, we find by multiplying both sides of the demand equation by u_t and summing, that

$$\sum_{t=1}^{T} x_t^d u_t = \alpha \sum_{t=1}^{T} u_t + \beta \sum_{t=1}^{T} p_t u_t + \sum_{t=1}^{T} u_t^2.$$

Statistical Demand Analysis

We use the previous equation and find that

$$\sum_{t=1}^{T} x_t^d u_t = 0,$$

and the assumption that $\sum_{t=1}^{T} u_t$ is zero. Then

$$\beta \sum_{t=1}^{T} p_t u_t = - \sum_{t=1}^{T} u_t^2.$$

Hence, it would not be reasonable to assume p_t and u_t independent if we start out with the assumption that u_t and $(v_t - w_t)$ are independent.

From this analysis we conclude that the demand function ought to be estimated from the least squares regression of p_t on x_t^d instead of the other way around. Essentially, the assumptions of the problem are the same as the assumptions used earlier, that supply is a predetermined variable with a one-way causation influence on price in the demand functions for perishable agricultural commodities. There we simply formed the regression of price on quantity without further specification of the probability characteristics of the model.

All agricultural commodities are not perishable, and the supply disturbances may not be dominated by meteorological variables. We may even introduce specific weather measures as exogenous variables in the supply equation and still be left with an error term. This term will definitely not be associated with these specific weather variables, and we may not want to use the assumption that u_t and v_t are independent. If the cobweb type pattern prevails, even though u_t and v_t are not independent, we can still manage to use a form of the least squares regression, but it will be slightly different from the preceding version.

First, we should form the regression of quantity on lagged price and specific weather variables, if they are measurable and available. Other exogenous factors important in determining yields such as the use of feed concentrates, fertilizers, or the prevalence of pests may be used in addition to the weather type variable. Next, to estimate the parameters of the demand function, we form the least squares regression of price on *computed* values of supply, that is, values of supply computed from the supply regression for the actual sample values of the explanatory variables in the estimated supply function, assuming no error term to be present.[26] These *computed* values of supply will be a linear function, with numerical coefficients, of lagged or exogenous variables. Hence, they will have a one-way causal influence on price.

In the cobweb model, if demand is posited to depend purely on current price and not on past price, and if supply is posited to depend purely on past price and not on current price, the basic conditions for identification in a linear system are readily seen to be fulfilled. Any linear combination of the two equations in the model (assuming the market clearing equation to be eliminated by substitution, as it contains no unknown coefficients) will provide a linear function depending on both current and lagged price. Such a derived or "mongrel" equation cannot be a supply equation because it depends partly on current price. Similarly, it cannot be a demand equation because it depends partly on lagged price. Identification is thus achieved, and the conclusion is not altered if some exogenous variables affecting yields are introduced in the supply equation in addition to lagged price. This step would only help to improve identification of the demand equation.

The simplest form of the cobweb model is of interest as a closed sequence model showing the dynamic development of a part of the economy. Apart from the obvious applications of results in statistical demand analysis for the purpose of assessing the magnitudes of various important elasticity parameters, there remains the interesting economic question on the properties of the evolution of prices, quantities, and similar magnitudes.

Let us return to the simple model and eliminate the market clearing condition by substitution. We shall drop the distinction between quantity supplied and demanded by virtue of this consolidation and simply neglect, for ease in notation alone, the effect on the error terms as a result of combination with w_t. The model is

$$x_t = \alpha + \beta p_t + u_t,$$
$$x_t = \gamma + \delta p_{t-1} + v_t.$$

For any starting value of price p_0, we obtain

$$x_1 = \gamma + \delta p_0 + v_1$$

---

[26] Short-cut methods for performing these computations can be used. See L. R. Klein, *et al.*, *An Econometric Model of the United Kingdom* (Oxford: Basil Blackwell and Mott, Ltd., 1961), esp. pp. 220-22.

Statistical Demand Analysis

as quantity in period 1. If we equate this to the value of quantity given by the demand curve in period 1, we obtain

$$\gamma + \delta p_0 + v_1 = \alpha + \beta p_1 + u_1,$$

$$p_1 = \frac{\gamma}{\beta} - \frac{\alpha}{\beta} + \frac{\delta}{\beta} p_0 + \frac{v_1 - u_1}{\beta}.$$

In period 2, we have

$$x_2 = \gamma + \delta p_1 + v_2$$

$$= \gamma + \frac{\delta}{\beta}(\gamma - \alpha) + \frac{\delta^2}{\beta} p_0 + \frac{\delta}{\beta}(v_1 - u_1) + v_2.$$

Price in period 2 is given by

$$p_2 = \frac{1}{\beta}(\gamma - \alpha) + \frac{\delta}{\beta^2}(\gamma - \alpha) + \frac{\delta^2}{\beta^2} p_0 + \frac{\delta}{\beta^2}(v_1 - u_1) + \frac{1}{\beta}(v_2 - u_2).$$

If this sequence is followed through, period after period, to the t-th period we can write, generally,

$$p_t = (\gamma - \alpha)\left(\frac{1}{\beta} + \frac{\delta}{\beta^2} + \frac{\delta^2}{\beta^3} + \ldots + \frac{\delta^{t-1}}{\beta^t}\right) + \frac{\delta^t}{\beta^t} p_0 + \frac{\delta^{t-1}}{\beta^t}(v_1 - u_1)$$

$$+ \frac{\delta^{t-2}}{\beta^{t-1}}(v_2 - u_2) + \ldots + \frac{1}{\beta}(v_t - u_t).$$

If the demand slope β is larger in absolute value than the supply slope δ, the influence of the initial value eventually fades away to nought since $(\delta/\beta)^t$ tends towards zero as t increases if δ/β is less than unity in absolute value. Moreover, the first term on the right-hand side also tends towards the finite value $(\gamma - \alpha)/(\beta - \delta)$ if δ/β is less than unity in absolute value. This would give the ultimate equilibrium value of the system if the disturbances v_t and u_t could be neglected. It is important to show how they are carried along in the sequence. Disturbances of more distant periods in the past receive decreasing weight. Thus, the dynamic path is seen to depend on the sizes of α, β, γ, and δ. The statistical estimates give us information about the plausible evolution of the system. In addition, estimates of the variances of v and u, also produced in the econometric analysis of the sample of observed data, give us the necessary information for making a probability judgement of the effect of disturbances on the dynamic position of the system. If the estimates show that δ/β is greater than unity in absolute value, we would have grounds for expecting an explosive evolution of the system over time.

A typical agricultural market in which the cobweb pattern is evident, the American onion market, has been subjected to econometric analysis by D. B. Suits and S. Koizumi.[27] The crop is nearly always harvested and demand is practically filled by domestic production.

The demand function is estimated as

$$\log p_t = 0.681 - 2.27 \log\left(\frac{x^d}{N}\right)_t + 1.31 \log\left(\frac{Y}{N}\right)_t.$$

The quantity demanded and the disposable income are both variables expressed per capita. Therefore, population (N) is divided into x^d and Y. x_t^d is in 10 million 50 pound sacks and Y_t is in billions of constant dollars. Price is measured in units of ten cents. Common logarithms are used. This equation was estimated from a least squares regression fitted to first differences of the variables over the period 1929-52. It gives an estimate of price elasticity at 0.4 and income elasticity at 0.6.

The supply function is estimated as

$$\log x_t^s = 0.134 + 0.0123(t - 1924) + 0.324 \log p_{t-1} - 0.512 \log c_{t-1}.$$

In this equation, a linear time trend, measured from zero in 1924 ($t - 1924$), and last season's cost index (c_{t-1}) are used as additional supply variables. The cost index is measured in units of ten index points from a base of 100. Climatic or other factors affecting yields are not introduced, but they probably are not negligible in the production of this crop. This equation, too, was fitted as a least squares regression from first differences of the variables over the sample period 1924-51. The price elasticity of supply is estimated as 0.324. Hence, with a reservation for sampling error, the basic stability condition of the demand parameter (an elasticity in this form of the equation) exceeding the supply parameter (also an elasticity) in absolute value is met with here. The time trend, population growth, and the cost variable influence the actual dynamic path of this system. It is not quite as simple as the two-equation system outlined in principle above.

At worst, 95 per cent of the crop is harvested in years for which

[27] D. B. Suits and S. Koizumi, "The Dynamics of the Onion Market," *Journal of Farm Economics*, Vol. XXXVIII, 1956, pp. 475-84.

data on harvestings are available. Nevertheless, Suits and Koizumi provide an estimate of the unharvested crop, U_t, as[28]

$$\log U_t = 1.84 - 1.71 \log p'_t + 0.22 \log w_t + 2.56 \log x^s_t.$$

In this equation they introduce the New York wholesale price p'_t, which is different from the farm price used in the demand and supply functions, and an index of the farm wage rate w_t. Their demand quantity x^d_t differs from supply x^s_t not only by unharvested crop U_t, but also by net exports, that is, exports less imports.

QUESTIONS AND PROBLEMS

1. Calculate the time path of price p and quantity q from the numerical cobweb scheme

$$q^d_t = 3.0 - 0.75 p_t,$$

$$q^s_t = 0.5 + 1.1 p_{t-1},$$

$$q^d_t = q^s_t.$$

q^d_t = index of quantity demanded in period t (say crop year t),

q^s_t = index of quantity supplied in period t,

p_t = index of price in period t.

Assume a starting value in the zero-th period

$$p_0 = 1.33.$$

(i) What is the equilibrium price in this system?
(ii) Is this a point of stable or unstable equilibrium?
(iii) Change the values of the coefficients so as to reverse your answer to (ii).
(iv) What are the roles of the constant terms in the linear equations in determining the time paths of p and q?
(v) Suppose that the system has some random disturbances
   a) demand disturbances such as changes in tastes,
   b) supply disturbances such as changes in production conditions,
   c) market disturbances such as random failures to equate demand and supply.

[28] This equation is not a least squares regression since there is no time lag in $\log p'_t$ and $\log w_t$. The causal pattern is not uni-directional. It is estimated by a technique called the method of instrumental variables.

Select some random numbers to represent the above disturbances and examine the numerical time path of p when the system is disturbed by these amounts.

Compare the amplitude and periodicity of the q-series with those of the p-series.

2. The cobweb model provides an elegant explanation of price dynamics in a closed agricultural market for perishables. Can you name five markets in which this model ought to give a good explanation of behavior? Outline extensions of the model to cover the following situations:

   (i) markets for nonagricultural commodities,
   (ii) open agricultural markets in which food imports are significant,
   (iii) agricultural markets for nonperishables in which storage stocks are significant.

3

Statistical Production and Cost Analysis

If a great deal of econometric research originated with an attempt to establish empirical foundations or describe the empirical implications of the theory of consumer behavior, it is natural that a similar development should have occurred in connection with the theory of the firm. In the case of consumer theory, we are faced with subjective magnitudes and relationships which pose intractable problems of measurement. Econometricians eschew the estimation of utility functions or marginal utility conditions, and confine their attention to *derived* relationships, namely, the demand functions, as discussed in the preceding chapter. In this connection, we also had occasion to consider the supply function, at least in the process of identifying the demand function. The supply function is *derived* from the theory of the firm in a manner analogous to the *derivation* of the demand function from the theory of the consumer. However, in the case of supply, we are able to unravel the chain of underlying relations into equations that are measurable.

The theory of the firm is developed in terms of production functions and marginal productivity equations as a consequence of profit maximization. Profit, production, and input are measurable ingredients of this theory, and it is possible to estimate relationships among them that are empirical counterparts of the economist's theoretical equations. At the head of this group of relationships stands the production function, and then follow the associated marginal productivity equations. Derived relations include cost and supply functions. These will also be discussed from an econometric point of view in this chapter.

THE PRODUCTION FUNCTION

In classifying the different relationships implied by the theory of the firm according to their degree of *autonomy*, we rate the production function in a very high position. By the *autonomy of a relation*, we mean the extent to which that relation will remain valid under differing circumstances. Particularly, if we are estimating statistical relations from a sample, we mean by an autonomous relation, one that will be valid in fresh samples that may be collected under environmental conditions different from those at hand in the sample being used for estimation.

The production function is a technical or engineering relation between input and output. As long as the natural laws of technology remain unchanged, the production function remains unchanged. Economic considerations involving prices, costs, and other *market* phenomena are not germane to the production function itself. We assume that an engineering decision analogous to an economic decision has been made in establishing the production function, namely, that for any given set of inputs, engineers design production processes to yield the greatest output. The schedule of maximum output for given inputs is the production function that we are trying to measure, but the variables and parameters of the function are entirely independent of market organization or market prices and costs.

The individual firm's production function, the clearest case from a conceptual point of view, is thus a technical relation showing how inputs are transformed into outputs. There may be a single product produced by the firm or we may have joint production. In traditional economic theory we usually think of land, labor, and capital as typical inputs and the finished product as the output. The production function is

$$x = f(n, k, a),$$
$$x = \text{output},$$
$$n = \text{labor},$$
$$k = \text{capital},$$
$$a = \text{land}.$$

Output is measured as a flow of goods and services during an accounting period. If labor is measured as the number of persons on the job, it is not measured as a flow but as stock in existence at a point of time, or averaged over several points within an accounting period. However, labor may be measured in terms of man-hours, in which case it is a flow variable in the same dimensions as output. In general, when man-hour measures are available, they are preferable from an econometric point of view. Capital and land are both stock, and not flow, variables. In some cases it is possible to measure capital consumption, machine-hours, or land depletion as estimates of input flows, but generally this is not the case. In any event, such measures, when they are available, are subject to wide margins of error. For the stock variables to be meaningful input factors, we implicitly assume a constant rate of capacity utilization.

Intermediate products which result as the output of other firms in the economy, or as imports, are not included explicitly in this production function. Explicit models dealing with intermediate goods will be taken up later in a general way; at this stage we shall consider only some specific aspects of this problem.

The production function of a single firm, although clearest conceptually, is not ordinarily the objective of econometric analysis even though it could be. It is the average firm in an industry or geographical area that is usually most interesting to the econometrician. If the geographical area covers an entire nation, we might think of intermediate products, aside from imports, as cancelling out, because they appear as inputs for some components of the average and outputs for others. For the aggregate of firms within a nation, output is measured customarily as *value added*, that is, as the gross value of output less the value of intermediate goods used up in the production process. In a similar way, the value of national product for a whole country excludes the value of imported intermediate goods. An aggregate production function thus differs from the individual firm's production function in that the output variable is defined in terms of value added instead of physical units produced. Not only is there a distinction between a net and gross concept involved, but there also is a distinction between a value and a physical quantity. By using indexes of physical quantities (industrial production indexes) or deflated values of net output, we may approximate physical flows, but the purity of the production function as a technological relation has been lost. It is an aggregation problem to show how the production function for the economy as a whole is related to those of single firms.

For the economy as a whole, if there is no undeveloped frontier, land is a fixed factor of production incapable of being changed by significant amounts. For this reason the aggregate production function is expressed as a relation between value added (in a constant price system), on the one hand, and labor and capital input, on the other. Most empirical work on aggregate production functions has proceeded along these lines.

A production function for the economy as a whole could possibly be written as

$$G(x_1, x_2, \ldots, x_m; n_1, n_2, \ldots, n_r; k_1, k_2, \ldots, k_p) = 0.$$

In this general form we have distinguished among m final outputs, x_i; r labor inputs, n_i; and p capital inputs, k_i. The m outputs form a vector of all the thousands and thousands of final commodities produced in the enterprises of the economy. There are many grades of labor and their separate man-hour inputs are represented by the vector $(n_1, n_2, \ldots, n_r)$. Similarly, there are numerous capital inputs, p in all, included in this economy. The function G shows the greatest amount of x_i obtainable in the economy from all the separate producing units when all other outputs $x_j (j \neq i)$ are held constant for any combination of inputs of labor and capital.

The G function would be an ideal concept of the production function for the economy as a whole, but it is not the concept used in econometric research. In actual statistical work, we choose single indexes to represent the vector variables,

$$x = (x_1, x_2, \ldots, x_m),$$
$$n = (n_1, n_2, \ldots, n_r),$$
$$k = (k_1, k_2, \ldots, k_p),$$

and establish an approximate relation among x, n, and k. Usually the index representations are weighted averages of the vector components. Of course, one need not reduce all the individual outputs or inputs to single outputs or inputs. More detail can be obtained by distinguishing among two, three, or some small number of different types of output, labor input, or capital input. But in any event, the result is highly aggregative and only approximates, in a rough way, the ideal type of production function.

The production function for the economy as a whole, when written in terms of individual inputs and outputs, has definite meaning for a given distribution of production techniques among firms or industries. In the aggregated form all different technologies are combined so that we have a conceptually complex notion behind this macroeconomic relation. The input-output variables and the technological parameters are aggregated.

An industry's aggregative production function has clearer meaning in this respect. Technological differences exist among firms in a given industry, but there is decidedly more homogeneity in the underlying techniques for the industry's than for the whole economy's production function. For many statistical purposes, the individual firm is a fine unit of analysis. We are generally interested in some statistical average, and an industrial average has many attractive natural attributes.

Although raw materials and other intermediate goods cancel as inputs and outputs for the economy as a whole, they do not cancel within an industry. Therefore, the industrial function should include materials, fuels, and similar intermediate goods among inputs. In many studies, however, value added, corrected for changes in the general price level, has been used as an output variable for an industry's function and has thus limited the explicit significance of intermediate inputs.

At all levels of aggregation, whether treating the firm, the industry, or the nation, the presence of technical change is a complicating factor in defining and estimating the production function. As technique changes, the parameters of the production function change, and an additional complication occurs in the measurement of capital input. The aggregation of capital would be like the aggregation of other economic variables were it not that different vintages of capital goods have different technical attributes. In a world of progress, it is difficult to measure, at successive instants of time, an aggregate of capital stock or input flow, where the different components of the aggregate consist of highly durable pieces of nonuniform quality.

The empirical solution to these problems caused by the phenomenon of technical change is to measure capital stock by the conventional techniques of national income statisticians and to introduce trend variables in the production function. In national income statistics, we are usually furnished with periodic estimates of gross investment in fixed capital and capital consumption or depreciation. The latter are usually based on book value accounting estimates and not actuarial estimates. Gross investment, less depreciation, gives net investment, and successively cumulated totals of the latter from some original asset levels give series of capital stock. The formula is

$$K_t = K_0 + \sum_{i=1}^{t} (I_i - D_i),$$

K_t = stock of capital at end of period t,

K_0 = initial asset value of fixed capital,

I_i = gross investment of the i-th period,

D_i = capital consumption of the i-th period.

To measure real capital from this formula, all the component variables must be expressed in a constant price system. We are still, however, faced with the problem of quality change and the fact that all the different vintages combined in this formula are of heterogeneous quality.

In some studies, alternative capital measures may be used. Direct physical estimates, such as horsepower ratings of equipment, may be used, but these are not representative for all capital. Measures of capacity may serve as measures of capital stock, in some industries, but the conceptual problems underlying such measures are fully as difficult as those for capital stock.

In order to take account of the influence of technical change, apart from the problems it causes in the measurement of capital, we might write an aggregative production function in the form

$$x_t = f(n_t, k_t, t).$$

The time variable may take the form of an additive trend, or a trend in some of the basic parameters such as those associated with marginal productivity measures. In the following sections we shall deal with specific trends introduced in empirical production functions to account for technical change.

The data used in production analysis

As in the case of statistical demand analysis, the samples of data used in the estimation of production functions are either time-series or cross-section samples.

The time-series samples could consist of periodic observations of outputs and inputs for any degree of aggregation. For an entire country, the appropriate output variable would be the statistics of the gross national product measured in constant prices. For the major industrial sector it would be the conventional index of industrial production. The former series measures value added. Therefore, one may not find any added statistical significance by including an input variable for intermediate goods in the production function. Man-hour employment in the whole economy or in the industrial sector would be an appropriate labor input variable. These may be derived from separate statistical series on the number of persons employed and the average length, in hours, of the working period. Statistics on capital stock could be obtained from series on net investment and initial assets, either for the economy as a whole or for the industrial sector. If there are periods of substantial under-utilization of capital during the sample range, it may not be desirable to use capital stock as an input variable. The estimates of capital consumption, if reliably computed so as to reflect actual use of capital, may serve as better input variables.

In the case of estimating the production function for a firm or an industry, it may be possible to measure output directly in physical units such as tons of cement, barrels of oil, bushels of wheat, tons of steel, and so on. If a limited number of different commodities are being jointly produced by the given process, we may deal with more than one physical output variable simultaneously. In highly diversified manufacturing, it may not be possible to do anything more refined than to use the series of output values corrected for average price changes over time.

Output values for a firm or industry may be either net (value added) or gross, depending on the source of available material, but in the case of firms both values are almost certain to be available. If gross value, corrected for price change, is used as the output variable, an intermediate input variable for materials and fuel should be included in the production function. Labor and capital measures are not likely to be essentially different in estimating the production function of a firm or industry than in estimating it for the whole economy.

Data in cross-section samples may refer to individual firms, industries, or geographical regions. The most suitable cross-section samples would seem to be a collection of output and input statistics for individual firms in a given industry. If physical amounts of different outputs are not available, gross value of production could serve as the output variable. Within an industry at a given point of time firm-to-firm variations in value of output are good indicators of firm-to-firm variations in physical output. Measures of fuel, materials, and other intermediate products in either monetary or physical units should be used as input variables. In addition, man-hours or employment and capital consumption or capital stock would be used as measures of input factors.

The appropriate cross-section data to choose from firms within an industry are fairly well defined and usually available. The case of inter-industrial variations is, however, less clear. The composition of outputs and inputs varies from industry to industry because of technological differences. Value figures must be used, but they are not as good an indicator of physical data as they are for firms within an industry. In some instances, it may not be possible to obtain separate data on values of gross output and intermediate inputs. Value added figures may have to be used, but, in any case, only one intermediate input variable can generally be inserted in the production function, namely, the total value of intermediate products used.[1]

Unlike individual firm data, which may be obtained directly from reports of the firms, industry data used in a cross-section sample of several industrial groups are usually obtained in a collection like a census of manufacturing or of business. In such a census, only limited types of data are available (sometimes number of employees, sometimes man-hours of work, and sometimes only the wages bill). Capital data are even more scarce and varied. It is not possible to generalize, but one should normally be able to obtain statistics on value added, wages bill, and asset values. These are fair approximations to indicators of physical output and factor input but are obviously inferior to data used in some of the other samples on which production function estimates are based.

Studies of the Cobb-Douglas production function

The statistical investigation into laws of production by C. W. Cobb and P. H. Douglas are among the most celebrated in the history of

[1] In special cases, intermediate goods can be grouped into separate meaningful groups for an inter-industry cross section. If all the industries in the sample use both fuels and other materials, it is possible to use valuations for each of these groupings as input variables.

econometrics.[2] They have proposed the general function

$$x = An^\alpha k^\beta u,$$

x = output,

n = labor input,

k = capital input,

u = random disturbance,

as a fairly universal law of production and estimated it in numerous samples of manufacturing industries throughout the world. This

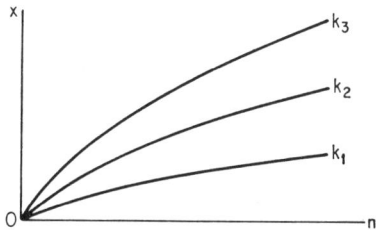

Fig. 3.1. The Cobb-Douglas production function

exponential type of production function has no more claim to general validity as a description of technology than other mathematical functions. However, it does have many interesting properties that make it a very convenient choice, and it graduates data on output and input well. This function is almost always referred to as the "Cobb-Douglas production function" when it appears, although other economists had used it independently, and even before the research of Cobb and Douglas.

The Cobb-Douglas function has constant elasticities of output variation with respect to labor or capital input.

α = elasticity with respect to labor input.

β = elasticity with respect to capital input.

The relationship is nonlinear. For constant levels of capital, the output-labor input relation is shown as the series of curved lines in Fig. 3.1. If either input is zero ($n = 0$ or $k = 0$), output is zero. Thus, both inputs are necessary to the production process. The curvature is such

[2] C. W. Cobb and Paul H. Douglas, "A Theory of Production," *American Economic Review*, Suppl., Vol. XVIII (1928) pp. 139-65.

(each elasticity assumed to be less than unity) that marginal productivity falls as input grows. There is no asymptotic level of output (or ceiling) beyond which production cannot grow, but the rate of increase decreases at high levels of input.

Although the function is nonlinear, it can be transformed with ease into a linear function by converting all variables to logarithms. In logarithms, the associated linear function is

$$\log x = \log A + \alpha \log n + \beta \log k + \log u,$$

or

$$x' = A' + \alpha n' + \beta k' + u'.$$

In terms of the primed variables we have a linear function. Scale changes in the basic units of measurement have no essential effect on any of the terms in this logarithmic formulation except the constant A'. Therefore, this function is convenient in international or inter-industry comparisons. Since α and β are elasticity coefficients, they are pure numbers and can easily be compared among different samples using varied units of measurement.

In a sense, one is able to capture the flavor of essential nonlinearities of the production process and yet benefit from the simplifications of calculation from linear relationships by transforming to logarithms. The logarithmic function is linear in the parameters, which is an essential point to the statistician. Other functions may give a similar type of curvature and keep linearity in parameters. A parabolic function would be an example.

$$x = \alpha_0 + \alpha_1 n + \alpha_2 k + \alpha_3 n^2 + \alpha_4 k^2 + \alpha_5 nk + u.$$

However, this type of equation uses many more parameters than does the Cobb-Douglas form. The latter is economical in the use of degrees of freedom, or parameters, and yet gives us nonlinearity.

The parameters of the Cobb-Douglas function, in addition to being elasticities, possess other attributes important in economic analysis. The sum of the exponents shows the degree of "returns to scale" in production.

$\alpha + \beta < 1$ decreasing returns to scale,

$\alpha + \beta = 1$ constant returns to scale,

$\alpha + \beta > 1$ increasing returns to scale.

Suppose that each input is increased by r per cent.

$$n \text{ increased to } n\left(1 + \frac{r}{100}\right),$$

$$k \text{ increased to } k\left(1 + \frac{r}{100}\right).$$

Then output is increased by less than r per cent, by r per cent, or by more than r per cent, according to whether there are decreasing, constant, or increasing "returns to scale." This is easily seen by substituting into the function

$$x = An^\alpha k^\beta u,$$

$$x\left(1 + \frac{r}{100}\right)^{\alpha+\beta} = A\left[n\left(1 + \frac{r}{100}\right)\right]^\alpha \left[k\left(1 + \frac{r}{100}\right)\right]^\beta u.$$

It is an important economic question whether the statistics of an investigation show $\alpha + \beta$ to be less than, equal to, or greater than unity. The sum of these coefficients shows the degree of "homogeneity" of the function. If $\alpha + \beta$ is equal to unity, we say that the production function is homogeneous of the first degree.

Marginal productivity of any factor is the slope of the function graphed in the output-factor input dimensions when all other inputs are held constant. In Fig. 3.1, we can visualize marginal productivity as the slope of an output-labor input curve for a given capital input. It was noted above that the marginal productivity changed as we moved along the curve at different levels of factor input. We noted, however, that the Cobb-Douglas function took on a linear form when expressed in logarithmic instead of arithmetic units. We can, therefore, write

$$\frac{\text{change in logarithm of output}}{\text{change in logarithm of labor input}}\bigg|_{\text{(capital input constant)}} = \alpha.$$

The change in the natural logarithm of some variable is the same thing as the percentage change. We can, therefore, also write

$$\frac{\text{percentage change in output}}{\text{percentage change in labor input}}\bigg|_{\text{(capital input constant)}} = \alpha.$$

A ratio of percentage changes is simply a ratio of absolute changes multiplied by the inverse ratio of levels of the two variables. The limiting value of absolute changes for infinitesimal increments is, however, our familiar concept of marginal productivity. We can, therefore, write

$$\left.\frac{\text{percentage change in output}}{\text{percentage change in labor input}}\right|_{\text{(capital input constant)}} =$$

$$\left(\frac{\text{labor input}}{\text{output}}\right) \text{(marginal productivity of labor)}$$

$$= \alpha.$$

This brings us to the important property of the function: marginal and average products are proportional, where the factor of proportionality is the associated exponent.

$$\text{Marginal productivity of labor} = \alpha \frac{\text{output}}{\text{labor input}}$$

$$= \alpha \text{ (average productivity of labor)}.$$

Similarly, we find

marginal productivity of capital = β (average productivity of capital).

The economic theory of competitive markets tells us that profit maximizing behavior by entrepreneurs leads to equality between marginal productivity and the real wage. Thus, we would have the relations

$$\alpha \frac{x}{n} = \frac{w}{p}, \qquad \beta \frac{x}{k} = \frac{q}{p},$$

$$p = \text{price of output},$$
$$w = \text{wage rate},$$
$$q = \text{price of capital inputs}.$$

A more revealing way of writing these relationships shows that the wage share of the value of output is constant.

$$\frac{wn}{px} = \alpha.$$

On a global level, the share of manufacturing or even national output value going into wages should tend toward constancy. The constant is identified with the exponent of the Cobb-Douglas function. This type of analysis and result is often cited as a rationalization of the empirical finding that "labor's share" tends to be constant. Douglas was struck by the numerical affinity between his estimates of the technical coefficients in the exponential production function and the independent aggregative statistics on factor shares in values of income streams. Not only do factor shares tend to be constant, but they also tend to give the same value as the production coefficient. In this respect, Douglas' research has been a test of theory (the marginal productivity theory of wages) as well as descriptions of production technology.[3]

In his presidential address before the American Economic Association in 1947, Professor Douglas summarized the results of a lifetime's academic career of research on the measurement of laws of production.[4] Both time-series and cross-section studies were made by Douglas and others for the manufacturing industry of the United States, Canada, Australia, New Zealand, and South Africa. Among the American studies we might select one time-series sample for the period 1899-1922 as typical for this type of data. The estimate is

$$x = 1.35 n^{0.63} k^{0.30}.$$

In this case, the variables are all defined as *deviations* from fitted trends. The estimated sampling errors associated with the exponents of labor and capital are 0.15 and 0.05, respectively. In six cross-section samples ranging from 1889 to 1919, Douglas found the average labor exponent to be 0.63 and the average capital exponent to be 0.34. In Australian studies, for the whole commonwealth and for the separate states of Victoria and New South Wales, the average exponents in nine cross-section samples (1912-1937) are 0.60 for labor and 0.37 for capital. Time-series samples for the separate states are, however, different.

$$x = 0.71 n^{0.84} k^{0.23} \quad \text{for Victoria, 1907-29.}$$

$$x = 1.14 n^{0.78} k^{0.20} \quad \text{for New South Wales, 1901-27.}$$

These time-series data were not adjusted for trend. A South African cross-section study yielded the estimate

$$x = 55.25 n^{0.65} k^{0.37}.$$

---

[3] The constancy of factor shares may not hold if imperfect competition is prevalent. Even if product demand and factor supply elasticities are constant, factor shares would not necessarily be equal to the production exponents as in the competitive theory outlined in the text above.

[4] Paul H. Douglas "Are There Laws of Production," *American Economic Review*, Vol. XXXVIII (1948) pp. 1-41.

On the whole, these results are all similar. The labor exponent is about two-thirds and the capital exponent one-third. There is slight evidence of decreasing returns to scale, but the exponent sums which do not reach unity are not significantly below unity if sampling errors are taken into account.

In the Australian state studies for Victoria and New South Wales, we find the time-series estimates somewhat different from the American study cited (the labor exponent being higher and the capital exponent being lower) but this is probably owing to the fact that no correction for trend was made in the Australian time-series investigations. When Douglas did not extract a trend from each of the American time-series (output, labor, and capital) he obtained results much like those of the Australian state studies. Professor Douglas argues that one should not be surprised by the differences between the time-series and cross-section estimates. He expects biases in indexes of output overtime, because of the introduction of new products and new processes, to lead to higher estimates of the labor exponent and to lower estimates of the capital exponent than in the cross-section samples. An exception occurs in the time-series sample where trends have been extracted from all the variables. In that case, the time-series and cross-section estimates agree more closely.

Similar studies in New Zealand and Canada, from both cross-sections and time-series, yield essentially different exponents. The exponents are nearly equal at one-half for labor and one-half for capital.

An implication of the Cobb-Douglas production function model is, as noted above, that labor's share of national production tends to be constant under competitive market conditions. The constant towards which labor's share should tend is the labor exponent in the production function. Although the estimate of this parameter is lower in Canada and New Zealand, we find the striking result that labor's share is also lower (at about the level expected on theoretical grounds). Likewise, agreement is good in the cases of the United States, Australia, and South Africa between labor's share and the estimated exponent of labor in the numerical production function. Douglas estimates the average labor exponent in cross-section Australian studies to be 0.60 and the average of labor's share in net value of product to be 0.58. The corresponding Canadian averages are 0.47 and 0.48, respectively, while for the United States they are 0.63 and 0.605. In some individual years the agreement is not close, but, on the average, the results seem to be satisfactory in testing this implication of the analysis.

Although Douglas has been a great pioneer and proponent of research into the laws of production, he has not overlooked the points at which his analysis is open to criticism. In association with our discussion of his work, however, it may be helpful to set out the major points of criticism that might be raised.

The data. Douglas' time-series data, and those of other research workers duplicating his efforts, usually consist of an index of physical production or deflated value of output, the number of employees or man-hours, and the value of capital in constant prices. Purely physical measures throughout would have been desired, but this is not possible, except for labor inputs, when aggregative data for all industry are used to estimate one macroeconomic function. The whole problem of aggregation as we developed it in the previous chapter for statistical demand analysis has been overlooked.

The output measure is usually a form of aggregate value added. This means that raw materials are not treated as a separate factor of production, but as an automatic subtraction from the total value of output. Raw materials, especially of the fuel variety, may not have the fixed relation to output that is implied by the use of the value added concept. We might illustrate this by the formulation

$$(x - m) = An^\alpha k^\beta,$$

or

$$x = m + An^\alpha k^\beta,$$

where m = materials input measured in the units of x.

Perhaps m should be treated in the same way as n and k in the production function. At different levels of productive operation there may be economies or dis-economies in the use of materials. Since the studies of the Cobb-Douglas function were often made for the manufacturing sector alone, raw materials do not cancel as intermediate goods produced and used within the same sector. Even for an economy as a whole, imported raw materials are significant factor inputs to be taken into account on the same footing as labor and capital inputs. In the Commonwealth countries studied, we find open economies where raw material imports are of great significance in the production process.

At the level of aggregation treated by Douglas, all labor is considered as a homogeneous input. This is again an index number or aggregation problem not taken up in this group of research studies. Douglas did, however, state clearly his preference for man-hour data over statistics on the straight count of employees and used the former wherever possible.

Capital measures, as pointed out earlier, are extremely difficult concepts to handle properly, either theoretically or empirically. Douglas' procedure in building up statistics of capital stock from cumulations of net investment is certainly the accepted practice. More recent attempts have perhaps been better as a result of having access to newer and superior data. Nevertheless, all the deficiencies in the depreciation estimates, changes in quality of fixed assets, and similar drawbacks should lead us to be conservative in appraising the accuracy of the numerical estimates of aggregate production functions. Douglas did not carry his American time-series studies beyond 1922 because of the complications of excess capacity in the use of capital stock as a measure of capital input.

In the cross-section samples, value of output (less the cost of materials and similar items), number of wage earners, and value of capital were the types of data used for the relevant variables. Since the cross-section studies are based on inter-industry rather than inter-plant or inter-firm variation within an industry, it was necessary to use monetary value statistics. This again introduces an aggregation problem. In the cross-section samples it was apparently not possible to use man-hour data instead of the count of men.

The samples. Apart from the pure data problems in the two types of samples, there are some other relevant points to be made. Professor Douglas' results fall into a neat pattern, for both time-series and cross-section analysis, for the United States in the period 1889-1922. There is some doubt whether his results would remain as satisfactory in later periods. He finds either slight tendencies towards decreasing returns to scale or nearly constant returns to scale. There is little evidence on the side of increasing returns. He is, of course, justified in being concerned about the problem of excess capacity affecting the capital input measure for the 1930's, but there are good reasons for believing that the American economy was functioning at a position of *increasing* returns to scale during a great deal of the period following Douglas' work.

We might argue that the true underlying curve of production

follows the usual S-shape. In this input-output relation there are phases of increasing, constant, and decreasing *marginal* returns. A sample of data usually approximates some portion of this curve in a limited range. From a limited number of observations, we do not actually estimate the entire curve but simply an approximate stretch of it. If a large cluster of sample observations is produced at an extreme region for a limited period of time, we actually estimate the portion of the curve associated with that particular sample. Although

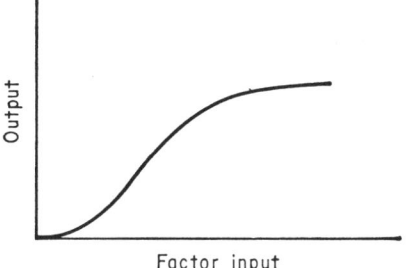

Fig. 3.2. Curve of production

the ordinary sample may be clustered in the region of decreasing returns, a sample heavily dominated by depression years may produce an estimated portion showing increasing returns. This is a possible interpretation of the results for the 1930's.

If there are increasing returns to scale, we cannot possibly have factor shares equal to corresponding exponents of the function because the sum of the exponents will exceed unity, and the sum of the shares cannot. However, the equalities between the shares and the exponents are based on the assumption of competitive markets. If there is monopoly and monopsony power, the relationship becomes

$$\text{factor share} = \text{exponent} \left[\frac{\left(1 - \frac{1}{\text{demand elasticity}}\right)}{\left(1 + \frac{1}{\text{factor supply elasticity}}\right)} \right].$$

Symbolically, we write for labor's share

$$\frac{wn}{px} = \alpha \frac{\left(1 - \frac{1}{\eta}\right)}{\left(1 + \frac{1}{\epsilon}\right)},$$

η = elasticity of demand for output,
ϵ = elasticity of supply of labor.

Depending on the relative sizes of η and ϵ, it would be possible to have α greater than unity and still have both sides of the equation less than unity.

The cross-section estimates of the Cobb-Douglas functions have usually been based on industry-to-industry variations. At least, that is the nature of the samples cited by Douglas in his grand review article on his lifetime work in this area. Most census returns would provide data of this type. Since the production process varies from industry to industry, one might interpret a sample of observations on average inputs and outputs for N industries as a scatter of points on N different production functions.

However, plant-to-plant or firm-to-firm variations within an industry would seem to provide more reasonable samples in which the nuisance variable, *technique*, is largely held constant. There is, of course, nothing in principle to prevent the use of data within, instead of between, industries for cross-section samples. In the case of an industry, however, one must take account of factors other than labor and capital. It is definitely true, in this case, that materials do not cancel mutually among firms in the sample using them as inputs and producing them as outputs. Just as Douglas has found that some countries indicate exponents of the order of (0.65, 0.35) while others show values of (0.50, 0.50), we find widely varying results among industries. Those industries employing relatively little labor and having a wage bill of much less than two-thirds of output value, will tend to have (under competition) exponents much less than the typical figure of two-thirds for the major portion of manufacturing. Thus, we get more information about the distribution of exponents among industries, as well as statistical results that are much easier to interpret, if we have samples of inter-plant or inter-firm variation within given industries instead of inter-industrial variation.

In the inter-industrial cross-section samples we encounter the problem of nonconstant technology, and a similar problem arises in the time-series sample. In the period-to-period variations over a long historical stretch, there will be much technical progress. In the cross-section sample, the nonuniform technology varies in a haphazard way, but in the time-series sample it changes gradually in a strictly chronological fashion. Two possibilities exist for dealing with this phenomenon. Explicit trend variables can be introduced in the equations, or trends can be extracted from each of the variables prior to the estimation of the parameters. In a completely linear relation with a linear

Statistical Production and Cost Analysis

trend variable or linear extraction of trend, the result is the same either way. In Douglas' work he extracted trends from the arithmetic value of variables and then fit a production function to the logarithms of adjusted values. This result is formally different from introducing a linear trend variable in the equation, but in a practical sense achieves the same results. Mechanical time variables and the extraction of mechanical trends are not the only devices for dealing with technical progress in time-series samples, but they are the most common and obvious.

Multicollinearity. As discussed in the preceding chapter on demand analysis, multicollinearity is frequently encountered in econometric time-series analysis. It may be expected that there would be high inter-correlation between capital and labor in the estimation of a production function. In cross-section samples we would expect large firms or industries to have large working forces and large capital assets and small firms or industries to have small working forces and small capital assets. This would make for high inter-correlation between labor and capital. In time-series samples we ought to find a fairly high degree of inter-correlation between labor and capital, but the former is probably more of a cyclical and the latter more of a trend variable. Therefore, the inter-correlation may not be as high as in cross-section samples.

Inter-correlation or multicollinearity is not necessarily a problem unless it is high relative to the over-all degree of multiple correlation among all variables simultaneously. Production functions with over-all correlations much in excess of 0.95, as often occur in practice, can be well-estimated with inter-correlations between labor and capital as high as 0.8 to 0.9. If these functions were not well-estimated, we would tend to find high sampling errors of the estimated coefficients. By conventional criteria, the estimated parameters of Douglas and his co-workers in this field, are large relative to sampling error. The coefficients are generally high multiples of sampling errors (certainly more than twice, which is the customary critical value for the five per cent level of significance). It does not appear that the Douglas type of research is open to the charge that the estimates are plagued by multicollinearity.

Least squares bias. In demand analysis, it was found possible to investigate a variety of interesting problems in which there was one-way causation in a single equation from one or more exogenous or lagged variables to one endogenous variable. This is, unfortunately, not the case with Douglas' study of production functions. Output, labor input, and capital input are all endogenous variables subject to simultaneous entrepreneurial decision. Associated with the technological production function are simultaneous relations involving marginal productivity conditions, possibly factor supply, and possibly product demand. Douglas' least squares regressions of output on labor and capital input assume implicitly that there is a causal flow from input to output and not vice versa. The assumption of this unique line of causation, when it is, in fact, not the case, will lead to statistical bias in the estimates of parameters. In some studies, one by R. J. Wolfson discussed below, a complete model is simultaneously estimated, taking into account several inter-relationships among the variables.[5] Wolfson confines his study to types of agricultural production, therefore his findings are not directly applicable to an assessment of bias in Douglas' studies of manufacturing production. At this stage we can only say that Douglas' results are open to the pitfalls of single-equation biases, but we are not able to judge the seriousness of this charge.

QUESTIONS AND PROBLEMS

1. Show that the Cobb-Douglas production function is a homogeneous function. Associate the order of homogeneity with the sum of the exponents. Write a linear production function that is homogeneous; that is not homogeneous.

2. Suppose that the production function is linear and suppose that the real wage is equated to marginal productivity. How would you make a statistical test of the model of production and marginal productivity? Criticize this model from an economic point of view.

3. What is the meaning of trend variables in statistical production functions? Can you suggest some *specific* trend variables? In the Cobb-Douglas function, labor and capital variables appear in the form n^α, k^β. Should the trend variable take the form t^γ?

4. Choose between the two possible probability models for fitting the Cobb-Douglas function

$$x_t = A n_t^\alpha k_t^\beta u_t$$

and

$$x_t = A n_t^\alpha k_t^\beta + u_t.$$

[5] See pp. 108-10 for a discussion of the model estimated by Wolfson.

Statistical Production and Cost Analysis

5. What mathematical properties would you impose on a production function? Consider some of the following: (a) slope, (b) curvature, (c) intercept, (d) number of variables, and (e) continuity.

6. How would you devise a statistical test for the existence of returns to scale in production (increasing, constant, decreasing)?

7. A time-series sample of U.S. statistics on aggregate production, employment, and stock of capital is given in the accompanying table. Plot scatter diagrams of production and employment and of production

TABLE 3.1

Year	Production ($bill 1929)	Employment (mill)	Capital ($bill 1929)
1921	59.6	39.4	236.2
1922	63.9	41.4	240.2
1923	73.5	43.9	248.9
1924	75.6	43.3	254.5
1925	77.3	44.5	264.1
1926	82.8	45.8	273.9
1927	83.6	45.9	282.6
1928	84.9	46.4	290.2
1929	90.3	47.6	299.4
1930	80.5	45.5	303.3
1931	73.5	42.6	303.4
1932	60.3	39.3	297.1
1933	58.2	39.6	290.1
1934	64.4	42.7	285.4
1935	75.4	44.2	287.8
1936	85.0	47.1	292.1
1937	92.7	48.2	300.3
1938	85.4	46.4	301.4
1939	92.3	47.8	305.6
1940	101.2	49.6	313.3
1941	113.3	54.1	327.4
1942	107.8	59.1	339.0
1943	105.2	64.9	347.1
1944	107.1	66.0	353.5
1945	108.8	64.4	354.1
1946	131.4	58.9	359.4
1947	130.9	59.3	359.3
1948	134.7	60.2	365.2
1949	129.1	58.7	363.2
1950	147.8	60.0	373.7
1951	152.1	63.8	386.0
1952	154.3	64.9	396.5
1953	159.9	66.0	408.0

and capital stock on ordinary arithmetic and double logarithmic paper. What type of production function would you fit to these data? Discuss problems of measurement of variables, multicollinearity, and identification with this sample in this problem.

Some problems in production analysis

Apart from the studies directly linked to the personal work of Douglas, there have been numerous statistical investigations making use, in one way or another, of an estimated Cobb-Douglas production function.

In a study of production functions for India, Murti, and Sastry take up the problem of aggregation of the Cobb-Douglas function.[6] From data on 320 individual firms they estimate a production function

$$x = 0.68 n^{0.53} k^{0.50}$$

for the year 1952. In their inter-firm cross-section they have used statistics on the net value of output x, wages and salaries n, and value of net assets k. Having made this estimate and similar estimates for separate industries, they ask how the results can be used to estimate the value of capital for all industry. For all industry, values of x and n are already estimated in standard sources as total values of net output and wage-salary payments.

If a Cobb-Douglas function for the i-th firm is written in logarithmic form

$$\log x_i = \log A + \alpha \log n_i + \beta \log k_i,$$

and added over all units, we find

$$\sum_{i=1}^{N} \log x_i = N \log A + \alpha \sum_{i=1}^{N} \log n_i + \beta \sum_{i=1}^{N} \log k_i$$

or

$$\frac{1}{N} \sum_{i=1}^{N} \log x_i = \log A + \alpha \frac{1}{N} \sum_{i=1}^{N} \log n_i + \beta \frac{1}{N} \sum_{i=1}^{N} \log k_i.$$

Arithmetic means of logarithmic values are logarithms of geometric means. Therefore, we have

$$\log g(x) = \log A + \alpha \log g(n) + \beta \log g(k),$$

[6] V. N. Murti and V. K. Sastry, "Production Functions for Indian Industry," *Econometrica*, Vol. 25 (1957) pp. 205-21.

where
$$g(x) = \text{geometric mean of } x \text{ values,}$$
$$g(n) = \text{geometric mean of } n \text{ values,}$$
$$g(k) = \text{geometric mean of } k \text{ values.}$$

Thus, we can rewrite our original production function in the form
$$g(x) = A[g(n)]^\alpha [g(k)]^\beta$$
or, in the Indian case,
$$g(x) = 0.68[g(n)]^{0.53}[g(k)]^{0.50}.$$

From a knowledge of $g(x)$ and $g(n)$, it would be possible to solve for a value of $g(k)$. The available data are for totals or arithmetic averages of x and n, not for geometric averages. Moreover, it is doubtful whether anyone is interested in having a figure on the geometric mean of capital value. The arithmetic mean or summed total is the required figure.

If the logarithms of x, n, and k follow the normal distribution, as is the case in many distributions of industrial variables throughout the world, we have a simple ratio relation between geometric and arithmetic means. Let $a(x)$ be the arithmetic mean of x and σ^2 the variance of logarithmic values of x. We then find
$$a(x) = g(x)e^{\sigma^2/2},$$
$$e = 2.71828 \ldots .$$

From the published arithmetic means of x and n, it is possible to estimate geometric means, provided σ^2 can be determined for each variable. Murti and Sastry fit logarithmic normal distributions to their three variables for separate industries and find it to give an acceptable graduation of their sample data. In this fitting process, they determine estimates of σ^2 for each variable and, consequently, are able to convert from arithmetic to geometric means. From their estimate of geometric mean capital for all industry, they derive an estimate of arithmetic mean or total capital.

With a sample of aggregative American data over the period 1909-1949, Solow has tried to isolate a measure of technical change.[7] His

[7] R. M. Solow, "Technical Change and the Aggregate Production Function," *The Review of Economics and Statistics*, Vol. XXXIX (1957) pp. 312-20.

measure is "neutral," that is, it is not specifically associated with either factor of production. His hypothesis is

$$x = A(t)n^{1-\beta}k^\beta.$$

The multiplying term A changes over time and causes output to change for any given factor inputs. He also uses the simplification of constant returns to scale. The exponents add to unity. Then his function can be written as

$$\frac{x}{n} = A(t)\left(\frac{k}{n}\right)^\beta,$$

or

$$\log\left(\frac{x}{n}\right) = \log A(t) + \beta \log\left(\frac{k}{n}\right).$$

If this equation holds at the t-th period, it also holds at the $t-1$st period. It will also hold for the differences between periods.

$$\Delta \log\left(\frac{x}{n}\right) = \Delta \log A(t) + \beta\Delta \log\left(\frac{k}{n}\right),$$

where Δ signifies the difference in value between two adjacent periods. Differences in (natural) logarithms are percentage differences. Therefore, we can write, approximately,

$$\frac{\Delta(x/n)}{x/n} = \frac{\Delta A(t)}{A(t)} + \beta \frac{\Delta(k/n)}{k/n}.$$

Equilibrium theory of the firm tells us that

$$\beta = \frac{qk}{px},$$

where

q = capital price,

p = output price.

Hence,

$$\frac{\Delta(x/n)}{x/n} = \frac{\Delta A(t)}{A(t)} + \frac{qk}{px}\frac{\Delta(k/n)}{k/n}.$$

From separate measurements for each year on

$\frac{x}{n}$ = nonfarm gross national product per man-hour,

$\dfrac{qk}{px}$ = share of property income in nonfarm national income,

$\dfrac{k}{n}$ = employed nonfarm capital per man-hour,

it is possible to compute $\dfrac{\Delta A(t)}{A(t)}$. For an arbitrary initial starting value, say 1.0, the computed series $\dfrac{\Delta A(t)}{A(t)}$ can be converted into a series on $A(t)$. This gives a separate measure of technical change. A correlation of $[\log (x/n) - \log A(t)]$ on $\log k/n$ in the production function gives an estimate of β, which works out at 0.353 for the American economy during the first half of the 20th century. This is fairly close to Douglas' own estimate.

Solow uses the Cobb-Douglas production function, together with the marginal productivity conditions of the theory of the firm, to develop a measure, indeed a whole time-series, of technical progress. Solow first estimates the technical change function $A(t)$ by making use of the marginal productivity condition and then uses the derived results to estimate β, the unknown parameter in the production function. The probability implications of his approach may suggest a preferred alternative approach to this problem.

Since β is a constant and qk/px is a variable, we might write, for the marginal productivity condition,

$$\beta = \dfrac{qk}{px} e,$$

where

$$e = \text{random error}.$$

In the computation of the time-series for $A(t)$, we would then have

$$\dfrac{\Delta A(t)}{A(t)} = \dfrac{\Delta(x/n)}{x/n} - \dfrac{qk}{px} \dfrac{\Delta(k/n)}{k/n} e.$$

It is important and necessary to carry along the error term in the computation of $A(t)$. The logarithm of $A(t)$ will have a cumulative error term of the form

$$\sum_t \left(\dfrac{qk}{px}\right)_t \left[\dfrac{\Delta(k/n)}{k/n}\right]_t e_t.$$

Therefore, the regression of $[\log (x/n) - \log A(t)]$ on $\log (k/n)$ does not admit of a simple interpretation. In the usual case, we would like to assume

$$[\log (x/n) - \log A(t)] = \alpha + \beta \log (k/n) + u,$$

where u is a random error unassociated with log (k/n) and with no serial dependence within its own time-series.

In a different application of the Cobb-Douglas type of production function, Wolfson has followed the probability implications of the economic model in a way that could be used more satisfactorily for Solow's problem.[8] Wolfson estimated the effect of weather on agricultural outputs, with strong analogies to Solow's problem of estimating technical change. His central substantive problem was the measurement of area differentials in marginal productivities to account for variations in farm wage rates. The measurement of weather effects on production was somewhat incidental.

Wolfson's model is developed in triplicate for three main agricultural crops: cotton, wheat, and the combination of corn and hogs. For each crop he has the production function

$$X_{0j} = A X_{1j}^{\alpha_1} X_{2j}^{\alpha_2} \ldots X_{nj}^{\alpha_n} W_j u_j,$$

where

X_{0j} = output in county j,

X_{ij} = i-th input in county j,

W_j = climatic factors affecting output in county j,

u_j = random error in county j.

The data in the sample consist of county averages of outputs and related inputs over restricted geographical areas. Within each of three major producing areas, a model is estimated for the predominant crop. This gives a high degree of homogeneity among "nuisance" variables in a cross-section sample.

The model contains, in addition to a production function, equations of marginal productivity for each of the factor inputs

$$\alpha_i = \frac{p_i X_{ij}}{\bar{p}_0 X_{0j}} v_{ij}, \quad i = 1, 2, \ldots, n.$$

In these equations the share of the i-th factor's payments in the value of output is set equal to the production elasticity coefficient, except for

---

[8] R. J. Wolfson, "An Econometric Investigation of Regional Differentials in American Agricultural Wages," *Econometrica*, Vol. 26 (1958) pp. 225-57.

random deviation v_{ij}. As in the ordinary cobweb example for agricultural supply, entrepreneurial planning is based on last season's price. In the marginal productivity equations, $\bar{p}_0$ denotes the price of output in the previous season. Prices and unit factor costs are assumed to be the same from county to county within a major crop area.

Unlike Solow's approach, Wolfson's procedure is to estimate the production elasticities from the marginal productivity equations and then substitute these estimated values into the production function to be used for studying the residual effects of climatic variables on production. Solow's procedure was to estimate a series on technological change from the marginal productivity equations and then use these values to estimate the output elasticities from the production function.

Wolfson's method is, however, more consistent in terms of the probability implications of his model. Assuming the logarithms of errors v_{ij} to be normally distributed about a zero mean value, an assumption that is tested in the analysis, Wolfson estimates α_i as

$$\text{est log } \alpha_i = \log a_i = \frac{1}{N} \sum_{j=1}^{N} \log \frac{p_i X_{ij}}{\bar{p}_0 X_{0j}} + \frac{1}{N} \sum_{j=1}^{N} \log v_{ij}.$$

The last term on the right-hand side is equated to zero, and the logarithm of the elasticity coefficient is estimated as the arithmetic mean logarithm of factor shares. Alternatively, we can view the a_i coefficients to be geometric means

$$\text{est } \alpha_i = a_i = \left(\prod_{j=1}^{N} \frac{p_i X_{ij}}{\bar{p}_0 X_{0j}} \right)^{1/N}.$$

The estimates a_i are substituted in the production function, and residuals of the form

$$\log X_{0j} - a_1 \log X_{1j} - \ldots - a_n \log X_{nj} = r_j$$

are regressed by standard multiple correlation techniques on measurable climatic factors in the individual counties of each major crop area separately. From the regression

$$r_j = b_0 + b_1 w_{1j} + \ldots + b_m w_{mj},$$

Wolfson finds estimates of the constant term and climatic factors in his production functions

$$\text{est log } A = b_0$$
$$\text{est log } W_j = b_1 w_{1j} + \ldots + b_m w_{mj}.$$

Individual weather variables measured in each county are represented by $w_{1j}, \ldots, w_{mj}$. They include such things as rainfall, temperature, number of days of sunshine, and so on.

The purpose of Wolfson's study was to measure marginal productivity differentials among the major crop areas to help explain wage differentials in agriculture among these same areas. The purpose of measuring the effects of climatic factors on production was to test the model as a whole, including the marginal productivity equations and the technical equations jointly, in explaining reality. He was interested in obtaining a model that deviated in all equations by random amounts from observed data. If we compare, however, this method of estimating the effects of W_j on production with Solow's estimates of the effects of $A(t)$ on production, we see that there is an important difference. Wolfson was able to measure explicitly the major components of log W_j, denoted by $w_{1j}, \ldots, w_{mj}$. These were individual county measures of climatic variables. Other than as a mechanical trend varying in some fixed chronological way, Solow did not have a direct measure of $A(t)$—a nebulous concept of technical progress.

In a study of Finnish industry, Niitamo has estimated Cobb-Douglas production functions in which a direct attempt is made to introduce an explicit measure of technical progress.[9] Niitamo used a variable called the "level of knowledge," measured by the ratio of each year's graduating class from lower secondary schools to the working population h. For the period 1925-52, using annual time-series data, he estimates

$$X = 1.011 n^{0.779} k^{0.221} w^{0.130} h^{0.545}.$$

This is a least squares multiple correlation estimate in which

x = index of industrial production,

n = index of man-years in industry,

k = index of machine capacity used in industry,

w = index of exports adjusted for trend,

h = ratio of graduating class from lower secondary schools to working population.

The equation is fit to the data under the restriction that coefficients of

[9] O. Niitamo, "The Development of Productivity in Finnish Industry, 1925-1952," *Productivity Measurement Review*, No. 15 (1958) pp. 1-12.

Statistical Production and Cost Analysis 111

n and k add to unity (constant returns to scale). The variable w is introduced as a cyclical factor affecting short-run changes in productivity, and h is intended to measure the long-run influence of changing technology. The elasticity coefficient associated with h is far from negligible.

QUESTIONS AND PROBLEMS

1. Suppose that you maintained the hypothesis that technical improvement was not neutral, that specific aspects of technical change were associated with labor and other aspects with capital in the production process. How would you make a statistical test of this hypothesis?

2. List some specific inputs that you would use as variables in Wolfson's production functions.

3. Should research investigators fit Cobb-Douglas production functions under the restriction of constant returns to scale or should they allow the sample data to determine the degree of returns to scale?

THE COST FUNCTION

The theory of the firm can be couched in terms of a production function, profit function, and conditions of marginal productivity, as we have done in the preceding parts of this chapter, or, alternatively, in terms of a cost function, profit function, and conditions of marginal cost. The cost function summarizes many of the factors that make up the theory in terms of production function and marginal productivity conditions. The production function is a multivariate relationship associating output with several inputs, whereas the cost function is usually a bivariate relationship associating output with total cost. If there are joint outputs, both the production and cost functions have added degrees of dimensionality on this account. Even though several conditions of marginal productivity are needed to describe entrepreneurial behavior, we can synthesize the theory of the firm in terms of one marginal cost condition, except in the circumstances of joint output.

The explanation of entrepreneurial behavior in terms of production constraints and marginal productivity conditions is, in a sense, more fundamental than the synthetic explanation in terms of a cost function and marginal cost conditions. One might say that the former exposition has a higher degree of autonomy than does the latter. Component parts of production and marginal productivity analysis remain valid under a wide variety of structural changes in markets or other economic institutions. However, cost functions are *derived* relationships that may change in a complicated way when economic institutions are altered.

The theory of the firm from the point of view of production and marginal productivity analysis can be outlined, under competitive conditions, as follows:

Production function $\quad x = f(n_1, n_2, \ldots, n_r)$,

$$x = \text{output},$$

$$n_i = i\text{-th factor input.}$$

Profit function $\quad \pi = px - (w_1 n_1 + \ldots + w_r n_r)$,

$$\pi = \text{profit},$$

$$p = \text{price of output},$$

$$w_i = i\text{-th factor cost.}$$

Profit maximization
subject to constraint
of production function

$$\text{real factor cost} = \text{marginal productivity.}$$
$$(i\text{-th factor}) \quad (i\text{-th factor})$$

In the profit function we find the concept of total cost expressed as $w_1 n_1 + \ldots + w_r n_r$. This may, however, be expressed as a cost function with the same results for the theory of the firm determined along a different chain of reasoning. Instead of finding the maximizing conditions jointly for outputs and inputs we proceed in two steps.

In the first step we minimize total cost for any *given* output level.

Minimize total cost $\quad\quad w_1 n_1 + \ldots + w_r n_r$.

Subject to production constraint $\bar{x} = f(n_1, \ldots, n_r)$,

$$\bar{x} = given \text{ output level.}$$

Ratios of factor costs = ratios of corresponding
marginal productivities.

Statistical Production and Cost Analysis

If we have r factors of production, there are $r - 1$ independent equations relating factor cost ratios to marginal productivity ratios. Each of these $r - 1$ equations can be written as

$$\frac{w_i}{w_j} = g_i(n_1, \ldots, n_r).$$

For if the production function depends on the r factor inputs, it will generally be true that the marginal productivity functions and their ratios also depend on these same inputs. We, therefore, have $r - 1$ marginal productivity equations and the production constraint

$$\bar{x} = f(n_1, \ldots, n_r).$$

This makes r equations in $r + (r - 1) + 1$ unknowns. The unknowns are the r factors, $r - 1$ ratios of factor prices, and some given level of output. Although the output level is assumed to be given for this step of the analysis, we do not know at which level it is given. Hence, it is included among the unknowns.

If all these equations are "well-behaved" in a mathematical sense, the r equations in $r + (r - 1) + 1$ unknowns can be rewritten, or transformed, in such a way that the r factor inputs are expressed as functions of the $(r - 1)$ factor cost ratios and the output level. Then the r equations would take the form

$$n_i = h_i\left(\frac{w_1}{w_r}, \ldots, \frac{w_{r-1}}{w_r}, \bar{x}\right), \quad i = 1, 2, \ldots, r.$$

All factor cost ratios are expressed with w_r in the denominator. This choice is arbitrary and of no essential importance. Next we multiply each n_i by its cost w_i and add to get

$$\sum_{i=1}^{r} w_i n_i = \sum_{i=1}^{r} w_i h_i\left(\frac{w_1}{w_r}, \ldots, \frac{w_{r-1}}{w_r}, \bar{x}\right)$$

or

$$C = F(w_1, \ldots, w_r, \bar{x}).$$

The function F is the total cost function, derived as a combination of the production function and conditions involving ratios of marginal productivities.

This completes the first step in this method of reaching equilibrium for the firm under competition. In the second step, we recognize that the cost function can be similarly derived for any *given* output level.

Therefore, we may remove the bar over the x-value and write more generally

$$C = F(w_1, \ldots, w_r, x).$$

The profit function is now

$$\pi = px - F(w_1, \ldots, w_r, x).$$

In competitive markets the only variable in the profit function is x because p and the w_i are assumed to be given to the individual firm. Thus, we have for conditions of profit maximization,

price = marginal cost.

In deriving the cost function, we made use of the functions $h_i\left(\dfrac{w_1}{w_r}, \ldots, \dfrac{w_{r-1}}{w_r}, \bar{x}\right)$ relating factor demand to relative costs and output. The h_i functions are homogeneous of degree zero in unit factor costs, that is, they are "real" functions and are invariant for proportional changes of all the w_i variables together. Proportional changes in all these factor costs will cancel from the numerator and the denominator of the cost ratios. However, the total cost function $F(w_1, \ldots, w_r, \bar{x})$ is not homogeneous of degree zero in the w_i variables; it is homogeneous of the first degree because it is obtained by multiplying functions of zero degree homogeneity by factor costs. The cost function, so derived, is a money cost function. A "real" cost function could be obtained by deflating total money costs by p, the price of output. The cost function of the form

$$C = \sum_{i=1}^{r} \frac{w_i}{p} h_i\left(\frac{w_1}{w_r}, \ldots, \frac{w_{r-1}}{w_r}, \bar{x}\right)$$

is homogeneous of degree zero in price and unit factor costs.

In the case of joint production, the analysis is similar, and a cost curve derived in the manner of the above will depend on factor costs and on each of the individual output variables simultaneously. The cost function will then take the form

$$C = F(w_1, \ldots, w_r, \bar{x}_1, \bar{x}_2),$$

where $\bar{x}_1$ and $\bar{x}_2$ are given levels of each of two joint outputs. For fixed unit factor costs, the cost function is no longer a simple bivariate relationship between total cost and total output.

Statistical Production and Cost Analysis

The cost function for the individual firm is based on technological conditions and factor supply conditions. It is independent of the state of the market for output. We may or may not have competitive conditions in the market for output. If, however, there are imperfections in the market for factor supply, the basic conditions for cost minimization become

$$\frac{w_i(1 + 1/\epsilon_i)}{w_j(1 + 1/\epsilon_j)} = \frac{\text{marginal productivity of } i\text{-th factor}}{\text{marginal productivity of } j\text{-th factor}}.$$

This is like the preceding set of equations except that each w_i is multiplied by the factor $(1 + 1/\epsilon_i)$, depending on the elasticity of factor supply ϵ_i. If supply elasticities are constant, there is no formal change in the general nature of the cost function. The parameters are affected, but the same variables are involved. The same is true in the case of variable elasticities, provided that the ϵ_i's are all homogeneous of the same degree in factor costs.

The principal point to be learned from this discussion is that the cost function depends on unit factor costs as well as on total output. The relevance of unit factor costs in this connection may be obscured by familiarity with the usual static diagrams in which a two-dimensional relationship between cost and output is assumed. Many of the samples of data on which cost analysis is based may not meet the *cet.par.* condition that other things remain equal in interpreting the correlation between cost and output as a structural cost function in the usual sense. Here we have a close analogy to the *cet.par.* condition of demand analysis and qualifications similar to those involved in treating price-quantity correlations as estimates of structural demand functions.

A second objective of the derivation of the cost function above, is to show clearly its relationship to the production function and marginal productivity. We may have situations in which the production function remains unchanged but structural changes in market conditions alter the equations between marginal productivity and factor rewards. In such cases, it is difficult to trace through the structural implications for the cost function without having the more *autonomous* set of relations consisting of the production function and equations between real factor rewards and marginal productivities. Technical change is always going on, and we may study that process directly in terms of the estimated production function. Solow's investigation, discussed above, is a specific example of the study of technical change in terms of the form of the production function. It is apparent that the cost function is related to the production function, and that parameters of technical change in the production function will have an effect on the cost function. However, a statistical analysis that cuts through the fundamental production relationship and initiates as a cost study may lose information about technical change. The *derived* or *less autonomous* nature of the cost function becomes apparent.

The cost function

$$C = F(w_1, \ldots, w_r, \bar{x})$$

is a total cost function. From it we may deduce the average and marginal cost functions. The U-shaped marginal and average cost

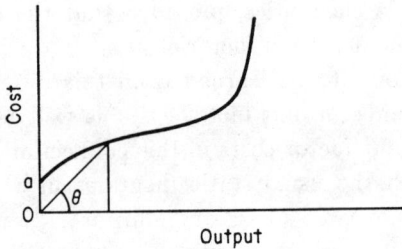

Fig. 3.3. Total cost function with diminishing and rising marginal cost

functions imply a nonlinear total cost function. A function that covers the whole range of diminishing and then increasing marginal costs would look like the graph in Fig. 3.3. The distance oa represents fixed costs that remain constant regardless of the level of output. In the lower ranges of output, the slope of the curve (marginal cost) is falling, and in the higher ranges it is rising. The average cost is measured by the tangent of the angle θ of the rays drawn from the origin to points along the curve. To reach points along the curve for successively higher output levels, it is evident that the angle must first decline and then rise. It is this property of the total cost function that makes the average cost curve U-shaped.

The range of diminishing marginal cost may be absent from the total cost curve, as in Fig. 3.4, in which case the marginal cost curve always rises, but average cost may first fall and then rise. Overhead or fixed costs, oa, are significant in determining the shape of the average cost function. If *oa* were nil, average costs would be continuously rising. There would be no falling portion because there would be no overheads to spread over increasing output levels.

Much of the research in the statistical analysis of cost has been concerned with the shape of the total cost function, particularly its departure from pure linearity. Conventionally, economic theory is based on a curved cost function like one or the other of the two graphed above. These are associated with U-shaped average cost curves and either U-shaped or rising marginal cost curves. These same curves are the type that fill the textbooks of economics. If the total cost function is, however, strictly linear, marginal cost will be *constant* because a straight line total cost function will have a constant slope.

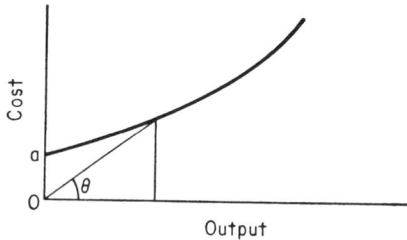

Fig. 3.4. Total cost function with rising marginal cost

The marginal cost curve simply becomes a horizontal straight line in a diagram with the usual axes of cost and output. The curve of average cost will be either hyperbolic (continuously falling in a curve) or constant (a horizontal line identical with the marginal cost line) depending on whether there are fixed costs or not.

Slight departures from linearity in total costs at extreme ranges of very low or very high output may produce nonconstancy of marginal costs only at implausible or rare output levels, leaving the bulk of interesting possibilities within the range of practically constant marginal costs. The implications of these possibilities, as well as the cases of strict linearity of total cost, are important for economic analysis, especially in settling disputes over marginal cost or marginal productivity pricing versus "full-cost" pricing. Just as Douglas' work on production functions was spanned by the broader question of the constancy of labor's share of output and marginal productivity theory of wages, so has Joel Dean's work on statistical cost functions been bound up with the wider implications of linear total cost functions.[10]

Before proceeding to Dean's and other cost studies it may be worthwhile to consider briefly the basic economic distinction between short- and long-run cost functions. Short-run average cost functions are drawn on the assumption of the existence of limitational factors, such as size of plant. In the longer run, this factor is not limited and can be generally varied. Although the short-run curves are drawn, logically, so that they have a U-shape, it is debatable whether the long-run curve ever turns up. See Fig. 3.5. If the long-run total cost function is linear with nonzero fixed costs, the long-run average cost function will not turn up. With this distinction in mind, the

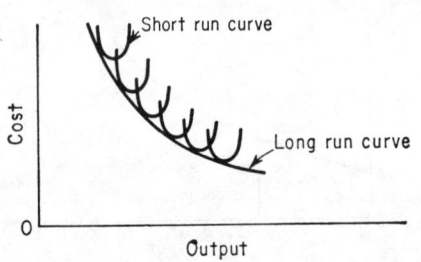

Fig. 3.5. Long- and short-run average cost curves

econometrician must settle clearly in advance whether he is going to extract cost data for his sample values from short-run cost items alone or from both short- and long-run costs.

In a firm's income statement there are both operating and nonoperating costs. Presumably, financial and other nonoperating costs are fixed costs. They may, however, be long-run costs such as interest on mortgage and bonded indebtedness, or they may be short-run costs such as interest on 90-day notes. Among operating costs there are costs of materials, cost of labor, and depreciation. Some labor and depreciation costs may vary with output levels and some may be fixed. If output is measured as "value added," material costs may not be taken into account in estimating the cost function. It would

[10] J. Dean, *Statistical Determination of Costs, with Special Reference to Marginal Cost* (Chicago: University of Chicago Press, 1936); *Statistical Cost Functions of a Hosiery Mill* (Chicago: University of Chicago Press, 1941); *The Relation of Cost to Output for a Leather Belt Shop* (New York: National Bureau of Economic Research, 1941) Technical Paper No. 2.

be preferable however to use a gross physical output measure instead of value added. In the short-run, for a plant of fixed size, depreciation costs might be neglected. They are, in any case, not easily measured with precision. It would, however, be wrong to neglect them in analysis of long-run costs.

In time-series examples of cost and output data over historical periods, it is necessary, as shown above, to take fluctuations in unit factor costs into account in estimating the function. In cross-section samples, the simplest and possibly the wisest choice would be to select cost and output data from a sample of plants that produce uniform outputs, use uniform accounting systems, pay identical factor prices, and have similar technological circumstances. Without these uniformities interpretation of the results will be difficult.

From this discussion it is clear that the econometrician embarking on a cost analysis has a considerable amount of theoretical formulation to keep in mind concerning the meaning of his fitted function. He also has a large number of corresponding decisions to make about the form of function to be fitted and the type of sample data to use.

QUESTIONS AND PROBLEMS

1. Derive cost functions that correspond to Cobb-Douglas production functions, assuming two inputs and one output. Do the same for quadratic production functions.

2. How could the fitting of statistical cost functions aid in the allocation of joint costs?

3. What mathematical properties would you impose on a cost function?

4. Accounting measures of cost in a manufacturing firm may be classified as:
  a) Prime costs
      i) direct materials
      ii) direct labor
  b) Manufacturing expenses
      i) indirect materials
      ii) indirect labor (supervisory and clerical)
      iii) other (rent, insurance, taxes, depreciation, maintenance, fuel, and so on)

c) Selling expenses
d) Administrative expenses
e) Nonoperating expenses (interest, fees, and so on)

Which components should be used in estimating a curve of variable costs? Which are fixed costs? How may they be used to determine parameters of a cost function?

5. How would you devise a statistical test of the constancy of marginal costs?

Some empirical cost functions

Among the many cost functions that have been computed for individual plants and industries, interesting studies are those of Joel Dean, who pioneered this type of research. Two of his cases are costs for a leather belt shop and for a hosiery mill.

In the leather belt study Dean collected cost records by four-week accounting periods, 1935-38. His function, measuring total cost C in thousands of dollars, output X in thousands of square feet of single-ply equivalent belting, and weight W in pounds per square feet of belting is given by the linear relationship

$$C = -60.178 + 0.77X + 70.181W.$$

In this total cost function, fixed costs are not estimated by the constant term alone since a value for W has to be specified. The variable W, in effect, gives an added dimension to the measures of output, showing that costs vary depending on the density of the final product. For a given value of W, marginal costs are $0.77 per square foot. Average cost falls in a hyperbolic arc and does not turn up from a minimum point on the basis of this total cost function. Dean tested for the existence of nonlinearity in the total cost relationship by fitting functions of higher degree in X, but found no evidence of statistically significant departures from a straight line relationship. This is a finding in favor of the full cost principle of pricing in the theory of the firm. The classical model requires the existence of increasing marginal cost in competitive markets.

A similar verdict on the linearity of the total cost function was suggested by the evidence in Dean's study of a hosiery mill. In this case he used monthly data over the period 1935-39. The variables were:

C = total costs in thousands of dollars,
X = output in thousands of dozen pairs,
t = time in chronological months.

The total cost function is estimated as

$$C = -13.635 + 2.068X + 1.308t - 0.022t^2.$$

For sample values of t, the level of the constant term, representing "fixed" costs, is positive, but the trend effect follows a parabolic arc first rising and then falling. The constant level of marginal cost is slightly over $2.00 per dozen pairs of hose.

Dean's findings do not imply that all total cost functions in all situations are linear. There is no doubt that his sample results suggest no evidence of significant departures from linearity, yet we must admit that other industries or firms may give a different result. In addition, he may have estimated cost functions from samples of limited range, that is, regions limited to areas in which segments of curves can be well-approximated by straight lines. The American economy was characterized by the existence of widespread excess capacity during the 1930's, and it would be best to consider samples drawn from periods when it is more likely that the scale of operations was pressing upon the capacity ceiling. For it is in the neighborhood of capacity that curvature (increasing marginal costs) would begin to appear.

Still another possibility exists. We frequently find in econometric research that more than one hypothesis is consistent with a given sample of data. In demand analysis, it is often hard to choose between a constant elasticity function, linear in the logarithms of variables, and a truly linear function. Both may give good graduations for the observed sample patterns, but they have different implications. The Cobb-Douglas production function has many neat, and convenient properties, but a purely linear relation between output and factor inputs may fit a given sample as well as a function that is linear in logarithms. We may be faced with a similar situation in cost analysis. Nonlinear cost functions may sometimes fit a given sample of data as well as a linear function. Nonlinearity is built into the constant elasticity demand functions or Cobb-Douglas production functions.

There is no question of testing for departure from linearity except by determining whether these functions fit sample data well or not.

In a cross-section study of costs for electric power stations, a particular form of nonlinear total cost function has been estimated. Its general shape is that shown above in Fig. 3.3, where the curve has consecutive ranges of falling and then rising marginal cost or slope. Many functions will depict this type of behavior, but one that is interesting and convenient is the cumulative frequency function, known as the *ogive* in statistics. Any ogive is confined to the range between 0 and 1.0, in terms of relative, and not absolute, frequency. The general pattern for a continuous variable is an S-shaped curve. This curve shows the percentage of cases in a distribution below some

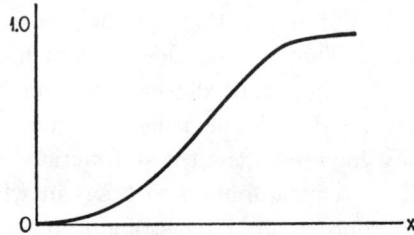

Fig. 3.6. Ogive or cumulative frequency function

value x. The variable x can take on values over the whole sample range. If the axes are interchanged in the ogive diagram, the curve has the appearance of the total cost function in Fig. 3.3, above, with fixed costs set at zero. Without interchanging axes, the curve has the shape of a production function, as in Fig. 3.6.

A special type of graph paper known as probability paper has been prepared, and is widely available, for plotting cumulative distributions of the *normal* frequency function in such a way as to produce a straight line instead of an S-shaped curve. The approach of plotted points to a straight line is an indicator of the approach to normality of a distribution. Logarithmic probability paper serves a similar purpose for functions following the logarithmic normal law, that is the law of distribution of variates whose logarithms follow the normal law. This is an important distribution in economics, especially for the industrial distribution of size characteristics of firms and plants.

We shall make use of the properties of logarithmic probability paper and the cumulative logarithmic normal distribution in the

Statistical Production and Cost Analysis 123

following way. Instead of measuring relative frequencies along one axis, we shall measure the ratio of output to *maximum possible output*. This ratio, like a probability figure, must always be confined to the interval between zero and unity. This ratio is not a true probability or empirical relative frequency. It is simply a fraction that is confined to the same range of variation as a probability measure and is plotted, by analogy, on the probability scale of probability paper. On the other axis we plot the logarithm of cost.

In the estimation of a normal distribution there are two unknown parameters that have to be empirically determined from the sample data. They are the mean and standard deviation, or variance, of the distribution. For the logarithmic normal distribution, the same two parameters defined in terms of logarithms of the sample variables must be estimated. In addition, a parameter defined as the *saturation* or maximum possible level of output must be determined. The estimation of these three parameters is not a simple exercise in the solution of linear simultaneous equations as is curve fitting in ordinary correlation analysis. A simple graphical method can, however, be used for obtaining approximate results.

If logarithm of cost and production as per cent of *saturation* output are plotted jointly on logarithmic probability paper, different plausible saturation values can be selected arbitrarily until one is found that makes this plotting of points scatter along a straight line path. In the graph shown in Fig. 3.7, cost and output data are plotted for electric power stations with a choice of saturation output, κ, at 10^{11} kwhr, which seems to straighten out the sample scatter. Alternative values above and below the chosen figure caused noticeable bends in the drift of points. It can be seen that the *saturation* value is chosen so large that actual production of the largest plant in the sample is less than ten per cent of this hypothetical maximum.

The sample data consist of cost and output statistics from individual plants burning coal exclusively, of conventional construction, and located in the Middle Atlantic or Southern New England States. The selection of the plants was controlled by these criteria in order to get a high degree of homogeneity in operating conditions and to minimize the effects of "nuisance" variables in a cross-section sample. The cost data are taken from a report of the Federal Power Commission in 1955. They are based, therefore, on a uniform accounting system. Operating costs alone are considered. These all vary with the scale of output. Therefore, fixed costs are not considered in this analysis. Output is measured in the homogeneous units of kwhr. The sample contains figures from 67 plants. The plant unit seems most relevant for establishing a cost function. An entire firm, that is, a possible collection of plants, would be less satisfactory.

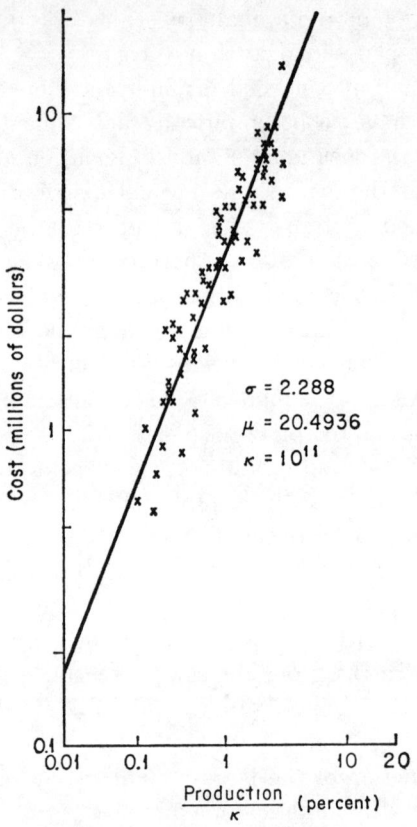

Fig. 3.7. Probit graph for electric power stations

The graph is drawn with the axes interchanged as compared with the usual ogive figure. On the horizontal axis the probability scale is made up to give the *normal deviate* corresponding to the indicated fraction (the ratio of actual output to *saturation* output). These are the pairs of figures given in the tables of the normal distribution. Once a value of saturation output has been selected, the two remaining unknown parameters can easily be obtained graphically. They

Statistical Production and Cost Analysis 125

are the values that satisfy the two linear equations

$$\log C_{p_1} = (\text{mean}) - n_{p_1} (\text{standard deviation}),$$
$$\log C_{p_2} = (\text{mean}) - n_{p_2} (\text{standard deviation}).$$

Everything but unknown mean and standard deviation is known in these two linear equations. p_1 and p_2 are two arbitrarily selected probability values in the horizontal scale of the graph. n_{p_1} and n_{p_2} are the associated normal deviates which can be read from a table of the normal distribution. Log C_{p_1} and log C_{p_2} are logarithms of corresponding cost values on the fitted curve and are read from the vertical scale of the graph as ordinates of a straight line drawn through the scatter of points. They are the ordinates for the two arbitrarily selected abscissae.

In this sample we estimate

standard deviation (σ) = 2.288 in units of natural logarithms,
mean (μ) = 20.4936 in units of natural logarithms,
saturation (κ) = 10^{11} kwhr.

These coefficients define a cost curve which is the cumulative of the density function

$$x = \frac{10^{11}}{c\sqrt{2\pi}\,(2.288)} e^{-\frac{(\log c - 20.4936)^2}{2(2.288)^2}}.$$

This gives output as a function of cost, that is, it reverses the order of dependent and independent variables in the ordinary cost function. The cumulative of this distribution will produce a curved cost function which has a U-shaped average cost curve.

The cost function estimated here is a cross-section estimate for individual firms. It can be aggregated into an industry function provided the distribution of firms within the industry is known. If we assume that firms' costs within the industry follow the logarithmic normal distribution, it is possible to make some very simple aggregations in terms of the parameters of the size distribution of costs, and properties of the industry cost curve can be conveniently studied. These aggregations, however, lead us into some complicated problems of distribution theory that we shall not pursue further in this introductory exposition.

THE SUPPLY FUNCTION

In a more complete statement of the theory of the firm under competitive market conditions, we summarize the results by saying that we follow through the implications of *maximizing profits subject to the production function constraint*. However, the cost function was found from the weaker prescription of *minimizing costs for a given output subject to the production function constraint*. The cost function, derived from the latter process, proved to be a relationship connecting two endogenous variables under the control of individual firms, namely, cost and output. Supply functions are different. They are derived from the first process implying the final equilibrium position of the firm and give a relation between output and market prices. The latter are outside the control of the individual firm under competitive conditions.

If we go back to the formulation of the theory of the firm written above, we have

real factor cost (i-th factor) = marginal productivity (i-th factor),

output = f (r factor inputs).

or

$$\frac{w_i}{p} = m_i(n_1, n_2, \ldots, n_r), \quad i = 1, 2, \ldots, r,$$

$$x = f(n_1, n_2, \ldots, n_r).$$

In the first set of equations we have real factor cost equated to marginal productivity, but marginal productivity will depend on the same variables as the production function. Therefore, we express it as $m_i(n_1, n_2, \ldots, n_r)$. There are r such marginal productivity functions, one for each factor. If, instead of writing each real factor cost as a function of all the inputs, we turn the equations about and express each input as a function of all the real factor costs, we have a set of equations[11]

$$n_i = q_i\left(\frac{w_1}{p}, \frac{w_2}{p}, \ldots, \frac{w_r}{p}\right).$$

---

[11] We made a similar rewriting in the course of deriving cost functions above. This inversion can generally be done if the marginal productivity functions are "well-behaved."

Substitution of each of the q_i functions into the production function would give us

$$x = f(q_1, q_2, \ldots, q_r) = S\left(\frac{w_1}{p}, \frac{w_2}{p}, \ldots, \frac{w_r}{p}\right).$$

This is a supply function. Like the cost function, it is derived from more basic relations involving the production function and marginal productivity conditions. It is subject to many of the same limitations that apply to cost functions. It depends on the whole group of unit factor costs and the price of output, although it is customarily drawn as a function of output price alone. Factor costs are held constant behind a two-dimensional diagram. It should also be noted that this function is homogeneous of degree zero in unit costs and price. It depends only on the factor cost-price ratio and not on the cost and price variables separately.

QUESTIONS AND PROBLEMS

1. What type of function and what variables would you suggest for estimation of statistical supply equations for (a) wheat, (b) beef, (c) machine tools, (d) cotton cloth?

2. In economic analysis of the labor market, it is hypothesized that the supply curve of labor has negative slope in a region of high wage rates, that is, "backward sloping supply curve." Suggest a mathematical expression for such a supply curve. What kind of data would you collect to make an econometric investigation of this hypothesis?

Some examples of supply functions

Agricultural markets with cobweb effects are useful examples for illustrating the estimation of supply responses to price because the lag structure effectively casts the relationship into a form suitable for a regression estimate of the one-way effect of past price on current supply. In addition, these markets usually satisfy the conditions of competition.

In the previous chapter, we have already had an example of an empirical supply function in a cobweb situation based on the onion market. Here we consider two examples in the cotton market. The *acreage* of Egyptian cotton for crop season years in the period 1899-1914 may be estimated from one of the three possible regressions:[12]

$$A_t = 90.25 + \underset{(0.116)}{0.055} (p_c)_t + \underset{(0.42)}{3.18t}, \quad R = 0.96$$

$$A_t = 85.74 + \underset{(0.11)}{0.25} (p_c)_{t-1} + \underset{(0.44)}{2.40t}, \quad R = 0.97$$

$$A_t = 117.82 - \underset{(0.04)}{0.16} \left(\frac{p_w}{p_c}\right)_{t-1} + \underset{(0.20)}{2.91t}, \quad R = 0.98$$

where

A = index of cotton acreage on 1900 base,

p_c = index of cotton price on 1900 base,

$\dfrac{p_w}{p_c}$ = index of ratio of wheat to cotton price on 1900 base.

The numbers under the estimated coefficients, in parentheses, are the computed sampling errors. The multiple correlation coefficients listed after each equation are adjusted for degrees of freedom used up in estimating the parameters in each of the equations.

The first of these equations is statistically unsatisfactory because the sampling error of the coefficient of p_c is large relative to the size of the coefficient itself. The variable $(p_c)_t$ is not statistically significant. This is not surprising since price is not dated for a previous crop year as it ought to be in a cobweb-type agricultural market such as this. In the second equation, we find an improvement in the ratio of the coefficient to its sampling error and an increase in the over-all degree of correlation simply as a result of replacing $(p_c)_t$ by $(p_c)_{t-1}$. This brings us closer to a realistic formulation of the supply function. In the third equation we make a further improvement by introducing an additional possibility. Planters have the choice of devoting acreage to wheat or cotton on the basis of last season's price. In effect, this introduces a unit "opportunity" cost, which gives us a ratio between a cost price and output price as we developed above in the general formulation of the theory of the firm. Among these three possibilities, the third function is the most suitable as an estimate of

[12] These illustrations are taken from the unpublished thesis of S. E. M. Shayal on "An Econometric Model of the Egyptian Cotton Market" (Oxford University, 1960).

the supply function. Other unit cost factors could also be introduced, as in the onion example, where the farm wage rate was used as a supply function variable, but these were not available.

Technical conditions of climate and environment show how acreages are translated into output. The equations above do not give output, they give acreage. Another part of the supply relation is estimated as

$$P_t = 153.11 + 0.44\ A_t - 0.85\ N_t, \quad R = 0.69$$
$$(0.12)(0.54)$$

P_t = index of cotton production on 1900 base,

N_t = index of maximum reading at Nile gorge on 1900 base.

Yields are estimated with much lower correlation than are acreages.

A similar acreage relation has been estimated from Brazilian cotton statistics over the period 1921-1940.

$$A_t = 54.36 - 0.65\ \left(\frac{p_s}{p_c}\right)_{t-1} + 10.34t, \quad R = 0.92$$
$$(0.24)\phantom{\ \left(\frac{p_s}{p_c}\right)_{t-1} + \ }(1.07)$$

A_t = index of cotton acreage on 1920 base,

$\dfrac{p_s}{p_c}$ = index of ratio of coffee (Santos) price to Brazilian cotton price on 1920 base.

In Egypt where cotton has been a dominant crop, supply elasticity appears to be smaller than in Brazil where coffee is more dominant and cotton is secondary.

INPUT-OUTPUT ANALYSIS

An entirely different econometric approach to the problems of production and cost analysis is associated with the work of Leontief under the heading of input-output models.[13] These models give numerical descriptions of production and cost relationships but not usually on the basis of the standard methods of statistical inference that we have been employing in the other work in this volume. Moreover, the models are of a special linear type.

[13] W. W. Leontief, *Structure of the American Economy, 1919-29* (2nd ed.) enlarged (New York: Oxford University Press, 1951).

The main purpose of input-output analysis is to show the interindustrial structure of production. The economy is divided into, let us say, n producing sectors. Each sector produces output that may be used as input in another sector or that may be used in final demand by an ultimate purchaser. For example, the agricultural sector produces some of its output for use as input in the food manufacturing sector (grain used for producing bread), some for use in the textile sector (cotton used for producing cloth), some for direct use in final consumption (fresh vegetables used for the home table), some for final export demand (tobacco used in the overseas cigarette industry). From the point of view of the domestic economy, the grain and cotton used in producing bread and cloth domestically are intermediate outputs to be used as inputs elsewhere in the industrial structure of production. The fresh vegetables and tobacco used in home consumption and export trade are final products sent to ultimate buyers as judged by domestic economic activity.

In more general terms we write:

x_i = total output of the i-th sector, $i = 1, 2, \ldots, n$,

x_{ij} = output of the i-th sector used as input by the j-th sector,

F_i = final demand for output of the i-th sector.

These variables are related in an identity

$$x_i = \sum_{j=1}^{n} x_{ij} + F_i,$$

which states that all output of the i-th sector ends up in some resting place, either as input in one of the sectors (including itself) or as a final demand. We shall define the sector of final demand to consist of personal consumption, capital formation (fixed and working), government expenditures for goods and services, and foreign export demand.

In addition to these definitions and identities there is the critical assumption that different input flows in any producing sector are used in fixed proportions and that output is proportional to each input. The proportionality factors are

$$a_{ij} = \frac{x_{ij}}{x_j}.$$

The a_{ij} are technical constants that show the amount of the i-th input required for each unit of the j-th output. That the inputs are assumed to be used in fixed proportions can be seen from the ratio

$$\frac{a_{ij}}{a_{kj}} = \frac{x_{ij}}{x_{kj}}.$$

Substitution of the input-output ratio into the identities above yields

$$x_i = \sum_{j=1}^{n} a_{ij} x_j + F_i, \quad i = 1, 2, \ldots, n,$$

which is a system of linear equations with constant coefficients associating n output flows to each other and to the bill of final demand $(F_1, \ldots, F_n)$.

The statistical procedures of Leontief are easy to understand although much work to carry out in practice. They consist of the calculation of the intermediate flows x_{ij} from accounting and production records. Ratios are formed between each x_{ij} and x_j to estimate the technical constants. A one-element sample is used for this purpose. The linear equations derived above are then given numerical form. For any assumed vector $F_1, \ldots, F_n$, it would be possible to compute the industrial composition of final output on the basis of numerical values for the a_{ij}. The analytical problem becomes one of solving a system of simultaneous linear equations. In principle this is a straightforward problem, but in practice it may raise considerable questions of a computational nature. If the whole economy is subdivided into 50, 100, or more individual sectors, it is a major problem to solve the resulting large system of simultaneous equations. A saving feature of the fine subdivision of the economy is that many specialized sectors will not trade with each other directly. Therefore, a helpful number of elements of the a_{ij}-matrix will be zero.

An example of a compact input-output scheme is illustrated in Table 3.2 which shows a 10-sector decomposition of the United Kingdom economy for the year 1954. This table is drawn up for an *open* economy. Hence, there is an extra row showing imports used up in each of the sectors (columns). The system is also "open" with respect to household activity. Therefore, labor input shown by income from employment (wages and salaries paid to labor factors of production) is also included as a separate row. Alternative treatments would be feasible for the foreign sector. We could subtract

TABLE 3.2
Input-Output Flows, United Kingdom, 1954[14]

Output from \ Input to	1	2	3	4	5	6	7	8	9	10	F final demand	X total output
1. Agriculture, forestry, and fishing		1	8		28	620	12			1	657	1327
2. Mining and quarrying	11	16	106	50	19	16	76	27	195	86	208	794
3. Chemicals and allied trades	129	73		198	57	60	118	48	25	223	711	1585
4. Metals, engineering, and vehicles	74	73	73		76	75	112	245	66	313	3567	4674
5. Textiles, leather, and clothing	8	6	10	58	2	14	110	2	2	50	1543	1803
6. Food, drink, and tobacco	214	1	14	2	2					45	2955	3233
7. Other manufacturing	22	41	100	501	68	164		274	19	121	670	1980
8. Building and contracting	40	26	5	25	15	10	10		3	100	1496	1730
9. Gas, electricity, and water	13	17	38	109	20	23	31	7		113	424	795
10. Other production and trade	150	45	210	445	155	235	260	175	80		5021	6776
Imports	91	8	285	346	466	490	271	52	10	277	1312	3588
Income from employment	303	494	217	2074	608	329	639	720	199	3026		8609

F = personal consumption + government purchases of goods and services + gross domestic capital formation + exports. It consists of public administration, defense, public services, dwellings, domestic services and services to non-profit bodies. The output of this sector is wholly consumed in final demand and does not flow to other sectors.
X = total output adjusted for stock appreciation (inventory revaluation).

[14] One sector has been omitted.

imports from exports. The latter are included in final demand. For each sector we could then show net exports, that is, its exports minus its imports, as a component of final demand. We could also treat imports as "competitive" with home production and distribute them together with domestic output along the rows of each industry producing the corresponding goods at home. In another formulation, we could have an 11th sector column for exports to match an 11th sector row for imports. This would involve subtracting exports from final demand and showing explicitly an export column and an F column.

It will be noticed that the main diagonal in this table is empty. That is because output is measured as the net of each sector's contribution to its own output. Agricultural output is measured by excluding things like domestically produced feed and seed from the total production flow.

The entries in the table correspond to the x_{ij} in the notation adopted above. A large part of agricultural output serves as input for the food, drink, and tobacco sector. The table shows that x_{16} amounts to £620 million, nearly half the total agricultural output. A good part of engineering output goes into construction ($x_{48} = 245$) and an even larger share goes into final demand ($F_4 = 3567$). The latter term is especially dominated by fixed capital formation and exports.

To derive the technical coefficients from this table, we divide each x_{ij} by x_j. As an example, we have

$$a_{29} = \frac{195}{795} = 0.25,$$

which implies that £25 of mining output, principally coal, are needed to produce £100 of gas, electricity, and water output. The numerator is x_{29}, the amount of mining output used up in the utility sector, and the denominator is x_9, the output of the utility sector. If all the entries in the first ten rows and columns are transformed into ratios by dividing by the appropriate output variables, we can construct the set of ten equations, for a given composition of final demand,

$$x_i = \sum_{j=1}^{10} a_{ij}x_j + F_i, \quad i = 1, 2, \ldots, 10.$$

In the import row, we can form a similar set of ratio coefficients. The first entry of this row should be divided by agricultural output

($\frac{91}{1327}$ = 0.07), the second by mining output ($\frac{8}{794}$ = 0.01), and so on. From the output results established as a solution to the above system of equations, we can then derive a set of import requirements, estimated as the product of the indicated ratios and the corresponding output value. A similar set of productivity coefficients estimated as output per unit of wage and salary payment, or its reciprocal, would indicate manpower requirements corresponding to a given set of output values.[15]

From a statistical point of view, we see clearly that the technical coefficients are derived by forming the ratio of two values, each a 1954 observation. If a similar table were constructed for a number of years we could estimate *average* coefficients from possible models such as

$$\frac{x_{ijt}}{x_{jt}} = a_{ij} + u_{ijt}, \quad \frac{x_{ijt}}{x_{jt}} = a_i u_{ijt},$$

or

$$x_{ijt} = a_{ij}x_{jt} + u_{ijt}.$$

All of these have different probability structures and lead to different methods of estimation, but once a particular scheme was adopted, a sampling model would be implied and methods of statistical inference could be applied to the whole body of analysis. It is not usual practice, in input-output work, to use such models. A nonprobabilistic approach is customarily followed.

Another model would be to view the linear system in total output as a stochastic scheme

$$x_{it} = \sum_{j=1}^{n} a_{ij}x_{jt} + F_{it} + u_{it}$$

and treat the problem as one of estimating the matrix of coefficients a_{ij} from a sample of observations on the x_{it} and the F_{it}.

The production function approach to the problems of inter-industry relations would involve the estimation of relationships such as

$$x_j = f_j(x_{1j}, x_{2j}, \ldots, x_{nj}, y_j, z_j) + u_j,$$

where x_j and x_{ij} are as defined above in connection with input-output

[15] A better set of labor input amounts for this purpose would be man-hours worked.

analysis

y_j = imported input in sector j,

z_j = labor input in sector j,

u_j = random error in sector j.

The Cobb-Douglas approach to the analysis of production was formulated in terms of output, labor, and capital. In fact, output was measured by them as "value added." Therefore, inter-industrial inputs were omitted as explicit factors of production, but there is nothing to stand in the way of a simple extension of their model to a situation in which output is measured as a gross flow, and inputs from other industries are treated as factors of production together with imports and labor. Capital, too, can be brought into both the input-output and production function model.

The empirical form of the production function could be linear in arithmetic values, linear in logarithmic values, or some nonlinear variety. The natural extension of the Cobb-Douglas form is, however, of particular interest in showing the relationship with the input-output method. The extended Cobb-Douglas function would be

$$x_j = A_j x_{1j}^{\alpha_{1j}} x_{2j}^{\alpha_{2j}} \ldots x_{nj}^{\alpha_{nj}} y_j^{\beta_j} z_j^{\gamma_j} u_j.$$

The marginal productivity conditions for a competitive economy take the form

production elasticity of factor i = factor i's share of output value

or

$$\alpha_{ij} = \frac{p_i x_{ij}}{p_j x_j}.$$

These are the same conditions noted above in connection with the Cobb-Douglas treatment of factor shares. In the table of inter-industry flows presented here, the entries are *values* of inputs and outputs. Therefore, the ratios derived as technical coefficients may be regarded as estimates of constant elasticity coefficients of extended Cobb-Douglas production functions.

We have two different theories of production. In one there are assumed to be fixed factor proportions

$$a_{ij} = \frac{x_{ij}}{x_j},$$

and

$$\frac{a_{ij}}{a_{kj}} = \frac{x_{ij}}{x_{kj}}.$$

This is the model of input-output analysis.

Isoquants for this model are of a rectangular shape permitting no substitution among factors of production. The expansion path of output is a straight line through the origin and the intersections of the isoquant arms.

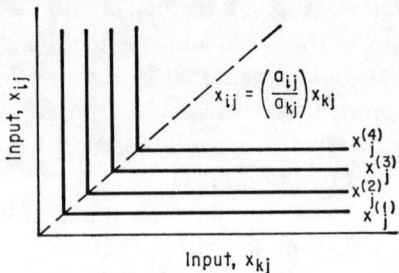

Fig. 3.8. Isoquants for the input-output model

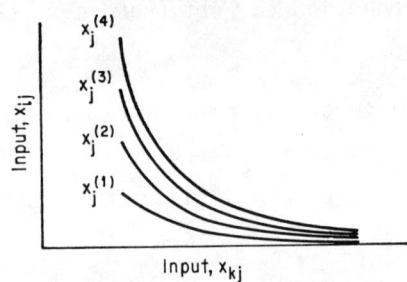

Fig. 3.9. Isoquants for the Cobb-Douglas function model

The corresponding figure for the Cobb-Douglas production function model is different. It is a pattern of exponential contours. The expansion path is derived from the ratio of two marginal productivity relations.

$$\alpha_{ij} = \frac{p_i x_{ij}}{p_j x_j},$$

$$\alpha_{kj} = \frac{p_k x_{kj}}{p_j x_j},$$

$$\frac{\alpha_{ij}}{\alpha_{kj}} = \frac{p_i x_{ij}}{p_k x_{kj}}.$$

If factor prices are in a constant ratio to one another, we find

$$x_{ij} = (\text{const}) \, x_{kj}.$$

Therefore, we could have the same expansion path as that implied by the input-output model. This constitutes the relationship between the two models.

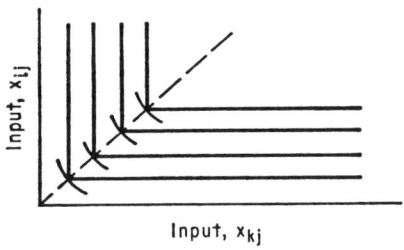

Fig. 3.10. Superposition of input-output and Cobb-Douglas isoquants (factor price ratios constant)

Input-output analysis can be equally well related to statistical cost analysis. Here the relationship is even more obvious and readily determined. For the j-th sector, total costs are

$$C_j = \sum_{i=1}^{n} p_i x_{ij} + q y_j + w z_j,$$

q = price of imports,

w = wage rate.

These factor prices may or may not vary by sectors. In addition to the inter-industrial technical coefficients, we shall assume the existence of two more

$$b_j = \frac{y_j}{x_j},$$

$$c_j = \frac{z_j}{x_j}.$$

Total costs can then be written as

$$C_j = x_j [\sum_{i=1}^{n} p_i a_{ij} + q b_j + w c_j].$$

This is a linear total cost function, as far as output variation is concerned, but it depends on factor prices as well. This is analogous to the linear cost function studied in connection with the general theory of the firm, although we did not use a process of minimization in deriving it.

We have been examining, in the preceding pages, the static input-output system. A dynamic system can be developed if capital formation is extracted from final demand and acceleration coefficients are introduced. Final demand is redefined to consist only of consumer goods, exports, and government expenditures. The basic equations then take the form

$$x_i = \sum_{j=1}^{n} a_{ij}x_j + F_i + \sum_{j=1}^{n} I_{ij},$$

I_{ij} = amount of investment goods sent from the i-th to the j-th sector.

Investment is defined as a flow. The corresponding cumulative measure is the stock of capital, defined as the summation of all past *net* investment. We could say that the rate of change of capital stock measures net investment

$$(K_{ij})_t - (K_{ij})_{t-1} = (I_{ij})_t.$$

Capital stock is dated as of the end of an accounting period.

The acceleration principle assumes a proportional relationship between capital stock and output

$$b_{ij} = \frac{(K_{ij})_t}{(x_j)_t}.$$

This is frequently called a capital-output ratio. From two such relations, one period apart, we derive

$$(K_{ij})_t = b_{ij}(x_j)_t,$$
$$(K_{ij})_{t-1} = b_{ij}(x_j)_{t-1},$$

and form their difference to obtain

$$(K_{ij})_t - (K_{ij})_{t-1} = b_{ij}[(x_j)_t - (x_j)_{t-1}],$$
$$(I_{ij})_t = b_{ij}[(x_j)_t - (x_j)_{t-1}].$$

We see the need for dating our variables now. The original set of equations can, by substitution, be written as

$$(x_i)_t = \sum_{j=1}^{n} a_{ij}(x_j)_t + (F_i)_t + \sum_{j=1}^{n} b_{ij}[(x_j)_t - (x_j)_{t-1}].$$

Statistical Production and Cost Analysis 139

This gives a dynamic system consisting of a set of linear difference equations of the first order with constant coefficients. Input-output analysis proceeds much as in the static case, once the a_{ij} and b_{ij} are determined from observed data. However, problems of dynamic evolution as well as of comparative statics can now be studied.

QUESTIONS AND PROBLEMS

1. Appraise some of the critical assumptions of the input-output model of production: (a) linearity, (b) fixed factor proportions, and (c) fixed product-mix (that is, fixed proportions among the joint output components of each sector).

2. In dynamic input-output systems, the ratios of capital stock to output are used to determine a set of capital coefficients. How are such estimates affected by the existence of excess capacity?

3. What are the probability assumptions and implications of statistical input-output calculations?

4

The Distribution of Income and Wealth

RELATIVE FREQUENCY, PROBABILITY, AND DISTRIBUTION

The ever present random errors in the relationships of econometrics are considered as drawings from probability distributions. For this reason, the idea of a statistical distribution needs elaboration and development in econometrics. We also encounter the concept of distribution in another context in this book, namely, in aggregating Engel curves of consumption or cross-section production functions. Income distributions are relevant in the aggregation of Engel curves, and these distributions are topics of econometric investigation in their own right. The explanation of the traditional skew pattern of income distribution is a classic study in econometrics on the level of researches into the laws of production and demand reviewed earlier.

Without reference to any particular economic phenomena, we can describe the idea of a distribution in abstract terms. The laws of probability define a distribution; a distribution lists probabilities showing the chance of occurrence of random events. In order to qualify as a probability distribution, the listing must (1) give only positive or zero probabilities of occurrence of any random event, (2) not allow the probability of any random event to exceed unity, and (3) make the sum of

The Distribution of Income and Wealth

probabilities of a mutually exclusive and exhaustive set of events equal to unity.

In flipping a fair coin, there are only two possible events—the appearance of a head (H) or a tail (T). These are *discrete* events, and the whole *distribution* can be summarized as,

$$\text{probability of heads} = P(H) = \tfrac{1}{2},$$

$$\text{probability of tails} = P(T) = \tfrac{1}{2}.$$

Obviously, these probabilities satisfy the criteria for a distribution. Graphically, we could portray this distribution as shown in Fig. 4.1. This probability distribution is pictured as a *density* function. It is a theoretical distribution. In any *sample* collection of statistical data, we could draw an empirical analogue of this theoretical function by

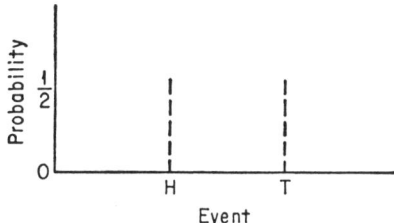

Fig. 4.1. Discrete function (fair coin)

calculating the relative frequencies of occurrence of the two events in a series of repeated trials of coin tossing. After hundreds and hundreds of actual trials, we shall have an observed sequence such as $HTTTHHTHTHHTT\ldots$. If we count through the sequence and compute the fraction of cases in which the coin turned up heads and in which the coin turned up tails, we shall have two numbers close to $\tfrac{1}{2}$ and $\tfrac{1}{2}$ but probably not precisely $0.5000000\ldots$ and $0.5000000\ldots$. The two numbers that are, in fact, obtained will add to unity and lie in the interval $(0, 1)$. They will be empirical counterparts of the concept of a probability distribution.

Three special properties of the distribution in the fair coin example distinguish it from those with which we shall typically be dealing in this chapter. They are: (1) the events are discrete, but we shall treat continuous phenomena, (2) the events are classificatory (H, T), but we shall deal with ordered numerical phenomena and, (3) the events are equally likely, but we shall deal with events of widely different probability.

The probability *density* function of a continuous variable typically follows a smooth, humped pattern. In a graph of such a function, we plot the different numerical values that the variable can assume horizontally. In the fair coin example, there was no particular reason for plotting H to the left of T, but in plotting the density function of a variable like income, we plot the lowest values to the left and the

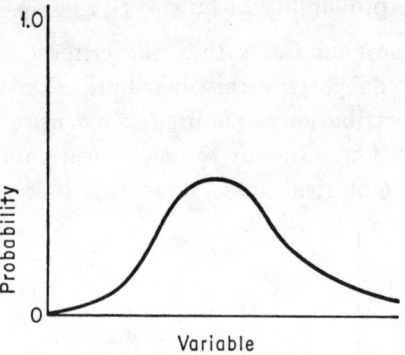

Fig. 4.2. Probability density function of a continuous variable

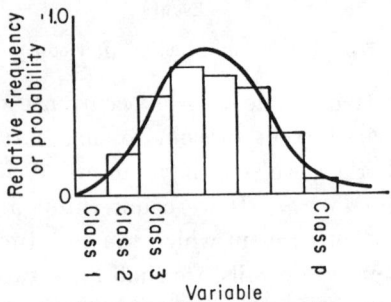

Fig. 4.3. Histogram of relative frequency distribution and associated theoretical density function

highest to the right. On the vertical axis we measure probability. A typical density function would appear as in Fig. 4.2.

This typical function as graphed has a single hump (*mode*), is smooth, and is symmetrical. It would not qualify as a probability density function unless it had the property that the area under the curve equals unity. This property follows from the condition that the sum of probabilities of a mutually exclusive and exhaustive set of events must be unity.

The Distribution of Income and Wealth

This latter point may perhaps be seen more clearly if we consider the relative frequency function corresponding empirically to this function. In actual observation, we would not see all possible values of a continuous variable. We would only have a finite sample of such values. Let us group the sample values into discrete classes, but let us order these classes by size of the variable being considered.

In Class 1	n_1 cases occur,
In Class 2	n_2 cases occur,
In Class 3	n_3 cases occur,
.	.
.	.
.	.
In Class p	n_p cases occur,
	Sum $= n$.

The relative frequencies for the successive classes are n_1/n, n_2/n, n_3/n, ..., n_p/n. By construction, these must add to unity. The graph of the relative frequencies (histogram) superimposed on the theoretical density function shows the relation between the two. We know that the total area under the histogram equals unity. If the relation between the theoretical curve and the empirical graph is such that areas of the vertical bars which are cut off above the curve just balance those gaps between successive bars under the curve, we would similarly have a unit area under the theoretical curve.

Another type of curve derived from the density or relative frequency distribution is known as the cumulative or ogive function.[1] The cumulative probability distribution function gives probability of events less than (greater than) each possible event. The probability of events less than or equal to the greatest possible event in the population is unity, and the probability of an event less than the smallest in the population is zero. The typical cumulative distribution function of a continuous variable looks like the curve plotted in Fig. 4.4. The empirical ogive curve derived from the summation of the relative frequency distribution would be a step-function closely graduated by the smooth theoretical S-shaped curve. If the cumulation occurred in the other direction (greater than instead of less than),

---

[1] This is the same curve that we used in the preceding chapter in connection with the estimation of nonlinear cost functions.

the curve would have a similar shape and fall from left to right between heights of unity and zero.

The curve of income distribution does not characteristically have the shape shown in the density function of Fig. 4.2. One of the basic facts of economic observation is that a wide variety of social situations yields a density curve of income distribution that is humped to the left—a skew distribution. An empirical relative frequency distribution of income superimposed upon a free hand graduation of a

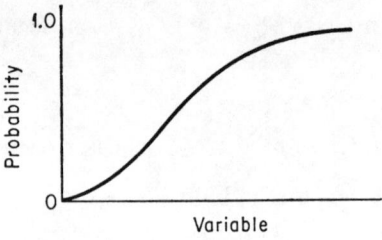

Fig. 4.4. Cumulative probability distribution function of a continuous variable

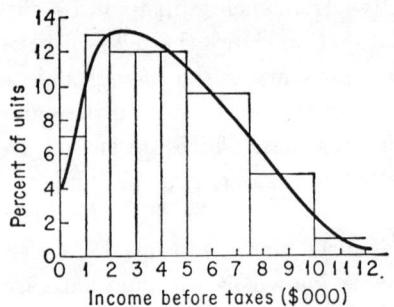

Fig. 4.5. Distribution of income, U.S.A., 1950

smooth density is shown in Fig. 4.5. A tabular presentation of this frequency distribution is given in Table 4.1. Both the relative frequencies corresponding to the graphed data and the cumulative frequencies corresponding to an ogive are given.

In the tabulation, the two extreme classes are open-end classes; that is, they do not have both lower and upper limits. Negative incomes, though rare, are possible. Business losses account for this possibility. The graph of the distribution begins with zero, but this is not strictly correct. Similarly, there is no limit given to the top of the highest income class. In the population there is a top consumer

The Distribution of Income and Wealth 145

unit, and the true ogive should reach unity at that income level. In drawing the histogram, the base of the last rectangle is indeterminate unless the highest income in the sample is known. For convenience in presentation, the class interval for grouping incomes in the distribution is widened as we go up the scale. As the bases of the successive rectangles are increased, their heights are proportionately reduced so that the area under the rectangle sums to 100 per cent.

TABLE 4.1
Distribution of Income Before Taxes among Spending Units, U.S.A., 1959.

Income class	Relative frequency in class (per cent)	Cumulative frequency (per cent)
Under $1000	7	7
$1000-1999	13	20
$2000-2999	12	32
$3000-3999	12	44
$4000-4999	12	56
$5000-7499	24	80
$7500-9999	12	92
$10,000 *and over*	8	100

The American income distribution follows the typical skew pattern. There is a single hump to the left and a long tail to the right. A main descriptive feature of such a distribution is its degree of inequality. Still another type of tabulation and graph brings out the degree of inequality. The Lorenz curve associated with a distribution gives a joint cumulation, both of the frequencies and of the variables being distributed. For example, the distribution of income may be cumulated to show the per cent of income received by the bottom class of spending units, by the bottom two classes of spending units, by the bottom three classes of spending units and so on. At the extremes, zero per cent of units receive zero per cent of income and 100 per cent of units receive 100 per cent of income. Between these extremes, we get a gradually varying amount. Distributions of American and British incomes are compared by this device in Table 4.2.

The diagonal line in Fig. 4.6 is the curve of equal distribution. Along it, X per cent of the spending units receive X per cent of total income at all levels. The departure of the actual curves from the line of perfect equality shows the degree of inequality. We observe that both countries have a similar degree of equality in their income distributions, but that incomes are slightly more equitably distributed in Great Britain than in the United States.

TABLE 4.2
Percentage of Total Income Received by Cumulated Deciles of Spending Units, U.S.A. and Great Britain, 1952.

Deciles of spending units	Cumulative per cent of total income received	
	U.S.	G.B.
Bottom tenth	1	2
Bottom two tenths	4	5
Bottom three tenths	9	10
Bottom four tenths	15	17
Bottom five tenths	23	25
Bottom six tenths	32	34
Bottom seven tenths	42	44
Bottom eight tenths	54	56
Bottom nine tenths	69	70
Ten tenths	100	100

These data are graphed in the Lorenz diagram in Fig. 4.6.

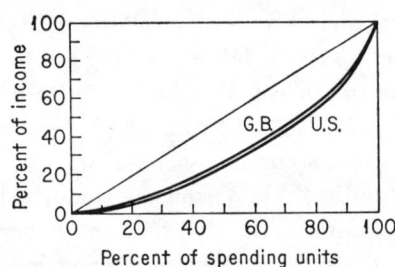

Fig. 4.6. Lorenz curves of income distribution, U.S. and Great Britain, 1952

A merit of the Lorenz curve technique is that it enables us to compare distributions in dissimilar units. Although the distributions are separately in terms of sterling and dollar variables, they can be compared as in Table 4.2 and Fig. 4.6 by transforming all data to percentages.

QUESTIONS AND PROBLEMS

1. What are the possible events in rolling a single die, a perfect cube with six faces? Make a graph of the density function. Suppose that

The Distribution of Income and Wealth

two dice are rolled together. Now list the possible events and make a graph of the density function.

2. What is the distinction between a theoretical probability distribution (density) function and an empirical relative frequency distribution?

3. Describe some economic processes or functional relationships that follow laws having the general shape of an ogive curve.

4. List as many uses as you can of the Lorenz diagram in the analysis of economic problems. Show specifically what data would be needed and how you would use the diagram.

5. The distribution of British income for 1953 is given in Table 4.3. It is based on a sample inquiry.
(a) Plot this distribution as a relative frequency function.
(b) Fit a smooth free-hand curve to the distribution.
(c) Plot the ogive or cumulative distribution.

TABLE 4.3

Income class	Percentage of income units
£0- 99	5.3
100- 199	15.3
200- 299	12.6
300- 399	16.3
400- 499	17.2
500- 599	12.3
600- 699	11.3
700- 799	2.6
800- 999	3.7
1000-1499	2.1
1500-1999	0.5
2000 *and over*	0.8

6. The distribution in the preceding question is not unimodal. Explain the meaning and significance of this fact. Can you suggest an alternative sample and universe that would be more likely to give a unimodal distribution?

Other skew phenomena in economics

Using the technique of distribution functions, we are able to see the skew nature of income distribution and its degree of inequality.

Other economic variables typically exhibit the same pattern, although not necessarily in an equal degree. Wealth, for example, is usually more inequitably distributed than is income. The distribution of consumers' net worth in Great Britain is tabulated in Table 4.4. The British income distribution has, as shown in Table 4.2, some of the characteristics of the American distribution. It too is a skew curve. Wealth, as represented by consumer net worth, is more highly skewed.[2]

TABLE 4.4
The Distribution of Consumer Net Worth, Great Britain, 1953.

Amount of net worth	Per cent of consumer units	Per cent of positive net worth held within each nonnegative net worth group
Negative	12.4	
Nil	22.2	0
£1-49	17.2	0.4
50-99	6.1	0.5
100-199	7.4	1.3
200-399	6.8	2.4
400-599	3.5	2.2
600-999	4.8	4.7
1,000-1,999	7.1	12.8
2,000-4,999	7.0	26.8
5,000 and over	2.9	48.9
Not ascertained	2.7	
	100	100

This distribution has a modal point at zero net worth, and the densities fall off sharply as we move up the wealth scale. It should be noted that the class width gets progressively larger. Were it not for this fact, the relative frequencies would fall much faster in absolute amount.

Comparison of the figures in the last column of Table 4.4 with the preceding column shows the great inequality in wealth distribution. The top 3.4 per cent of nonnegative wealth holders owned 48.9 per cent

[2] Net worth is measured as the difference between assets and liabilities. The assets included are bank accounts, securities, real estate, car, and unincorporated business. The liabilities are consumer credit, bank overdrafts, and mortgages.

The Distribution of Income and Wealth

of net worth.[3] The top 11.6 per cent of wealth holders owned 75.7 per cent of net worth. When this figure is compared with the per cent of income going to the top tenth of income receivers (Table 4.2), which is 30 per cent for Great Britain, the greater concentration of wealth ownership is evident. The striking distance between the curves of income and net worth distribution on a Lorenz diagram, Fig. 4.7, show this difference throughout a whole range of values.

Another example of skew distributions in economics is given by industrial size characteristics. Firms or plants within an industry

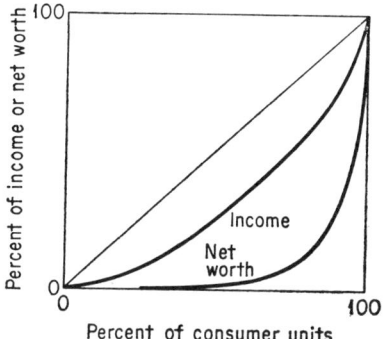

Fig. 4.7. Lorenz curves of income and net worth, Great Britain, 1953

tend to be distributed in a skew manner when classified by number of employees, total assets, total sales, or some other size characteristic. While the income distribution has proved to be important in aggregating Engel curves from cross-section data on individual families, the size distributions of industrial characteristics have similarly proved to be important in aggregating cross-section estimates of production or cost functions. Examples of such aggregations were given in Chapter 3.

From American industrial statistics, we find actual examples of skew distributions. Manufacturing industries, when classified by number of employees, show a marked skew pattern. In Table 4.5, we have listed the percentage of establishments of different size in some typical manufacturing sectors.

[3] The figure of 3.4 per cent is estimated by re-distributing all but negative and **not** ascertained holders to add to 100 per cent.

$$.034 = \frac{2.9}{84.9}.$$

There are so many firms with only a few employees that these appear to be continuously falling frequency distributions. They do not, as in the case of income, rise to a modal peak and then decline. They begin with a modal peak and decline throughout. They do, however, exhibit the typical long right-hand tail of the skew distribution.

TABLE 4.5
Distribution of Manufacturing Establishments by Number of Employees, U.S., 1955
(Per cent)

	Number of employees				
	1-99	*100-249*	*250-499*	*500-999*	*1000 and over*
Primary metals	74	11	7	4	4
Nonelectrical machinery	91	5	2	1	1

The Pareto distribution

Particular forms of distribution functions have occupied as prominent a role in econometrics as have such well-known functions as the Cobb-Douglas production function or the constant elasticity demand function. The Pareto law of income distribution asserts:

> The logarithm of the percentage of units with an income in excess of some value is a negatively sloped linear function of the logarithm of that value.

Symbolically, this takes the form

$$\log P(y) = \log A - \alpha \log y,$$

$$P(y) = A y^{-\alpha},$$

where

$P(y)$ = percentage of units with income in excess of y,

y = income level,

A, α = parameters of the distribution.

This is a cumulative distribution function, but cumulated in a direction opposite that in Fig. 4.4. This is the usual way in which the Pareto function is written. The corresponding density function for representing relative frequencies is

$$p(y) = \alpha A y^{-(\alpha+1)}.$$

The Distribution of Income and Wealth

As income levels approach zero, the relative frequency, $p(0)$ in the above formula, approaches infinity. As incomes get larger and larger, the frequency falls towards zero. A graph of this function does not give the usual picture of a single humped curve. Like the last example of the preceding section, it portrays a long tail to the right. The Pareto distribution is usually assumed to represent the distribution of incomes or other economic phenomena at upper levels or, at least, above some low values. In the case of income distributions, it does not graduate the distribution of low incomes well. We might think of it as a law of graduation of the distribution of incomes among taxpayers. Those income units receiving less than the exempt levels for purposes of taxation are not included. In practice, the Pareto distribution has been fit to such bodies of data.

The parameter A, in the distribution, may then be defined as

$$A = y_0^\alpha,$$

where y_0 is some low level of income above which the Pareto law graduates the rest of this distribution. The Paretian frequency function is then

$$p(y) = \frac{\alpha}{y_0} \left(\frac{y_0}{y}\right)^{\alpha+1}.$$

This function holds for $y > y_0$. If $y \leq y_0$, the frequency is assumed to be zero. The cumulative function is then

$$P(y) = \left(\frac{y_0}{y}\right)^\alpha \quad \text{for } y > y_0.$$

If y_0 is arbitrarily selected as some low value of income such as the modal value, or the upper limit of tax exemption, or some other a priori value, we see that the distribution depends on only one parameter, α. If $\alpha > 1$, as we find in empirical work on income distribution, the mean income of a Paretian distribution is given as

$$\text{mean} = \frac{\alpha y_0}{\alpha - 1}.$$

To determine whether a body of economic data follows the Pareto distribution, we plot, on a double logarithmic graph, the percentage of units with income (or some other variable) in excess of each of a series of values against these same values. If the resulting scatter of points lies along a negatively inclined straight line to a good approximation, we conclude that the distribution is Paretian. Of course the validity of the approximation must be tested by standard statistical methods.

The upper tail of the British tax distribution (incomes liable to surtax, that is, taxable incomes in excess of £2,000) affords a good example of a Paretian graduation of the upper tail. This tail, roughly speaking, covers the upper one per cent of the income distribution. The percentages of this restricted population in each of several income classes are presented in Table 4.6.

TABLE 4.6
Distribution of Income Liable to Surtax
U.K., 1953-54

Income	Percentage of tax returns
£2,000-2,499	28.6
2,500-2,999	19.9
3,000-3,999	21.7
4,000-5,999	16.8
6,000-9,999	8.8
10,000 and over	4.2
	100

This distribution is cumulated, by incomes in excess of each successive level, and plotted on a double logarithmic scale in Fig. 4.8. According to the Pareto theory, this graph ought to be a straight line. It appears to be nearly straight but is not perfectly so. If the two end points in the plotting are joined by a straight edge, it can be clearly seen that there is a bend among the middle points. This gives a systematic departure from strict linearity. Nevertheless, the scatter is nearly linear with a slope coefficient of about -1.9. We would write the cumulative function as

$$P(y) = \left(\frac{2,000}{y}\right)^{1.9}.$$

From the formula given above for the mean of a Pareto distribution, we compute

$$\text{estimated mean income} = \frac{1.9(2,000)}{0.9} = £4,222.$$

From the actual data in the distribution of Table 4.6, we estimate, using mid-points of class intervals and the actual mean of the open-end group,

computed mean income = £4,197.

In an average sense, the Paretian graduation appears to be good.

The graphs of the Pareto distribution required the logarithm of income along one axis, but such a value cannot be computed for

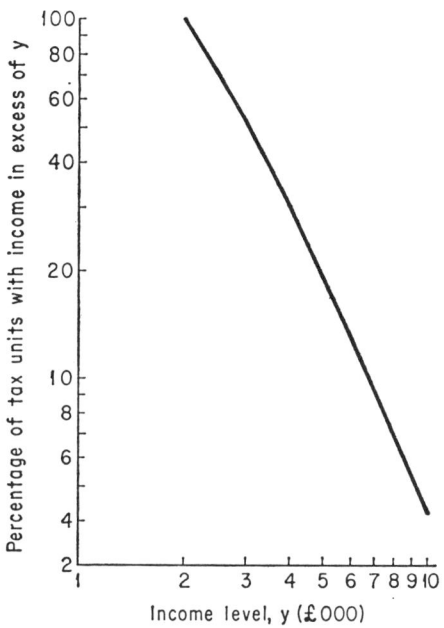

Fig. 4.8. Distribution of surtax incomes, United Kingdom, 1953-54 (double logarithmic scale)

negative numbers. It was remarked above that incomes *can* be negative. In many American sample surveys of family income, we find negative values as a result of business or farm losses. Most other forms of income are strictly positive. If from each income value being considered we subtract the lowest income (or some smaller value) the resulting values will all be positive. Thus we may denote the income value by $(y - \beta)$, where β is a parameter having as a value the smallest income in the *population*. All values of the transformed variable, $y - \beta$, will be nonnegative. If we subtract one more unit from $y - \beta$, we shall have all positive values, and the theory may be applied to the transformed magnitude instead of to y directly. This procedure adds another unknown parameter to the function, and it must be estimated together with the α parameter.

The Pareto distribution applies most suitably to the upper tail of the distribution, where all magnitudes are clearly positive, so that in practice, it should not be necessary to deal with negative values in studying this particular graduation of income statistics.

The lognormal distribution

Another popular parametric form of skew distribution in economics is the lognormal. Instead of using the well-known normal distribution to graduate a set of numerical statistics such as income, we might use the same distribution function to graduate the logarithms of the numerical values. It is assumed, of course, that only positive values of the original data are considered.

Towards the greater end of a logarithm table given differences in arguments are associated with small differences in logarithms. At the smaller end the same differences in arguments are associated with larger differences in logarithms. The logarithmic scale thus *compresses* the distribution of income at higher levels and *stretches* the distribution at lower levels. This transformation is one that would be likely to change a skew curve with a right-hand tail into a symmetrical curve.

The formula for the lognormal distribution can be derived by first considering the ordinary normal distribution of the logarithm of some variable. Call it $\log y$. The density function is

$$\frac{1}{\sqrt{2\pi}\,\sigma} e^{-\frac{1}{2\sigma^2}(\log y - \mu)^2}.$$

An area under this density function between two values of $\log y$ gives probability or frequency (see Fig. 4.3). This element of area has as its base,

$$\log y_2 - \log y_1 = \log \frac{y_2}{y_1},$$

where $\log y_2$ and $\log y_1$, are two values chosen on the logarithmic scale. In other words, differences on the logarithmic scale are functions of ratios on the arithmetic scale. The percentage change between the same two values on the arithmetic scale is given by

$$\frac{y_2 - y_1}{y_1} = \frac{y_2}{y_1} - 1.$$

It, too, depends on the ratio, y_2/y_1.

Therefore, we find that the probability density on the arithmetic scale must be based on given percentage changes to correspond with precisely the same absolute changes on the logarithmic scale. If we multiply the lognormal density function by $1/y$, and associate this function with absolute changes in y, we obtain the same relative frequencies that we would get by associating the lognormal function with absolute changes in $\log y$. The density function on the scale of y is

$$\frac{1}{\sqrt{2\pi}\,\sigma y}\, e^{-\frac{1}{2\sigma^2}(\log y - \mu)^2}.$$

This function plotted along the scale of y is a skew curve.

The parameters of this distribution are μ and σ. The "true" or population mean of $\log y$ is μ, and the population variance of $\log y$ is σ^2. The mean of logarithms is the logarithm of the geometric mean. Therefore, μ may be regarded as the logarithm of the geometric mean of y. In this distribution there follows a simple relation between arithmetic and geometric mean. This was used in an application in the preceding chapter. It is

$$\text{arithmetic mean } y = \text{geometric mean } y(e^{\frac{\sigma^2}{2}}).$$

This preserves the celebrated general inequality, for positive numbers, that states that the geometric mean is less than the arithmetic mean.

We deal with negative incomes in the context of the lognormal distribution in the same way as we did for the Pareto distribution. We subtract the least value of income from all incomes. This makes the transformed values nonnegative.

To fit a normal distribution to a body of data, we compute two sample statistics, the arithmetic mean and the standard deviation (or variance). For the lognormal distribution, we make similar calculations

$$\text{est } \mu = \frac{1}{N} \sum_{i=1}^{N} \log y_i = \overline{\log y}$$

$$\text{est } \sigma^2 = \frac{1}{N} \sum_{i=1}^{N} (\log y_i - \overline{\log y})^2.$$

The sample size is N, and the mean is denoted by an overhead bar. These would be maximum likelihood estimates, but for small sample estimation it would be advisable to replace N by $N - 1$ in the variance estimate. If the minimum income in the universe is not known, the three-parameter form of the lognormal distribution must be used, and it is more difficult to estimate.

Graphically, the lognormal distribution can be readily examined and estimated as was done for the probit function (cost function for electric power stations) in the preceding chapter. The cumulative function when plotted on logarithmic probability paper should fall along a straight line path. This corresponds to the linearity criterion for the Pareto function when the cumulative distribution is plotted on double logarithmic paper.

Both the lognormal and Pareto distributions have simple properties in terms of the Lorenz diagram. The usual measure of income inequality, that is, the ratio of the area between the Lorenz curve and the line of equal distribution to the area of the triangle under the line of equal distribution, depends in the Paretian case on α and in the lognormal case on σ. Inequality varies inversely with α, in the one case, and directly with σ, in the other. If a line is drawn perpendicularly from the line of equal distribution to the lower right-hand corner of the Lorenz diagram, we find that it divides symmetrical parts of the Lorenz curve corresponding to the lognormal.

Other distributions

The Paretian and lognormal distributions are by far the most usual descriptions or graduations of income distributions. There is a tendency towards the view that the Pareto distribution gives a better explanation of the upper tail and that the lognormal distribution gives a better explanation at lower income values.

Other curves have also been suggested for the description of income distributions or, more generally, of skew phenomena in economics. Karl Pearson proposed a whole system of frequency distributions corresponding to different parametric assumptions in the evolution of a basic differential equation. Among the several types of distributions in his family of functions, we find the Pareto distribution as a special case of Type VI. The Pearson Type III is, however, a skew curve that can be used in graduating income distributions. Its formula, as a frequency function, is

$$p(y) = Ae^{-\gamma y}\left(1 + \frac{y}{k}\right)^{k\gamma}.$$

The range of this distribution on the (income) y scale is from $-k$ to ∞, that is, from some finite negative income at the bottom end to infinitely large values at the top. A range restricted at one end is typical of a skew distribution. With γ and k positive, this distribution is unimodal (one hump).

Some authors have proposed other distributions that tend to more standard forms in limiting conditions. It is customary to have these other distributions tend to the Pareto form as income increases. Champernowne's distribution has the form, as a cumulative function,

$$P(y) = \frac{1}{\theta}\tan^{-1}\left(\frac{\sin\theta}{\cos\theta + (y/y_0)^\alpha}\right),$$

where $P(y)$ represents the percentage of incomes exceeding y.[4] The parameters of his distribution are α, y_0, and θ. For high incomes, this expression is closely approximated by a function proportional to $y^{-\alpha}$, and thus merges into the Paretian form.

An alternative function that is similarly asymptotic to the Paretian distribution is given by Simon, as

$$p(y) = AB(y, \rho + 1),$$

where $B(y, \rho + 1)$ is known as the Beta function of y, $\rho + 1$. Actually, Simon has revived interest in the explanation of this skew distribution for problems in sociology, biology, and economics. It was originally introduced by Yule.[5]

QUESTIONS AND PROBLEMS

1. Plants or firms within an industry, when distributed by size (number of employees), tend to show a skew pattern. We say that industrial size distributions are skew. What other industrial size

[4] D. G. Champernowne, "A Model of Income Distribution," *Economic Journal*, Vol. LXIII (1953) pp. 318-51.

[5] H. A. Simon, "On a Class of Skew Distribution Functions," *Biometrika*, Vol. 42 (1955) pp. 425-40. G. U. Yule, "A Mathematical Theory of Evolution, Based on the Conclusions of Dr. J. C. Willis, F.R.S.," *Philosophical Transactions*, Vol. 213 (1924).

distributions besides those of the number of employees would you expect to be typically skewed?

2. What class of mathematical functions do you associate with the Pareto distribution in cumulative form? What class do you associate with the Pareto distribution in density form?

3. Do the data in Table 4.5 follow the Pareto distribution?
Hint: Plot the appropriate cumulative distribution on a double logarithmic graph.

4. Choose parameter values

$$\mu = 0, \quad \sigma = 1.$$

Plot the corresponding density function of the lognormal distribution with the horizontal axis scaled in units of log y and in units of y.
Hint: Use tables of the normal distribution ordinates.
Repeat this problem using

$$\mu = 3.4, \quad \sigma = 3.0.$$

5. For the parameter values assigned in the previous question

$$\mu = 3.4, \quad \sigma = 3.0,$$

what is the geometric mean of population values? Common logarithms are used. If the variable being considered follows the lognormal distribution, what is the arithmetic mean of population values?

6. Describe the shape of the cumulative lognormal distribution when plotted with the horizontal axis scaled in units of log y and in units of y.

7. Show that the Pearson Type III distribution is a skew curve.

Distribution functions and aggregation

In Chapter 2 on demand analysis, the relation between individual and market demand was studied as a problem in aggregation. The relation of Engel curve calculations to aggregative time-series analysis was also considered. Either highly restrictive assumptions must be made, or some knowledge of empirical frequencies of income and similar explanatory variables must be used in order to make the necessary aggregations. If relationships are purely linear with constant coefficients for all units in the society, or if all incomes (or prices) change in the same proportion, aggregative relationships are simply derived from individual relationships. The highly restrictive assumptions are often not valid, and a more general approach to aggregation is needed.

Linear and higher order polynomial relationships can be aggregated in a simple way for any class of distribution functions in terms of moments of the distributions. An example was given earlier for a quadratic function, in which the variance or second moment of the income distribution was introduced as a separate variable. Much of empirical economics involves, however, logarithmic relationships. In demand theory, these are constant elasticity functions, and in production theory they are variations of the Cobb-Douglas function. Aggregation of individual functions expressed as logarithms results in macroeconomic relationships among geometric means, but macroeconomic statistics consist of arithmetic means or totals. It is at this stage of analysis that specific distributions such as the Pareto, the lognormal, the Champernowne, or similar distributions make an important simplification, for they provide analytical expressions of the relation between arithmetic and geometric means. In the case of aggregating the Cobb-Douglas production function for Indian manufacturing industry in Chapter 3, the relationship between arithmetic and geometric mean for the lognormal distribution was used.

Thus, we find an intimate connection between the classical parametric forms of econometric relationships and the classical parametric forms of distribution theory. A striking connection between the Pareto distribution and the Cobb-Douglas production function has been discovered by Houthakker.[6]

He considers the derivation of an aggregate production function for an industry made up of numerous production units (or cells). Production units may be plants firms, assembly lines, or even machines. For each production unit, he assumes constant production coefficients of the input-output type discussed in Chapter 3. The j-th unit will have coefficients a_{1j}, a_{2j}, and so on to show the amount of x_1, x_2 and so on needed to produce a unit amount of x_0, the output quantity. Houthakker assumes the existence of a competitive market with profit per unit of output given by

$$p_0 - a_{1j}p_1 - a_{2j}p_2,$$

[6] H. Houthakker, "The Pareto Distribution and the Cobb-Douglas Production Function in Activity Analysis," *The Review of Economic Studies*, Vol. XXIII (1955) pp. 27-31.

if there are just two inputs. If this expression is positive, the j-th production cell will push its scale of operation to full capacity limits. He then considers all combinations of a_{1j} and a_{2j} over different cells for which production is profitable. The sums of the outputs and inputs over all profitable combinations are aggregative measures of the variables X_0, X_1, and X_2. These sums will depend on the way in which a_{1j} and a_{2j} are distributed among production cells. His principal result is the following: If the distribution of technical coefficients is of a generalized Pareto type

$$p(a_1, a_2) = A a_1^{-\alpha_1 - 1} a_2^{-\alpha_2 - 1},$$

the aggregate production function will be of the form

$$X_0 = C X_1^{\gamma_1} X_2^{\gamma_2},$$

where the constants of the production function are defined in terms of the parameters of the distribution function, $p(a_1, a_2)$.

If there were more than two input factors being considered, the results would generalize readily

$$p(a_1, a_2, \ldots, a_n) = A a_1^{-\alpha_1 - 1} a_2^{-\alpha_2 - 1} \ldots a_n^{-\alpha_n - 1},$$

$$X_0 = C X_1^{\gamma_1} X_2^{\gamma_2} \ldots X_n^{\gamma_n}.$$

The joint distribution function is a product of individual Pareto distribution functions, while the production function is a natural extension of the Cobb-Douglas type to one with many inputs.

Houthakker's result is a neat synthesis of two classical parametric formulas in econometrics, the Paretian formula for distribution and the Cobb-Douglas formula for aggregate production. The Pareto distribution has been widely studied in connection with the distribution of industrial characteristics, particularly the size of firm. It has not been studied in connection with the distribution of technical coefficients over an industry. Houthakker merely assumes that this distribution correctly describes the distribution of a_{1j}, a_{2j}, and so on.

THE GENERATION OF INCOME DISTRIBUTIONS

The Pareto and lognormal distributions graduate income, wealth, plant size, and other skew distributions in economics well, but is this mere empirical observation without foundation in theory? An econometric problem, of considerable interest, that has exercised fine minds for many years, is to devise random processes that would, in fact, give rise to these two or other distributions frequently encountered in economics. The normal distribution occupies a central role in statistical theory because very general random processes give rise to this type of distribution. Averages or general linear functions of random variables tend asymptotically towards normality even though the original components are not necessarily normal. In addition to this abstract Central Limit theorem of probability theory, many physical processes with a chance element are known to generate normal distributions. Brownian motion phenomena are typical.

The simplest economic process constructed to generate a skew income distribution is the "law of proportional effect," giving rise to the lognormal distribution. Suppose that an individual begins with income y and that this income undergoes a series of chance proportional changes. One might think of this as the generation of capital gains (or loss) income as the result of random movements in unit price applied to a fixed initial investment. After t periods of random shock, the original income of y_0 will have become

$$y_t = y_0(1 + r_1)(1 + r_2)(1 + r_3) \ldots (1 + r_t),$$

$r =$ random disturbance.

The logarithm of income will become

$$\log y_t = \log y_0 + \sum_{i=1}^{t} \log (1 + r_i) = \log y_0 + \sum_{i=1}^{t} u_i,$$

$$u_i = \log (1 + r_i).$$

By the Central Limit theorem, if all the u_i are mutually independent, their sum will tend towards normality. This makes $\log y_t$ tend towards normality, and we have the lognormal distribution for y_t. This simple scheme was criticized by Kalecki since the variance of a sum is the sum of variances, and we get[7]

$$\text{var} (\log y_t) = \sum_{i=1}^{t} \text{var} (u_i).$$

With the passage of time, the variance of $\log y_t$ should grow steadily, but this phenomenon has not been observed in empirical economics.

If we modify this process and assume

$$y_t = A y_{t-1}^{\sqrt{\rho}}(1 + r_t),$$

[7] M. Kalecki, "On the Gibrat Distribution," *Econometrica*, Vol. 13 (1945) pp. 161-70.

we get
$$\log y_t = \log A + \sqrt{\rho} \log y_{t-1} + \log(1 + r_t)$$
or
$$Y_t = \alpha + \sqrt{\rho}\, Y_{t-1} + u_t.$$

This recurrence formula can be easily solved by building up successive values of Y_t from an initial value, Y_0:

$$Y_1 = \alpha + \sqrt{\rho}\, Y_0 + u_1,$$
$$Y_2 = \alpha + \sqrt{\rho}\, Y_1 + u_2 = \alpha + \sqrt{\rho}\,\alpha + (\sqrt{\rho})^2 Y_0 + \sqrt{\rho}\, u_1 + u_2,$$
$$Y_3 = \alpha + \sqrt{\rho}\, Y_2 + u_3 = \alpha + \sqrt{\rho}\,\alpha + (\sqrt{\rho})^2\alpha + (\sqrt{\rho})^3 Y_0$$
$$+ (\sqrt{\rho})^2 u_1 + \sqrt{\rho}\, u_2 + u_3.$$

If we continue this procedure to the t-th value of Y, we obtain
$$Y_t = \alpha[1 + \sqrt{\rho} + (\sqrt{\rho})^2 + \ldots + (\sqrt{\rho})^{t-1}] + (\sqrt{\rho})^t Y_0 + (\sqrt{\rho})^{t-1} u_1$$
$$+ (\sqrt{\rho})^{t-2} u_2 + \ldots + \sqrt{\rho}\, u_{t-1} + u_t,$$
or
$$Y_t = \alpha \frac{1 - (\sqrt{\rho})^t}{1 - \sqrt{\rho}} + (\sqrt{\rho})^t Y_0 + (\sqrt{\rho})^{t-1} u_1 + (\sqrt{\rho})^{t-2} u_2$$
$$+ \ldots + \sqrt{\rho}\, u_{t-1} + u_t.$$

The logarithm of income Y_t is made up of two terms depending on parameters and initial conditions, followed by a linear function of random variables. It is the cumulation of random variables that gives rise to the stochastic nature of Y_t. We calculate

$$\operatorname{var}(Y_t) = \operatorname{var}(u)(1 + \rho + \rho^2 + \ldots + \rho^{t-2} + \rho^{t-1})$$
$$= \operatorname{var}(u)\left(\frac{1 - \rho^t}{1 - \rho}\right).$$

If $\sqrt{\rho}$ is a positive fraction, $0 < \sqrt{\rho} < 1$, the powers of this quantity after the t-th value, where t becomes large, will tend to become negligible. We may write

$$\lim_{t \to \infty} Y_t = \frac{\alpha}{1 - \sqrt{\rho}} + \sum_{i=1}^{t} (\sqrt{\rho})^{t-i} u_i,$$

$$\lim_{t \to \infty} \operatorname{var}(Y_t) = \operatorname{var}(u)\left(\frac{1}{1 - \rho}\right).$$

In this process, the variance of the logarithm of y_t does not grow progressively larger with the passage of time. The linear sum of disturbances u_t is like a moving average and does not have more and more terms of effective size with the passage of time because the coefficients $(\sqrt{\rho})^{t-i}$ get smaller and smaller as t grows. After a certain point, a term in the linear sum is effectively dropped $[(\sqrt{\rho})^{t-i}u_i]$ while a new one is being added (u_t).

Lydall has described an extremely simple process that gives rise to the Pareto distribution.[8] He is mainly interested in the explanation of the distribution of employment income. For property income, "the law of proportional effect," or some more sophisticated generalizations seem appropriate to him. Lydall assumes that employees within a firm are arranged in a pyramid formation. At the top is a director with control over a small number of subordinates. These, in turn, control a larger number of assistants, and so on. At the base are the lowest grade of the mass of production workers under the supervision of foremen. He assumes that people in any grade (except the bottom) control a fixed number of persons in the next lower grade.

$$\frac{y_i}{y_{i+1}} = n,$$

where y_i = number of persons in the i-th grade. The constant ratio n is made independent of i. His next assumption is that the total income paid in any grade is proportional to the total paid in the next lower grade.

$$\frac{x_{i+1}}{nx_i} = p,$$

where x_i is employee's income in the i-th grade. The factor of proportionality p is independent of i.

These two assumptions produce the Pareto distribution. A *double-logarithmic* graph of the number of persons in each grade y_i plotted against the income level of the corresponding grade x_i will produce a straight line with negative slope under these conditions. The slope is defined as

$$\frac{\log y_{i+1} - \log y_i}{\log x_{i+1} - \log x_i} = \frac{\log y_{i+1}/y_i}{\log x_{i+1}/x_i} = \frac{\log 1/n}{\log np}.$$

[8] H. F. Lydall, "The Distribution of Employment Incomes," *Econometrica*, Vol. 27 (1959) pp. 110-15.

This slope is a constant since n and p are constants. Thus, we have a measure of the Pareto coefficient of the frequency distribution

$$-\alpha - 1 = -\frac{\log n}{\log np}.$$

This is the parameter of the frequency distribution since y_i is not a cumulative frequency but simply the number in a given grade level.

QUESTIONS AND PROBLEMS

1. A demand function for the i-th individual is

$x_{it} = A y_{it}^{\epsilon} p_t^{\eta} u_{it},$

x_{it} = quantity consumed by the i-th individual at time t,

y_{it} = real income of the i-th individual at time t,

p_t = relative price of x at time t,

u_{it} = random disturbance of i-th individual's demand at time t.

The parameters A, ϵ, and η are assumed to be constant for all individuals and time periods. Assume that y_{it} and u_{it} follow a fixed lognormal distribution for all time periods. Derive the aggregative relation associating the macroeconomic quantities

$$x_t = \frac{1}{N} \sum_{i=1}^{N} x_{it}, \quad y_t = \frac{1}{N} \sum_{i=1}^{N} y_{it},$$

$$u_t = \frac{1}{N} \sum_{i=1}^{N} u_{it}, \quad \text{and } p_t.$$

2. Think of a physical experiment, with random processes in it, that would produce a normal-type distribution. What modification in the physical design would cause the resulting distribution to become skew?

3. Prepare a critique of Lydall's theory of income distribution.
  i) Does it cover all types of income?
  ii) Are his parameters, n and p, really constant?
  iii) Does it allow properly for the diversity of personal abilities and talents?
  iv) Does it allow for the institutional structure of employment (that is, personnel policies of management and trade unions)?

4. Suppose that a process of income generation is given by

$$y_t = A y_{t-1}^{\rho_1} y_{t-2}^{\rho_2} (1 + r_t).$$

Under what conditions would you expect the limiting distribution of y_t to be lognormal? Develop a formula for the variance of log y_t.

A more general process

The examples of the preceding section are simple schemes that produce the lognormal and Pareto distributions. Another approach, known as Markoff processes, can be used more generally to describe the generation of income and other distributions.

Suppose that we have income distributions for identical economic units in two adjacent time periods. Of course, there are births, deaths, and modifications of family units in any period of time, but our theoretical model will assume a constant population of income receivers. From these two distributions, we can construct Table 4.7.

TABLE 4.7

	Income Class Period t \ Period $t+1$	1	2	Class 3	...	n	Row total
Class	1	N_{11}	N_{12}	N_{13}	...	N_{1n}	N_{1t}
	2	N_{21}	N_{22}	N_{23}	...	N_{2n}	N_{2t}
	3	N_{31}	N_{32}	N_{33}	...	N_{3n}	N_{3t}
	.	.	.	.		.	.
	.	.	.	.		.	.
	.	.	.	.		.	.
	n	N_{n1}	N_{n2}	N_{n3}	...	N_{nn}	N_{nt}
	Column total	$N_{1,\,t+1}$	$N_{2,\,t+1}$	$N_{3,\,t+1}$	...	$N_{n,\,t+1}$	N

The entries in the body of the table N_{ij} show the number of income receivers moving from class i (t-th period) to class j ($t+1$-st period). The right-hand column, showing row totals, is the frequency distribution of period t. The bottom row is, accordingly, the frequency distribution of period $t+1$. The total number of recipients in both periods is N. This table looks very much like an input-output table of the preceding chapter. Indeed, much of the following analysis closely parallels the structure of input-output analysis.

We may write the identity

$$N_{j,\,t+1} = N_{1j} + N_{2j} + \ldots + N_{nj}.$$

This is a repetition of the column summation in Table 4.7. It says that the occupants of class j in $t+1$ came from all possible classes in t. Define

$$p_{ij} = \frac{N_{ij}}{N_{it}}.$$

These are the percentages of units in class i (t-th period) who move into class j ($t+1$-st period). These are called *transition probabilities*. We can rewrite the identity, after substitution of the p_{ij}, as

$$N_{j,\,t+1} = \sum_{i=1}^{n} p_{ij} N_{it}.$$

If we assume the transition probabilities to be constant through time, we have a set of linear simultaneous equations showing how the distribution at time t is transformed into the distribution at time $t+1$. The assumption of constancy of p_{ij} parallels the assumption of constancy of a_{ij} in input-output analysis.

In many respects this model resembles an input-output model, but there are some differences. There is nothing corresponding to *final demand* of the input-output system. The set of linear equations with transition probabilities as constants are nonhomogeneous equations but only because they are dynamic with different numbers in classes at time t and $t+1$. For a given set of numbers within classes at time t, the equations give a basis for *expecting* the numbers to be found in each class at $t+1$. An interesting question concerns the end result of this dynamic process. Does the system eventually come to rest at a final limiting distribution? If it did, the values in any class at $t+1$ would be unchanged from those in corresponding classes at t. We would have

$$N_j = \sum_{i=1}^{n} p_{ij} N_i,$$

or

$$(p_{11} - 1)N_1 + p_{21}N_2 + \ldots + p_{n1}N_n = 0$$
$$p_{12}N_1 + (p_{22} - 1)N_2 + \ldots + p_{n2}N_n = 0$$
$$\vdots$$
$$p_{1n}N_1 + p_{2n}N_2 + \ldots + (p_{nn} - 1)N_n = 0.$$

The Distribution of Income and Wealth

This is a system of homogeneous linear equations and requires examination to see if a meaningful solution exists, that is, whether there is a solution other than $N_i = 0$ ($i = 1, 2, \ldots n$). The solution can easily be examined in full for the two-dimensional case. Assume $n = 2$. We then have

$$(p_{11} - 1)N_1 + p_{21}N_2 = 0,$$
$$p_{12}N_1 + (p_{22} - 1)N_2 = 0.$$

By the method of construction of the transition probabilities we can see that

$$p_{11} + p_{12} = 1,$$

and

$$p_{21} + p_{22} = 1.$$

We can therefore write the equation system as

$$(p_{11} - 1)N_1 + (1 - p_{22})N_2 = 0,$$
$$(1 - p_{11})N_1 + (p_{22} - 1)N_2 = 0.$$

From the first equation we find

$$\frac{N_1}{N_2} = \frac{p_{22} - 1}{p_{11} - 1}.$$

From the second, we similarly find

$$\frac{N_1}{N_2} = \frac{1 - p_{22}}{1 - p_{11}} = \frac{p_{22} - 1}{p_{11} - 1}.$$

The ratio N_1/N_2 is consistently estimated from either equation. This is the special condition that must prevail for a meaningful solution to exist from this homogeneous system. This condition has been easily examined in a 2 by 2 equation system, but is less apparent in larger systems.[9]

We thus can determine the relative frequency N_1/N_2 for our system. This value in conjunction with the requirement that the universe be fixed

$$N_1 + N_2 = N$$

[9] By more advanced mathematical methods it can be shown that a meaningful solution exists for the general n by n system, where $\sum_{j=1}^{n} p_{ij} = 1$.

completely defines the distribution.

$$N_1 = \frac{p_{22} - 1}{p_{11} - 1} N_2.$$

Therefore,

$$\frac{p_{22} - 1}{p_{11} - 1} N_2 + N_2 = N.$$

$$\frac{N_2}{N} = \frac{1}{\dfrac{p_{22} - 1}{p_{11} - 1} + 1} = \frac{p_{11} - 1}{p_{22} + p_{11} - 2},$$

and

$$\frac{N_1}{N} = \frac{p_{22} - 1}{p_{22} + p_{11} - 2}.$$

The limiting distribution is given by these two values for N_1/N and N_2/N. A significant aspect of this solution is that the limiting distribution depends only on the transition probabilities and *not on the initial distribution*. Starting from any initial point, the transition probabilities completely specify the final outcome. What we have worked out in detail for the two-dimensional case, generalizes readily for n classes.

Markoff processes with 12 income classes have been studied empirically in sampling investigations where transition probability matrices can be computed. In the Oxford savings survey, a group of identical respondents were interviewed in 1953 and 1954. From reports on income in each of two years by identical income units, transition probabilities were calculated for a 12 by 12 square array.[10] Of these 144 possible cells of joint income in the two years, over half were empty. These probabilities were estimated as zero.

It was assumed that the way units shuffled about between 1953 and 1954 would give rise to an endless process repeated year after year. From the actual income distributions for these two years in which there were general improvements on a large scale throughout the British economy and substantial inflation, the implied probability process would be one in which most people would ultimately shift into the upper brackets of the income distribution. To avoid giving an unrealistic picture of the extent of upward movement, income was multiplied at all levels in 1953 by 1.09 so that the mean of the dis-

---

[10] Peter Vandome, "Aspects of the Dynamics of Consumer Behavior," *Bulletin of the Oxford University Institute of Statistics*, Vol. 20 (1958) pp. 65-105.

The Distribution of Income and Wealth 169

tribution would equal the mean of the 1954 distribution. By this adjustment the process shows changes in the *relative* distribution of incomes instead of the *absolute* distribution of incomes.

Table 4.8 gives the results of the 1953-54 transition process carried on indefinitely until a stationary distribution is reached in which there is substantial, but not overwhelming, movement into the upper income classes.

TABLE 4.8
British Income Distributions, 1953 and 1954, and Stationary Distribution
(Income before Tax)
(percentages of income units)

Income class	1953	1954	Stationary
£0-99	3.5	3.4	3.4
100-199	13.6	14.1	13.9
200-299	12.5	12.4	11.5
300-399	15.3	15.8	15.3
400-499	17.1	13.0	11.4
500-599	11.2	15.5	14.6
600-699	13.3	13.5	13.3
700-799	4.5	3.5	3.1
800-999	5.1	4.5	3.7
1,000-1,499	2.6	3.0	4.3
1,500-1,999	0.5	0.4	0.9
2,000 *and over*	0.8	1.0	4.6

These general Markoff processes for generating income distributions do not explain anything as specific as the Pareto or lognormal distribution unless some restrictions are imposed on the system of transition probabilities. Champernowne has analyzed such processes on the assumption that the transition probabilities p_{ij} depend on the spread between the two associated classes $j - i$, only.[11]

$$p_{ij} = q(j - i),$$

for $j \neq 1$. The interval 1 is a special residual interval defined as

$$p_{i1} = 1 - \sum_{j=2}^{\infty} q(j - i).$$

He further assumed that income classes are designed so that the upper limit of each class is a constant multiple of the lower limit. The class limits thus grow in geometric progression. With these assumptions

[11] D. G. Champernowne, *op. cit.*

he proves a fairly general theorem that the limiting distribution of such a process will be of the Pareto type.

Aitchison and Brown have shown that slight modifications of Champernowne's assumptions produce the lognormal as a limiting distribution.[12] They divide the income scale into intervals of equal *arithmetic* width. The class limits form an arithmetic progression in their model. Instead of assuming that p_{ij} depend only on $j - i$, they assume that the transition probabilities depend only on j/i,

$$p_{ij} = q(j/i),$$

with a similar definition for $j = 1$.

$$p_{i1} = 1 - \sum_{j=2}^{\infty} q(j/i).$$

With these assumptions, they deduce a theorem showing that the limit distribution is lognormal.

QUESTIONS AND PROBLEMS

1. Compare and contrast the Leontief input-output system with the Markoff transition probability scheme.

Hints: Take up open and closed systems, the meaning and size of column sums, constancy of coefficients, dynamics and statics.

2. The joint class frequencies of income in two successive periods is given in Table 4.9. Compute the transition probabilities. What is the distribution of income in period t? What is the distribution of income in period $t + 1$?

TABLE 4.9

t \ $t+1$	0-999	1000-1,999	2000-2,999	3000-4,999	5000-9,999	10,000 and over
			Income class			
0-999	168	75	42	10	0	0
1,000-1,999	18	403	89	75	2	0
2,000-2,999	11	6	532	125	16	3
3,000-4,999	2	3	60	347	88	8
5,000-9,999	0	0	16	63	204	25
10,000 *and over*	0	0	6	13	15	75

[12] J. Aitchison and J. A. C. Brown, *The Lognormal Distribution* (Cambridge: Cambridge University Press, 1957).

3. Would you expect transition probabilities for income classes to be constant? How would you design a sample of incomes so as to estimate reliable transition probabilities?

SYSTEMATIC FACTORS IN THE DISTRIBUTION OF INCOME

Income distributions have been considered as parametric types among classes of skew distributions and as the outcome of chance processes. There is another approach to the income distribution problem which treats it like many other problems in econometrics.

What are the determinants of a person's income? This question can be asked in much the same way as what are the determinants of a person's spending or saving? We use Engel curve analysis and extensions of that approach to answer such questions. There is no reason why the same approach cannot equally well be used to explain income. In family-budget studies from cross-section samples we find that spending on a certain class of goods usually depends on family income, family size, parental age, marital status, occupation, geographical location, and other variables. Some of these variables might be called "nuisance" variables, apart from income level, yet their effects are important and must be simultaneously estimated if we are to obtain a suitable estimate of income effects on the spending in question.

Similarly we might explain income variation from family-to-family in terms of such "nuisance" variables. Education, occupation, race, sex, age, and variables like these would seem to be of significance in explaining income variability. If the income distribution is to be built from a chance process, the chance factors must be properly isolated. Thus, the measurement of "nuisance" variables and their influence on income are important in getting estimates of the random influences.

In the United States, occupation, age, education, sex, and race would appear to be obvious demographic variables influencing a person's income. A regression of income level, for individual units in a cross-section sample, on these variables would be suggested except for the fact that some are not naturally quantifiable. Classificatory variables like occupation, sex, and race could be scaled arbitrarily or tested by a statistical technique known as *analysis of variance*. Chronological age or number of years of education completed can be readily measured, but these may not be appropriate scales of measurement. A regression approach that is equivalent to the *analysis of variance* is the following:

$$Y_i = \alpha_1 j_{1i} + \alpha_2 j_{2i} + \ldots + \alpha_{n_j} j_{n_j i} + \beta_1 a_{1i} + \beta_2 a_{2i} + \ldots$$
$$+ \beta_{n_a} a_{n_a i} + \gamma_1 e_{1i} + \gamma_2 e_{2i} + \ldots + \gamma_{n_e} e_{n_e i} + \delta_1 s_{1i} + \epsilon_1 r_{1i} + u_i,$$

where

Y_i = income of the i-th (family) unit,

j_{1i} = 1 if the i-th unit is in occupation class 1
      = 0 otherwise,

j_{2i} = 1 if the i-th unit is in occupation class 2
      = 0 otherwise, and so on,

a_{1i} = 1 if the i-th unit is in age class 1
      = 0 otherwise,

a_{2i} = 1 if the i-th unit is in age class 2
      = 0 otherwise, and so on,

e_{1i} = 1 if the i-th unit is in education class 1
      = 0 otherwise,

e_{2i} = 1 if the i-th unit is in education class 2
      = 0 otherwise, and so on,

s_{1i} = 1 if the i-th unit is headed by a male
      = 0 if the i-th unit is headed by a female,

r_{1i} = 1 if the i-th unit is headed by a white
      = 0 if the i-th unit is headed by a nonwhite,

u_i = random disturbance.

These constructed variables that assume values of zero or unity can be used like any other numerical variables in a regression calculation. Their drawback is that they require many associated parameters. There must be separate parameters to be estimated for each class, and if there are several classes, the computing problem can rapidly become large. The analysis of variance technique with a proper sample design can be used to streamline the calculations considerably, but the sense of the problem is shown by the equivalent regression.[13]

[13] Possible combinations of variables into "interaction" classes can also be formed. This adds to the calculations.

The constructed or "dummy" variables illustrated above contain zero-unity combinations for all but one class. If variables are assigned values in every class but one, the variable corresponding to that one class is known. For example, there are two sex classes. If a person is unity for s_1, *he* must be *zero* for s_2. Similarly, if a person is *zero* for s_1, *she* must be *unity* for s_2.

Demographic determinants of American income levels have been studied from sample survey data.[14] Adams has estimated a regression equation and made variance analyses of the American Surveys of Consumer Finances, 1950-53. He took sex and race variables into account by selecting only white males. He studied the variation in their wage and salary income alone. This makes his distribution quite specific. In the analysis of variance, he finds the following factors significant in explaining income variation among recipients: occupation, age, education, number of months worked per year, geographical region, and city size. A specific regression equation was also estimated, but it did not contain the large number of parameters of the type illustrated above, for Adams made an arbitrary scaling of all his variables. His equation for 1949 income data is

$$\log Y = 2.65 + .20A - .027A^2 + .056E + .14J + .055L + .060C + .21P.$$
$$(.02) \quad (.003) \quad (.012) \quad (.01) \quad (.014) \quad (.009) \quad (.01)$$

The numbers in parentheses under each coefficient are estimated sampling errors. From a statistical point of view, all these variables appear to be quite significant. The coefficients are large in comparison with sampling errors.

The definitions of variables are:

A = 1, 18-24 years of age,
 = 2, 25-34,
 = 3, 35-44,
 = 4, 45-54,
 = 5, 55-64,
 = 6, 65 or over.

[14] F. G. Adams, "The Size of Individual Incomes: Socio-Economic Variables and Chance Variation," *The Review of Economics and Statistics*, Vol. XL (1958) pp. 390-98.

E = 1, low education (high school or less for white collar, grade school or less for blue collar),
  = 2, high education (college for white collar, high school or above for blue collar).

J = 0, unskilled and service occupation,
  = 1, semi-skilled, skilled, clerical and sales,
  = 2, managerial and professional.

L = 0, southern region,
  = 1, nonsouthern region.

C = 0, open country,
  = 1, community of fewer than 50,000 persons,
  = 2, community of 50,000 or more persons.

P = 0, worked fewer than 11 to 12 months in 1949,
  = 1, worked full year in 1949.

All these variables have the expected positive association with income size, except age which has a significant parabolic relationship with income. This is to be expected because of the decline of earning power during old age.

The over-all multiple correlation coefficient for this equation is 0.66. Therefore, a substantial amount of income variability remains unaccounted for by the variables used. Instead of applying some sort of probability reasoning to the raw income data, as was done in the preceding sections, one might think of applying it only after systematic influences of some demographic and economic variables have been removed. The residuals are possibly better suited to analysis by chance processes than is actual log Y. Under the simple lognormal hypotheses, the residuals ought to fit a normal distribution. This particular question was not pursued in Adams' study.

A similar approach to variance analysis of British incomes from the data of the Oxford Savings Survey was carried out by Hill.[15] He used data on wage and salary income of male employees, taken from the 1954 Survey, which covered the results of the financial year April 1, 1953 through March 31, 1954. Racial distinctions are not of importance in Great Britian. Therefore, Hill singled out a group of British earners comparable with Adams' group of American earners. Hill's sample produced a unimodal distribution with the usual skewness.

[15] T. P. Hill, "An Analysis of the Distribution of Wages and Salaries in Great Britain," *Econometrica*, Vol. 27 (1959) pp. 355-81.

The Distribution of Income and Wealth

He used the methods of variance analysis by means of a regression with classes for different variables assigned values of zero or unity. The variance analysis can be symbolized as

$$y = M + O_i + A_j + R_k + T_l + I_m + (OA)_{ij} + (OR)_{ik} \\ + (OT)_{il} + \text{error.}$$

M = general parameter,

O_i = occupation divided into 9 classes, $\quad i = 1, 2, \ldots, 9,$

A_j = age classes, $\quad j = 1, 2, \ldots, 6,$

R_k = region, $\quad k = 1, 2, 3, 4,$

T_l = town size, $\quad l = 1, 2, 3,$

I_m = industry, $\quad m = 1, 2, \ldots, 10,$

$(OA)_{ij}$ = occupation and age jointly classified, $\quad i = 1, 2, 3,$
$\quad j = 1, 2, \ldots, 6,$

$(OR)_{ik}$ = occupation and region, $\quad i = 1,$
$\quad k = 1, 2, 3, 4,$

$(OT)_{il}$ = occupation and town size, $\quad i = 1,$
$\quad l = 1, 2, 3.$

In the regression formulation of the variance analysis, the term O_i takes the form

$$\alpha_1 O_1 + \alpha_2 O_2 + \ldots + \alpha_8 O_8.$$

$O_i = 1$ if a particular individual is in occupation class i,

$\quad = 0$ if a particular individual is not in occupation class i.

Each of the other variables of the variance analysis are replaced by a similar linear expression with unknown coefficients and zero-unity variables. In addition to the five main variables (occupation, age, region, town size, and industry) there are three *interactions*, that is, joint classifications by occupation and age (or region or town size). Adams did not find significant interactions of these simple types in the American samples.

There are nine occupation classes and six age classes. These give rise to 54 possible joint OA classes, but Hill grouped his nine occupation classes into three relevant classes for this particular interaction and, therefore, considered only 18 possible joint classes. In the *OR* and *OT* joint classes he considered only one occupation giving four possible joint classes in one case and only three possible joint classes in the other. Even with these simplifications, there are 58 unknown parameters to be estimated in the regression. This poses a formidable computational problem that he was able to solve only by iterative approximations.

The regression was estimated in two forms, one using arithmetic values of income with a linear function of explanatory variables, and the other using logarithmic values of income with a linear function of explanatory variables.[16] In either form, the regression equation accounted for about one-half the total variance of the dependent income variable. The residuals from the logarithmic model were nearly symmetrical when arrayed in a frequency distribution and had fairly uniform variance (homocedastic) from class to class. The other model produced a skew distribution of residuals and strong heteroscedasticity.

Under a lognormal hypothesis, we might expect the distribution of residuals in the logarithmic model to be normal. The main departure from normality is excessive *peakedness* of the residuals near the mode (leptokurtosis). Hill shows that the merging of two normal distributions with unequal variance produces such leptokurtosis. The

TABLE 4.10
Logarithmic Model, British Incomes, 1953-54
Distribution of Residuals

Size of residual	Percentage of cases	Size of residual	Percentage of cases
−0.40 *and less*	0.9	0.00 *to* 0.05	19.9
−0.30 *to* −0.40	0.3	0.05 *to* 0.10	14.5
−0.20 *to* −0.30	2.7	0.10 *to* 0.15	8.3
−0.15 *to* −0.20	4.3	0.15 *to* 0.20	3.9
−0.10 *to* −0.15	6.3	0.20 *to* 0.30	3.1
−0.05 *to* −0.10	13.4	0.30 *to* 0.40	0.7
0.00 *to* −0.05	21.4	0.40 *and over*	0.2

[16] In the logarithmic form the occupation variable takes the form $O_1 \log \alpha_1 + O_2 \log \alpha_2 + \ldots + O_9 \log \alpha_9$. The variables O_i as before assume values of zero or unity. When anti-logarithms are formed, the O_i variables appear as exponents of the α_i parameters. The other variables are treated in the same way.

The Distribution of Income and Wealth

distribution of salary earners has a larger variance than does that of wage earners. The former distribution of residuals from the logarithmic model is nearly normal, but the wage earner group produces nonnormality. It is possible that further subdivisions within the wage earner group would yield normality.

In contrast with these calculations of residual income after the extraction of demographic influences, the British distribution of income for each group separately was very close to being lognormal. The total distribution of wage and salary earners fused together gave a good fit to the Pareto distribution in the upper tail. In Table 4.6 and Fig. 4.8, we saw that the upper tail of *total* British incomes was nearly Paretian.

The merging of distributions

The techniques of Adams and Hill, by isolating a number of systematic socioeconomic factors influencing the level of an individual's income, attempt to uncover a residual distribution that is symmetrical and possibly normal either in arithmetic or logarithmic values of income. Instead of using regressions or variance analysis in their approach, we could simply subdivide samples of individuals into fine groups and study the distribution of income within groups. For example, an American sample of male, White, wage earners, in the age group, 35 to 40 years, living in Northeastern urban areas, and having completed high school education, would form a fairly homogeneous group of people whose income differences may be attributed largely to random causes.

The distribution for each such group should appear to be more symmetrical than that of the total of all such groups amalgamated into one over-all distribution. It is possible that none of the studies made so far has gone far enough in subclassification to bring out a truly symmetrical distribution of random forces.

If several symmetrical distributions, which have different means and dispersions, are merged into a single distribution, we may find a highly skewed distribution as the result. If the groups with the high means are comparatively rare in the population, the resultant merged distribution is likely to have the typical skewness of total income distributions.

A thesis proposed by Miller, is that male-female differences in income level and occupational differences are largely responsible for the skewness in the American distribution.[17] The long right hand tail of the distribution is made up principally of males in professional, managerial, or entrepreneurial occupations. Distributions of male persons in separate occupational groups are much less skewed, and nearly symmetric, while the whole distribution is highly skewed in the usual way.

In actual practice, many people derive income from more than one occupation or source. Wages and salaries do not make up the whole of each person's income, and all persons cannot be unequivocally placed in an unique occupational group. Mandelbrot has remarked on some interesting properties of the Pareto distribution that help to take account of these difficulties.[18] The Pareto law of distribution, like the normal law, possesses a property of "reproduction." A sum of Pareto variables follows a Pareto distribution if the parameter α of the cumulative form of the distribution lies in the interval

$$0 < \alpha < 2.$$

Mandelbrot restricts his attention to cases in which α lies in the range

$$1 < \alpha < 2,$$

which is frequently found in practice to be an interval containing the Paretian coefficient although some cases are known in which the parameter exceeds two. As $\alpha \to 2$, the distribution approaches normality.

Also like the normal distribution, the Pareto distribution with,

$$1 < \alpha < 2,$$

serves as the limit distribution of sums of random variables. Mandelbrot implies that if the sum of many income variables, making up total income, is not normal, as is definitely observed to be the case, then it will tend towards the Pareto distribution. If the total distribution is skewed and has a finite variance, he would conclude that it is Paretian. Thus we have another type of appeal to probability theory rationalizing Pareto's empirical insight.

[17] H. P. Miller, *Income of the American People* (N.Y.: John Wiley and Sons, Inc., 1955).

[18] B. Mandelbrot, "The Pareto-Levy Law and the Distribution of Income," *International Economic Review*, I (May, 1960) pp. 79-106.

QUESTIONS AND PROBLEMS

1. Name some variable that might affect individual income levels in addition to those covered in the text.

2. What occupational subdivisions would be necessary to derive symmetrical (normal-type) distributions of personal income.

3. Compare and contrast arbitrary scaling of classificatory variables in regression analysis with the system of zero-unity "dummy" variables for each subclass.

4. What are the determinants of individuals' wealth holdings?

5

Statistical Models of Economic Growth and Trade Cycles

AGGREGATIVE ECONOMIC SYSTEMS

Another great field of application of econometric techniques has been in the construction of models of the economy as a whole. This might be called *macroeconomics*. Underlying statistical demand analysis, we have the microeconomic theory of consumer behavior, and underlying statistical production, cost, or supply analysis we have the microeconomic theory of the firm. Macroeconomics is an essentially different branch of economic theory, and similarly, econometric model construction in the field of aggregative economics has a few of its own distinctive characteristics.

The theories of consumer and entrepreneurial behavior have implications as to the form of the relationships assumed in demand, supply, or cost analysis. These theories suggest where relationships should depend on relative prices, absolute prices, real incomes, money incomes, other specific prices, and so on. In some studies, theory has been used to make more explicit specifications about the form of the relationship. Macroeconomic models are, however, more intuitive and less rigidly tied to a theory of rational behavior. It is possible to try to aggregate the traditional relationships of microeconomics into specific, implied aggregative systems, but the usual procedure is to develop an aggregative model from a more global and less closely reasoned argument. Sometimes the models are in money terms and sometimes in real terms. Sometimes they contain price variables (relative or absolute) and sometimes not. Some are dynamic, some are static. Some are in aggregative totals, some are scaled by population factors (per capita variables) or other indicators of size. There are few acceptable rules limiting the scope and variety of such systems. In demand, production, or cost analysis, theory and knowledge of economic institutions combine to give some a priori information about the structure of the relationships. The a priori information is much less in aggregative systems. In practical work, it is probably true that institutional information will prove to be relatively more important in the statistical estimation of macroeconomic models; the contribution of traditional theory will be limited.

The original econometric discussion of single equation biases in the estimation of relationships was formulated in terms of a simple aggregative model.[1] Aggregations over time, space, and commodities tend to introduce a higher degree of simultaneity in equation systems and reduce the frequency of uni-directional chains of causation. In narrowly defined markets, with short time periods, and highly specific variables, ordinary least squares regression methods, applied to single equations, have their greatest chance of leading to unbiased results. Haavelmo was originally inspired to take up the problem of simultaneous estimation of a whole system of equations as a result of Tinbergen's effort to build a complete aggregative model of the American economy for the League of Nations.[2]

The goals of aggregative economics

Tinbergen's main interest in constructing the first aggregative statistical models was to study the characteristics of the trade cycle and to test various cyclical hypotheses. He was interested in the possibility of constructing a statistical dynamic system that would

[1] T. Haavelmo, "The Statistical Implications of a System of Simultaneous Equations," *Econometrica*, Vol. 11 (January, 1943) pp. 1-12.

[2] J. Tinbergen, *Statistical Testing of Business Cycle Theories, II, Business Cycles in the United States of America, 1919-1932* (Geneva: League of Nations, 1939). See also J. Tinbergen, *An Econometric Approach to Business Cycle Problems* (Paris: Hermann et Cie, 1937). The latter volume contains a model of the Dutch economy.

generate cycles of activity or price levels that we commonly associate with the elusive phenomenon known as *the business-cycle*. Various mathematical theories had already shown that self-contained systems could be constructed that would oscillate and grow in a way similar to the actual economy. Tinbergen's question was more numerical and specific. He wanted to see if a system with numerical, or statistical coefficients determined from actual economic data would exhibit the ordinary cycle with damped or steady oscillation. He wanted to measure the cyclical characteristics implied by a system with numerically estimated coefficients and from this possibly devise a scheme for stabilization of the economy.[3]

An outgrowth of what might be called neo-Keynesian, or post-Keynesian, economic analysis was the focus of attention on influencing the level of activity at any moment of time rather than the study of the whole temporal shape of a cycle. The theory of the level of employment is so intimately tied up with exogenous, or control, variables in the public sector of the economy, that the future time shape of important variables cannot be specified without explicit knowledge of the future development of the exogenous forces. *Multiplier* analysis, which shows the current effect of policy decisions on variables representing economic activity, requires a system that will show the levels of these variables at any desired point of time. In a general sense, the problems of business-cycle analysis and employment policy seem to be mutually consistent and are both studied on the basis of the same parent models. Yet, as will be developed below in the discussion of the applications of empirical models, the two methods use the parent system in different ways and have different emphases.

In order to make short run policy decisions on such typical questions as tax rates, government spending, or monetary policy, it is necessary to have reliable short-run forecasts of the main economic magnitudes. A model that produces useful current forecasts, regardless of its longer run cyclical implications, or regardless of the uncertainty of its eventual cyclical course, is the type of model that has been developed in much of the post-Keynesian discussion.

Forecasting is important in other applications of models, besides its

---

[3] In the United States, the ordinary cycle shows a period of about four years, on the average, over the course of modern business history. At the time of Tinbergen's study for the League of Nations, the average cycle length was taken to be about 40 months. The cycle estimated from his model was 4.8 years.

Statistical Models of Economic Growth and Trade Cycles   183

use in public policy formation. Business firms or industrial groups have need of forecasts of their own industry and of an entire national or international economy. They are probably not forecasting for purposes of economic control; they are forecasting in order to determine their adaptive policies to the economic environment in which they must operate. In spite of the fact that they occupy a microeconomic status, they must make careful macroeconomic studies, and for this reason the techniques discussed in this chapter have relevance for private business as well as for general, economic research.

A MODEL OF GROWTH—THE GREAT RATIOS OF ECONOMICS

In economic discussion one or another celebrated ratio is frequently used as though it were a stable parameter. The parametric nature of these ratios is established either as an empirical observation or as a basic pattern of rational behavior. These celebrated ratios are:

1. the savings-income ratio (propensity to save),
2. the capital-output ratio (acceleration principle),
3. labor's share of output (income distribution),
4. the ratio of cash to income (reciprocal of velocity of circulation),
5. the capital-labor ratio (fixed factor proportions).

Together, these ratios constitute a system of equations that might serve to explain trend growth for an economy. The constancy or stability of the ratios is not absolute; they do fluctuate, especially over the trade cycle. Therefore, they are most useful in a growth model and not in a business-cycle model.

The model implied by this system of ratios is an exceedingly simple model which is typical of those studied in macroeconomics. This model is so simple that it serves as a starting point to our excursion into the econometrics of aggregative systems.

Let us assume a simple closed economy with no explicit government activity. We have the following aggregative variables:

S = savings, w = wage rate,
Y = income or output, p = price level,
K = capital stock, N = employment,
I = net investment, M = cash balances.

The five ratios, together with a definition relating change in capital stock to investment and an equilibrium condition adjusting savings and investment, determine a complete system; provided it is assumed that the stock of cash is under the autonomous control of the monetary authorities. The system is written symbolically as

$$\frac{S}{Y} = \alpha, \qquad \frac{K}{N} = \delta,$$

$$\frac{K}{Y} = \beta, \qquad K - K_{-1} = I,$$

$$\frac{wN}{pY} = \gamma, \qquad S = I.$$

$$\frac{M}{pY} = \kappa,$$

The solution of this simple system may be carried out in separate steps. The first two ratios and the last two equations may be condensed into

$$\alpha Y = \beta(Y - Y_{-1}).$$

This is the familiar Harrod-Domar growth equation combining the multiplier $1/\alpha$ and the accelerator β. For a given initial value of income, it determines the growth path. This equation could be rewritten as

$$Y = \frac{\beta}{\beta - \alpha} Y_{-1}.$$

If we start with an initial value Y_0, for successive periods we get

$$Y_1 = \frac{\beta}{\beta - \alpha} Y_0,$$

$$Y_2 = \frac{\beta}{\beta - \alpha} Y_1 = \frac{\beta}{\beta - \alpha} \left(\frac{\beta}{\beta - \alpha}\right) Y_0 = \frac{\beta^2}{(\beta - \alpha)^2} Y_0,$$

$$Y_3 = \frac{\beta}{\beta - \alpha} Y_2 = \frac{\beta}{\beta - \alpha} \left[\frac{\beta^2}{(\beta - \alpha)^2}\right] Y_0 = \frac{\beta^3}{(\beta - \alpha)^3} Y_0,$$

$$\cdot$$
$$\cdot$$
$$\cdot$$

$$Y_t = \frac{\beta^t}{(\beta - \alpha)^t} Y_0.$$

From the last line, it is clear how the value of Y, for any time period, can be determined if the initial value Y_0 is given. In this sense, the savings-investment equilibrium condition determines the level of activity, or value of Y, in this system. Also, the time path of output or income in this system is one of positive trend growth with ever increasing levels of activity in prospect. The growth coefficient $\beta/(\beta - \alpha)$ is expected to be greater than unity, as β is probably a positive number in excess of unity, whereas α is a positive number less than unity. For example, if β were 3.0 when α were 0.1, the coefficient would be $3.0/(3.0 - 0.1) = 3.0/2.9$, which, when raised to the t-th power, would increase without limit for larger and larger values; that is, with the passage of time.

If output were determined, the quantity equation or velocity constant would give a value of p, the absolute price level for any particular monetary policy with respect to M. In the equation

$$\frac{M}{pY} = \kappa,$$

p is the only unknown. M is determined by monetary policy, and Y is determined from the previous step.

From the original form of the accelerator equation

$$\frac{K}{Y} = \beta,$$

the only unknown is K; therefore the stock of capital can be determined. Knowing this value, the labor-capital ratio can be used to determine N, as it is the remaining unknown quantity in

$$\frac{K}{N} = \delta.$$

In the equation for labor's share, employment, output, and the price level values from previous equations can be inserted. The result is the value for w, the wage rate

$$\frac{wN}{pY} = \gamma.$$

The solution is completed by determining S from the first equation, the propensity to save, and I from the last, the savings-investment equilibrium value.

This is an interesting and plausible system. The present illustrative purposes will not be served by an exhaustive defense of this model in an appeal to economic analysis. It is merely a simple case of the general type of system studied in macroeconomics.

Identifiability might be questioned in connection with this model. Can a savings function and an investment function, both dependent in some form on income, be separately identified? This model raises questions similar to those discussed earlier in demand analysis. There we came up against the problem of estimating

$$\text{demand} = \text{linear function of price},$$
$$\text{supply} = \text{linear function of price},$$
$$\text{supply} = \text{demand}.$$

Our present situation can be stated as

$$\text{savings} = \text{linear function of income},$$
$$\text{investment} = \text{linear function of income},$$
$$\text{savings} = \text{investment}.$$

In demand analysis, further specification of the model into a cobweb pattern or the introduction of particular exogenous variables assured us of identification. In an analogous manner, the specification that savings depend on current income level alone, whereas investment depends on the change in income level alone, assures us of identifiability in the present case. Any weighted combination (with nonzero weight) of

$$S = \alpha Y \quad \text{and} \quad I = \beta(Y - Y_{-1})$$

cannot be identified as the savings function, because it would contain the variable Y_{-1} which does not appear in the savings equation. However, such a combined function cannot be identified as the investment function because it would not depend on Y and Y_{-1} in the particular way required, that is, as two variables with coefficients equal in magnitude but opposite in sign. If it is not possible to obscure one of the basic relations by developing another, through linear combination processes, that has the same appearance, we say that the equations are identified. This is, in fact, true of the entire model.

Statistical Models of Economic Growth and Trade Cycles 187

The econometrics of measurement and estimation in the model of growth

The model as presented above is in the general form in which it would be used in theoretical economics. The *econometrician* must be more specific and more realistic. On taking up the problem of estimating any of these relationships from observed data, he has to deal with many thorny questions.

The five basic ratios comprising the system have all been, at one time or another, the object of separate investigation. Different authors, solving their own special problems, have used statistical data that seemed best suited to the purpose at hand. We are, however, engaged in the task of estimating the system implied by these ratios as coherent units of mutually consistent parts; therefore, we shall not always use precisely the same series that are historically associated with studies of these ratios separately.

Most of the empirical studies of these ratios have found some degree of cyclical variability. Also some have found trends. We shall not try to account for cyclical movements in this investigation, but will try to estimate some of the trends. Some obvious reasons can be readily cited for most of the cyclical movement. The savings-income ratio contains a numerator that can be either positive or negative. Savings are the most adjustable component of a consumer's budget in extraordinary conditions; therefore, we should expect fluctuations in the ratio to reveal low values, in some cases even negative values, during depressions or recessions and high values during booms. The capital-output ratio rises during a general economic decline because output falls during such a phase while the stock of capital remains nearly stable. It can, at most, fall no faster than depreciation. Similarly, it takes time to increase capital during an upswing while output is growing rapidly; hence, the ratio falls in this phase. For similar reasons the capital-labor ratio will vary inversely to the state of trade over the business-cycle. The work force can be adjusted in accordance with business conditions, but capital stock cannot be altered as readily. Labor's share of output will vary cyclically; largely because nonlabor income includes an important volatile compensatory factor, namely, profits. Like savings, they can be either negative or positive. Their fall during a depression raises labor's share, and their rise during prosperity takes away from labor's share. The velocity ratio, or its reciprocal, will vary cyclically, depending on the relative movements of M and pY. Historically, velocity has varied positively with the level of activity. It may be argued that the stock of cash balances, like the stock of capital, cannot be adjusted to changing business conditions as readily as the income flow pY. Subtle analyses of banking policy and people's asset preferences are needed to explain fluctuations of this ratio in terms of interest rates, price levels, and other money market variables.

The first equation of the model states that savings are proportional to income. How are savings and income to be measured? Shall we use the statistics on personal savings alone or should we combine personal, business, and government savings? Should the government sector be separated from the rest of the system through the use of exogenous decision variables under the control of public authorities? If so, the endogenous variables should refer to the private sector alone. Similarly, the income variable may be personal, private, or national depending on the choice for the savings variable. In addition, it is necessary to decide whether to measure income before or after taxes. Should savings and income be expressed in current or constant prices? If a common price unit or price deflator is used for each, it makes no difference, in a strictly proportional relation, whether the variables are expressed in real or current money terms. The common deflator will cancel from the numerator and denominator of the ratio. If different deflators are used, a decision about the appropriateness of each deflator must be made.

For purposes of the simplest type model—not necessarily the most realistic—we choose the most global forms of measurement. Savings will be measured as total savings (personal, corporate, and government) and income as total net national product.[4] Both will be expressed in a constant price system. Later we shall present details of a more complicated short-run model of the trade cycle in which quite different decisions are made.

Economists and statisticians have long been impressed with S.

---

[4] As will be explained later, some of the computations were made on the basis of the consumption-income ratio instead of the savings-income ratio. Implicitly, savings are defined as the residual after subtracting current consumption from net national product. The consumption variable is given unusual treatment by S. Kuznets, whose compilations we use, so that it includes some government current expenditures as well as personal expenditures. By using national product instead of disposable personal income, we include business savings in our residual estimate of savings.

Kuznets' findings that the percentage of American income saved by persons has tended to be constant in the long-run, when measured by decade averages which iron out short-run business-cycle movements.[5] Goldsmith's more recent study of yearly savings since the beginning of this century show a similar stable trend in the *personal* savings-income ratio.[6] His series show fluctuations over the course of the trade cycle, but they have no discernible trend. For the most part, people accept this great stable ratio of economics as an empirical fact, representing the free outcome of personal choice, but M. Friedman has gone to considerable length to attempt to justify it as a basic pattern of behavior to be expected as a result of rational consumer choice.[7]

The actual numerical estimation of the parameter α in the savings-income relation will depend on the probability assumptions that are put into the model. To this point the system has been treated as an exact model, but all the component parts involving unknown parameters are subject to error. Three possible error assumptions are:

$$\frac{S}{Y} = \alpha + u,$$

$$\frac{S}{Y} = \alpha u,$$

$$S = \alpha Y + u.$$

Each case implies a different statistical calculation for the estimate of α. In the first case, the savings-income ratio is assumed to deviate randomly above and below a central value. The arithmetic average of sample values of S/Y would give a desirable estimate of α. In the second case, the ratio is assumed to deviate above and below a central value with deviation proportional to size of the ratio. The geometric average of the ratios would seem to be suggested, but this method is not generally applicable since S/Y can be either positive or negative. In years of serious economic depression the ratio may turn negative, and geometric averages of negative members have no meaning for us. In

---

[5] S. Kuznets, *Uses of National Income in Peace and War* (N.Y.: National Bureau of Economic Research, 1942) p. 30.

[6] R. W. Goldsmith, *A Study of Savings in the United States*, Vols. I, III (Princeton: Princeton University Press, 1955, 1956).

[7] M. Friedman, *A Theory of the Consumption Function* (Princeton: Princeton University Press, 1957).

the third case, we have the ordinary linear regression model with zero intercept. If Y is an endogenous variable, not independent of u, the technique for the estimation of α will be more complicated than in the usual case of least squares regression.

In many cases, we cannot decide upon one probability model or another, but careful study of the data may help to fix our choice. Not only do we want a close fit between mathematical theory and statistical fact, but we want to have an estimate that is consistent with the probability assumptions of the model. One assumption that is usually made is that the distribution of points in a scatter diagram have uniform variability about the estimated, or fitted, function. If residuals about a computed line

$$S = aY$$

in the (S, Y)-plane show a tendency towards increasing dispersion as income increases (the phenomenon of heteroscedasticity or nonuniform variance), the model

$$\frac{S}{Y} = \alpha + u$$

would be suggested, and the arithmetic average of S/Y would serve as an estimate of α. However, the closeness of fit and the distribution of residuals for a semi-logarithmic model, if applicable, should be compared to see if they are more satisfactory.

In our global model, data are used that cover a long time span (from 1900 to 1953) and that fit together in nearly a closed system. Government spending is lumped with private spending. We have used some series prepared by S. Kuznets to show the trend growth of the American economy in this century. In his framework, government expenditures are, to a large extent, intermediate, and not final, purchases. In terms of the input-output table of the preceding chapter, much of government purchasing is like the intermediate purchase of materials by one industrial sector from another. Government construction is placed with private investment as a *final* expenditure in the national product accounts, and a part of the remaining expenditures by government are attributed to consumption. A large part of expenditures in the growing government sector is omitted, and Kuznets' estimates of national product, in recent years, are considerably lower than those of the U.S. Department of Commerce.

Instead of examining the savings-income ratio, where income is defined as net national product, we examine the consumption-income ratio in order to have all variables positive. We can derive the savings equation from the consumption equation by using the identity

$$\text{savings} + \text{consumption} = \text{income},$$
$$S + C = Y.$$

Both consumption and income are expressed in dollars of 1929. The series used are given in the accompanying table.

TABLE 5.1
Consumption and Net National Product, U.S.A.
(billions of 1929 dollars)

	Consumption	Net national product		Consumption	Net national product
1900	27.8	33.0	1927	74.2	83.6
1901	30.5	36.3	1928	76.3	84.9
1902	30.9	36.8	1929	80.3	90.3
1903	32.9	38.8	1930	75.9	80.5
1904	33.3	38.1	1931	73.2	73.5
1905	34.9	40.7	1932	66.4	60.3
1906	38.3	45.4	1933	65.0	58.2
1907	39.7	46.7	1934	68.6	64.4
1908	38.1	42.6	1935	73.1	75.4
1909	41.4	47.8	1936	80.8	85.0
1910	42.1	48.2	1937	84.4	92.7
1911	43.2	47.9	1938	83.0	85.4
1912	42.8	48.5	1939	87.0	92.3
1913	44.7	51.3	1940	91.7	101.2
1914	47.1	49.8	1941	97.9	113.3
1915	48.2	53.7	1942	96.2	107.8
1916	49.4	58.8	1943	98.8	105.2
1917	50.8	59.0	1944	102.2	107.1
1918	49.6	55.4	1945	109.1	108.8
1919	52.2	61.1	1946	122.3	131.4
1920	54.2	62.2	1947	124.9	130.9
1921	57.0	59.6	1948	127.5	134.7
1922	59.2	63.9	1949	130.7	129.1
1923	64.3	73.5	1950	138.7	147.8
1924	69.0	75.6	1951	139.8	152.1
1925	67.1	77.3	1952	143.9	154.3
1926	72.5	82.8	1953	149.4	159.9

A graph of the ratio of consumption to income, together with the other Great Ratios in our system, are given in Fig. 5.1. In the early years of this century consumption was less than nine-tenths of net national product; recently it has been more than nine-tenths. When defined in this way, instead of purely as personal consumption and personal disposable income, we find a definite upward trend in the

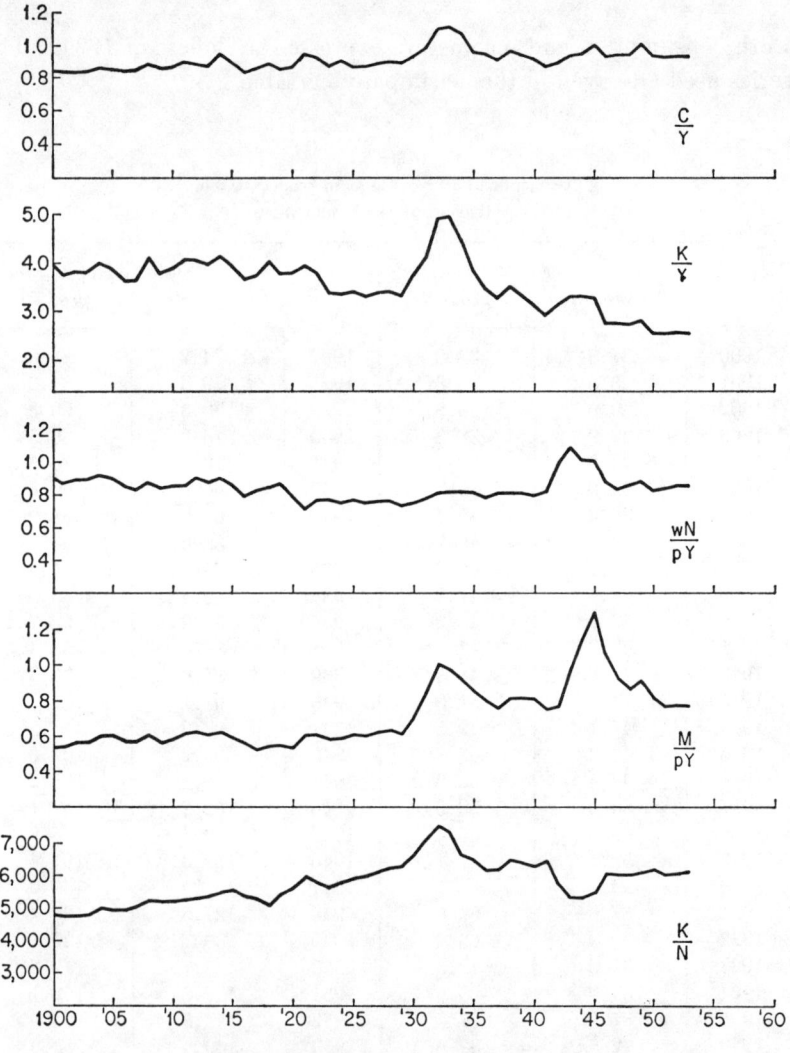

Fig. 5.1. The great ratios of economics

consumption-income ratio or a downward trend in the savings-income ratio.

Either a linear arithmetic or linear semilogarithmic trend would fit these data well and be simple to compute. For the logarithmic case, we estimate

$$\log \frac{C}{Y} = -0.03933 + 0.00054t,$$

or

$$\frac{C}{Y} = 0.9134(1.0013)^t.$$

Time is measured chronologically, centered at January 1, 1927. A unit change in t is six months; therefore we have

.
.
.

1924	$t = -5$,	1927	$t = +1$,
1925	$t = -3$,	1928	$t = +3$,
1926	$t = -1$,	1929	$t = +5$.

.
.
.

For the midpoint of the sample period, the trend value of the consumption ratio is 0.9134. It advances with time at a compound interest rate of about $\frac{1}{8}$ of one per cent semi-annually. The estimated advance is statistically significant in the sense that the coefficient of t in the semilogarithmic equation is more than five times as large as its estimated sampling error.

The second equation of the model contains the capital-output ratio, or the accelerator. In the most aggregative form, capital will be defined to include both private and public stocks of productive wealth. It is important to make the capital concept consistent with the investment concept. Investment includes private capital formation (housing, inventory change, business construction, and private producers' equipment) and public capital formation. In order to equate the rate of change in the capital stock to investment, the latter must be measured *net*, that is, after capital consumption allowances have been subtracted from gross investment expenditure. The output variable in the capital-output ratio must, for consistency, be measured *net*. It is net national product.

Capital is actually measured as the cumulation, from a fixed starting value, of annual net investment. This is most readily done in constant dollars, giving a cumulated figure measured in real terms. Similarly, output will be measured as net national product in constant dollars. Although both series are comprehensive for the economy as a whole, alternative measures covering private capital, or private fixed capital, and net private product would be reasonable.

It may appear to be a matter of indifference whether one estimates the capital-output ratio from the sample data and derives the accelerator equation of investment or estimates the latter and derives the former. A proper consideration of the probability structure of the system will, however, show that a real decision has to be made. If one assumes, as the probability model for the capital-output ratio,

$$\frac{K_t}{Y_t} = \beta + u_t,$$

where $u_1, u_2, \ldots$ are *mutually independent* random variables, it would be natural to estimate β as the arithmetic mean of K_t/Y_t. If, however, one assumes

$$\frac{I_t}{(Y_t - Y_{t-1})} = \beta + v_t,$$

where $v_1, v_2, \ldots$ are *mutually independent* random variables, β should be estimated as the arithmetic mean of $I_t/(Y_t - Y_{t-1})$. The probability model for this form of the investment process says that investment is proportional to income change except for a random error. More specifically, it says that the ratio of I_t to $Y_t - Y_{t-1}$ fluctuates randomly about a constant value. This random fluctuation is expressed by the variable v_t. In the other form, we assume that the ratio of K_t to Y_t fluctuates randomly about the same constant value, but that the random error u_t is different from v_t. The assumptions are quite different in the two cases since

$$v_t = \frac{Y_t u_t - Y_{t-1} u_{t-1}}{Y_t - Y_{t-1}}.$$

We derive this expression as follows: Multiply both sides of the capital-output ratio model by Y_t.

$$K_t = \beta Y_t + Y_t u_t.$$

Write the same equation for period $t - 1$.

$$K_{t-1} = \beta Y_{t-1} + Y_{t-1}u_{t-1}.$$

Subtract the lower from the upper equation. We obtain

$$K_t - K_{t-1} = \beta(Y_t - Y_{t-1}) + Y_t u_t - Y_{t-1}u_{t-1}.$$

Divide both sides by $(Y_t - Y_{t-1})$ to get

$$\frac{K_t - K_{t-1}}{Y_t - Y_{t-1}} = \frac{I_t}{Y_t - Y_{t-1}} = \beta + \frac{Y_t u_t - Y_{t-1}u_{t-1}}{Y_t - Y_{t-1}}.$$

Mutual *independence* among the values of u will generally be associated with mutual *dependence* among the values of v.

Kuznets in a comprehensive study of many facets of the American economy has computed the capital-output ratio directly as K/Y, that is, not in the accelerator form.[8] From 1879 to 1944 his calculated ratio rises from 2.83 to 3.19. There are, however, noticeable cyclical fluctuations within this period, giving rise, especially, to high values during the great depression. Annual estimates by Goldsmith in the same volume confirm the general pattern.[9] Goldsmith's ratios show predominately cyclical fluctuations from 1897 to 1939. During and after World War II, however, the ratio appears to have been at lower levels. In very recent years, with the postwar investment boom, it shows a tendency to rise somewhat.

Kuznets' more recent data on net investment, cumulated through time from a starting value of capital stock, show a generally declining ratio to net national product where both numerator and denominator are estimated in prices of 1929. The data are tabulated in Table 5.2 and graphed in Fig. 5.1. From these statistics, we have estimated as before in the case of the consumption-income ratio,

$$\log \frac{K}{Y} = 0.54699 - 0.00152t$$

or

$$\frac{K}{Y} = 3.523(1.0033)^{-t}.$$

---

[8] S. Kuznets, "Long Term Changes in the National Income of the United States of America Since 1870," *Income and Wealth*, Series II (Cambridge: Bowes and Bowes, 1952).

[9] R. W. Goldsmith, "The Growth of Reproducible Wealth of the United States of America from 1805 to 1950," *ibid*.

This trend formula estimates that the capital-output ratio has been falling at the rate of about one-third of one per cent semi-annually. This drop is statistically significant. The coefficient of t is estimated to be about seven times as large as its sampling error. At January 1, 1927 ($t = 0$) the trend value was 3.5. It should be remembered that

TABLE 5.2
Capital Stock and Net National Product, U.S.A.
(billions of 1929 dollars)

	Capital stock	Net national product		Capital stock	Net national product
1900	131.57	33.0	1927	282.61	83.6
1901	136.71	36.3	1928	290.20	84.9
1902	142.27	36.8	1929	299.42	90.3
1903	147.72	38.8	1930	303.30	80.5
1904	152.20	38.1	1931	303.42	73.5
1905	157.65	40.7	1932	297.12	60.3
1906	164.50	45.4	1933	290.12	58.2
1907	171.25	46.7	1934	285.43	64.4
1908	175.31	42.6	1935	287.78	75.4
1909	182.05	47.8	1936	292.11	85.0
1910	187.86	48.2	1937	300.33	92.7
1911	192.45	47.9	1938	301.38	85.4
1912	198.04	48.5	1939	305.58	92.3
1913	204.38	51.3	1940	313.32	101.2
1914	207.28	49.8	1941	327.41	113.3
1915	210.36	53.7	1942	338.98	107.8
1916	215.70	58.8	1943	347.08	105.2
1917	220.26	59.0	1944	353.46	107.1
1918	223.94	55.4	1945	354.13	108.8
1919	229.37	61.1	1946	359.43	131.4
1920	235.13	62.2	1947	359.30	130.9
1921	236.19	59.6	1948	365.19	134.7
1922	240.15	63.9	1949	363.21	129.1
1923	248.87	73.5	1950	373.73	147.8
1924	254.47	75.6	1951	385.95	152.1
1925	264.08	77.3	1952	396.47	154.3
1926	273.94	82.8	1953	408.01	159.9

these statistics of Kuznets include government capital together with private capital in K and also use a smaller denominator than would be the case if the official series on national product were used. By estimating from the capital output ratio, instead of the investment-output change ratio, we used only positive numbers in our calculations.

The measurement of labor's share is an exercise frequently encountered in empirical economics. Many versions of this ratio have been prepared by authors studying the distribution question. In our particular context we do not have much latitude in choosing a denominator. For consistency with the output measure in other equations of the model, we use net national product, the only difference being that it is measured here in current, rather than constant, dollars. It may be considered desirable to use *national income* or *personal income*, instead of *national product*, in the denominator of this ratio. This would ordinarily necessitate the introduction of a tax-subsidy function into the model to explain the difference between income, at factor costs, and product, at market prices. Complications like these are introduced in larger, more practical models. As it happens, Kuznets' particular concept of national product used here does not differ from national income.

The choice of a numerator in the expression for labor's share is more open to question. Should wages include contributions to pension funds, high salaries of executives, the drawings of small shopkeepers and farmers? The cyclical stability of labor's share has been investigated for a variety of concepts over the interwar period by J. T. Dunlop.[10] His charts show no statistical grounds for choosing among alternatives, and the long-run stability of the ratio persists with substantial cyclical variation, in spite of a variety of plausible definitions. His results do, however, reveal important differences between wages and salaries and among industry groups. The most stable numerical finding appears to be absence of a trend in the ratio for the economy as a whole during the interwar period. D. G. Johnson has attempted to impute a wage to farm operators and entrepreneurs.[11]

Over a longer time period Johnson finds labor's percentage of national income growing by about five points from the first decade of this century to the post World War II period. Were he to exclude the adjustment for the labor content of entrepreneurial income, the increase would be about twice as large.

I. B. Kravis cites the comparative inelasticity of labor's response to increased demand in a growing economy as a reason for the rise in

---

[10] J. T. Dunlop, *Wage Determination under Trade Unions* (New York: Augustus M. Kelley, Inc., 1950) Chapter VIII.

[11] D. G. Johnson, "The Functional Distribution of Income in the United States 1850-1952," *Review of Economics and Statistics*, Vol. 36 (1954) pp. 175-82.

labor's share.[12] The rural-urban population shift may also be an important factor influencing this upward trend in the ratio for the economy as a whole. Labor's share is lower in agriculture than in industry; therefore an occupational shift may affect the national ratio.

TABLE 5.3
Earned Income and Net National Product, U.S.A.
(billions of current dollars)

	Earned income	Net national product		Earned income	Net national product
1900	14.9	16.4	1927	63.0	83.1
1901	15.8	18.0	1928	64.6	85.0
1902	16.8	18.8	1929	65.9	90.3
1903	17.9	20.0	1930	58.3	76.9
1904	18.3	19.9	1931	48.4	61.7
1905	19.5	21.7	1932	36.4	44.8
1906	21.0	24.8	1933	35.1	42.6
1907	22.1	26.5	1934	41.3	50.3
1908	21.1	24.1	1935	47.7	58.2
1909	23.6	28.1	1936	53.4	68.3
1910	24.9	29.0	1937	60.6	75.1
1911	24.7	28.6	1938	56.1	68.8
1912	27.2	30.2	1939	59.7	73.8
1913	27.9	32.1	1940	65.1	81.8
1914	28.3	31.6	1941	82.2	99.0
1915	30.1	35.2	1942	109.2	106.5
1916	34.3	43.5	1943	137.8	113.2
1917	44.5	53.9	1944	150.9	118.7
1918	49.5	58.2	1945	154.0	124.2
1919	56.5	65.2	1946	154.3	160.5
1920	59.6	75.7	1947	164.3	179.0
1921	44.4	61.8	1948	181.2	192.8
1922	48.7	63.0	1949	176.4	185.8
1923	57.0	74.1	1950	191.7	215.0
1924	56.6	75.2	1951	222.3	238.1
1925	60.8	78.6	1952	237.2	245.6
1926	63.2	84.6	1953	249.5	258.8

Similarly, the growth of the government sector has tended to increase the ratio since, by national accounting convention, all *national income* originating in government is wages. Not having disaggregated in this global model, we form the ratio of labor's share from statistics of the economy as a whole. Apart from occupational movements and differ-

[12] I. B. Kravis, "Relative Income Shares in Fact and Theory," *American Economic Review*, Vol. XLIX (1959) pp. 917-49.

ences, trends may be imposed on the ratio by such forces as growing trade union strength and social welfare legislation.

Most long-term investigations of labor's share in the output of the American economy show a positive trend, but we have altered the form of the ratio so that near constancy is obtained. The numerator of our ratio is the sum of employee compensation and the total income of self-employed persons. The scope of our series is wider than a series, like that of Johnson, that includes merely an imputed wage component from the total income of self-employed. To be consistent with the total employment variable of our model, it is desirable that the scope of the numerator be extended to include self-employed persons as well as employees. The imputations of wage components in self-employed factor rewards are difficult to make; therefore, we have constructed essentially an *earned* income variable. The other forms of income in the total national dividend are rewards for the holding of property.

The graph of the ratio of the figures on earned income and net national product, both measured in current prices, shows no significant trend in the twentieth century.[13] Were we to limit the numerator to statistics of employee compensation alone, there would be a pronounced trend in the ratio.

A formal calculation of the trend estimate is

$$\log \frac{wN}{pY} = -0.07369 + 0.000082t$$

or

$$\frac{wN}{pY} = 0.8439(1.00019)^t.$$

This is a tiny trend, not statistically significant, compared to the others in this model. The coefficient of t is less than one-half its estimated sampling error. For practical purposes we ignore it and assume the trendless ratio,

$$\frac{wN}{pY} = 0.8439.$$

The most celebrated ratio in our model is that between cash and income. Our parameter, κ, represents the reciprocal of income velocity. It may be called the *Cambridge "k."* Velocity may be

[13] A peculiarity of Kuznets' definition of national product is that in some wartime years it is less than total factor payments.

defined in terms of total monetary transactions, personal income, total national income, or total national product. We have chosen the last-mentioned form to achieve consistency with the output measure used in the other equations. Cash is used in final purchases covering the full price, inclusive of indirect taxes less subsidies; therefore, national product at market price is a suitable measure here as well as being consistent with usage in the other ratios of the model. As in the equation of labor's share, the denominator is measured in current dollar prices. In the wide variety of velocity estimates prepared in other investigations by monetary theorists, an income (at factor costs) concept is frequently used.

The definitions of cash balances are more varied. Strict transactions cash, consisting of demand deposits and circulating currency, is the narrowest concept. A choice may be made among personal, business, and government holdings and even between holdings by financial and other companies, but we shall, in the present model, confine ourselves to the most aggregative concepts including all personal, business, and government holdings together, as long as they are owned outside the banking system.

To the total of demand deposits and circulating currency, we add time deposits. Some students may include similar holdings in savings and loan associations, credit unions, or other banking institutions. The notion of *liquid assets* includes government bonds, at least those redeemable at a fixed price on demand. We have not included government securities in our total of cash but have drawn the line at the total of bank deposits (demand and time) and currency.

A recent authoritative summary of velocity statistics computed by many authors is given by Selden.[14] Selden's own measure includes, in cash balances, total deposits, plus currency outside banks, plus Treasury cash, plus Treasury deposits with Federal Reserve Banks, and money held in the Treasury. His transactions variable is national income. His velocity estimates range between 0.75 and 1.76 covering the years from 1919 to 1951. He notes both a trend and cycle in velocity and is largely concerned with explaining cyclical fluctuations of velocity in terms of money market variables. Evidence in favor of velocity or its reciprocal as a stable parameter is not very strong.

[14] R. T. Selden, "Monetary Velocity in the United States," *Studies in the Quantity Theory of Money*, M. Friedman, ed. (Chicago: University of Chicago Press, 1956) pp. 179-257.

Nonetheless, for purposes of illustration, we assume the ratio to fluctuate randomly about a constant value or, at worst, a steady trend.
Our estimate of the trend is

$$\log \frac{M}{pY} = -0.15500 + 0.0025t$$

or

$$\frac{M}{pY} = 0.6998(1.0057)^t.$$

The reciprocal of the velocity ratio turns out to have the strongest trend, in the sense measured, among all five ratios of the model. The estimated coefficient of t is more than ten times its sampling error.

TABLE 5.4
Cash Balances and Net National Product, U.S.A.
(billions of current dollars)

	Cash balances	Net national product		Cash balances	Net national product
1900	8.9	16.4	1927	52.2	83.1
1901	10.0	18.0	1928	54.7	85.0
1902	10.8	18.8	1929	55.2	90.3
1903	11.5	20.0	1930	54.4	76.9
1904	12.0	19.9	1931	52.9	61.7
1905	13.2	21.7	1932	45.4	44.8
1906	14.1	24.8	1933	41.7	42.6
1907	15.1	26.5	1934	46.0	50.3
1908	14.7	24.1	1935	49.9	58.2
1909	15.8	28.1	1936	55.1	68.3
1910	17.0	29.0	1937	57.3	75.1
1911	17.8	28.6	1938	56.6	68.8
1912	18.9	30.2	1939	60.9	73.8
1913	19.4	32.1	1940	67.0	81.8
1914	20.0	31.6	1941	74.2	99.0
1915	20.7	35.2	1942	82.0	106.5
1916	24.2	43.5	1943	110.2	113.2
1917	28.2	53.9	1944	136.2	118.7
1918	31.4	58.2	1945	162.8	124.2
1919	35.6	65.2	1946	171.2	160.5
1920	39.9	75.7	1947	165.5	179.0
1921	37.8	61.8	1948	167.9	192.8
1922	39.0	63.0	1949	167.9	185.8
1923	42.7	74.1	1950	173.8	215.0
1924	44.5	75.2	1951	181.0	238.1
1925	48.3	78.6	1952	191.0	245.6
1926	50.6	84.6	1953	197.6	258.8

From the capital-output ratio, we determine the stock of capital after output has been determined by the savings-investment equilibrium. The stock of capital appears in the numerator of our final ratio—the capital-labor ratio. In the ratio showing labor's share, we use the wage bill in the numerator; otherwise, the amount of employment does not enter the system. For a given wage rate, the wage bill determines the level of employment; or, for a given level of employment, the wage bill determines the level of the wage rate. We have chosen the latter approach for measurement. The denominator of the capital-labor ratio is determined from a direct series on total employment including self-employed businessmen and farmers as well as paid workers. This makes the scope of the labor input variable consistent with the factor share variable used above. The wage rate is determined by dividing the wage bill by the total number employed.

This particular ratio has received considerably less attention in economic literature than have the four others in our system. Kuznets has, however, computed and analyzed it in his long-run statistics of the American economy.[15] His estimates of the capital-labor ratio show nearly a tripling from 1879 to 1944. In the last 30 to 40 years the trend has not been marked, but a rapid growth took place just before and after the turn of the century. This is the traditional picture of the increasing industrialization or capitalization of the United States economy.

The annual statistics of the present model show a steady upward growth of the capital-labor ratio from about $5,000 per person engaged at the turn of the century, to about $6,000 after World War II. This amounts to a compound interest growth of slightly less than one-fourth of one per cent semi-annually. The trend formulas are

$$\log \frac{K}{N} = 3.76126 + 0.0010t$$

or

$$\frac{K}{N} = 5771(1.0023)^t.$$

As in the previous cases, we give the values of the numerator and denominator of this ratio in Table 5.5. The ratio itself is plotted

[15] S. Kuznets, *op. cit.*

against time in Fig. 5.1. The appearance of an upward trend is confirmed by the statistical significance of the computed coefficient of t, which is more than six times its estimated sampling error.

TABLE 5.5
Capital Stock and Persons Engaged, U.S.A.
(billions of 1929 dollars and millions of persons)

	Capital stock	Persons engaged		Capital stock	Persons engaged
1900	131.57	27.3	1927	282.61	45.9
1901	136.71	28.4	1928	290.20	46.4
1902	142.27	29.6	1929	299.42	47.6
1903	147.72	30.5	1930	303.30	45.5
1904	152.20	30.4	1931	303.42	42.6
1905	157.65	31.8	1932	297.12	39.3
1906	164.50	33.1	1933	290.12	39.6
1907	171.25	33.8	1934	285.43	42.7
1908	175.31	33.1	1935	287.78	44.2
1909	182.05	34.8	1936	292.11	47.1
1910	187.86	35.7	1937	300.33	48.2
1911	192.45	36.3	1938	301.38	46.4
1912	198.04	37.3	1939	305.58	47.8
1913	204.38	37.9	1940	313.32	49.6
1914	207.28	37.5	1941	327.41	54.1
1915	210.36	37.7	1942	338.98	59.1
1916	215.70	40.1	1943	347.08	64.9
1917	220.26	41.5	1944	353.46	66.0
1918	223.94	44.0	1945	354.13	64.4
1919	229.37	42.3	1946	359.43	58.9
1920	235.13	41.5	1947	359.30	59.3
1921	236.19	39.4	1948	365.19	60.2
1922	240.15	41.4	1949	363.21	58.7
1923	248.87	43.9	1950	373.73	60.0
1924	254.47	43.3	1951	385.95	63.8
1925	264.08	44.5	1952	396.47	64.9
1926	273.94	45.8	1953	408.01	66.0

The last two equations of the model hold as accounting identities. We measure net investment I and stock of capital K in such a way that the rate of change in the latter must equal the former. The investment series includes private and public capital formation. The other accounting identity can be expressed in two ways—as an equality between savings and investment, or as an equality showing that total output is a sum of component parts. In the latter form, it is

$$C + I + B = Y.$$

C, I, and Y are already defined in the model. B is an exogenous variable denoting the net foreign balance. It is a small magnitude over the sample period studied. This accounting identity is often expressed with a separate component measuring government purchases of goods and services. With Kuznets' definitions, however, that we are using, government current expenditures (if for final goods) are included in consumption, and government capital expenditures are included in investment. Intermediate purchases by government are

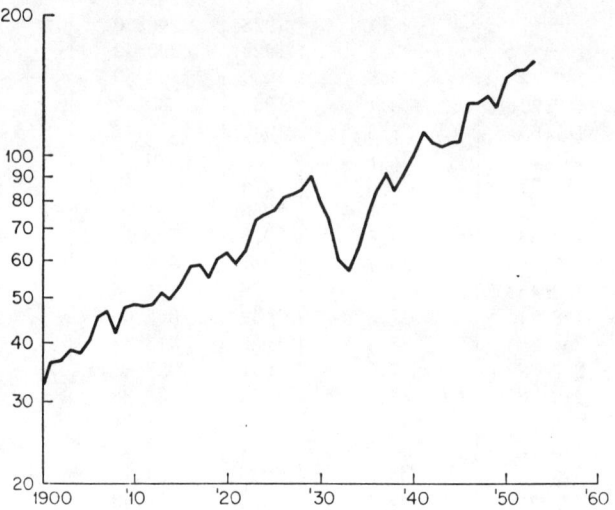

Fig. 5.2. Net national product, 1900-1953 (billions of 1929 dollars-logarithmic scale)

excluded entirely. Thus, except for a small foreign balance, consumption plus investment exhaust national income, which is the form of the accounting identity used in most pedagogical models. This form suits the global simplicity of the present analysis. If the savings-investment form of the equation were used, we would have

$$Y - C = I + B.$$

The left hand side gives a residual definition of savings as the difference between net national product Y and consumption C—both components following Kuznets' particular definitions.

From the consumption and investment ratios, together with the accounting definition of total income, we find, except for the small

foreign balance,
$$Y = 0.9134(1.0013)^t Y + 3.523(1.0033)^{-t+1}[(1.0033)^{-1} Y - Y_{-1}]$$
or
$$Y = \left[\frac{3.523(1.0033)^{-t+1}}{0.9134(1.0013)^t + 3.523(1.0033)^{-t} - 1}\right] Y_{-1}.$$

If the economic ratios were all constant instead of following trends, we would have the ordinary multiplier-accelerator recurrence formula
$$Y = \left[\frac{3.523}{0.9134 + 3.523 - 1}\right] Y_{-1} = 1.025 Y_{-1}.$$

The period-to-period rate of growth of real output is $2\frac{1}{2}$ per cent. This would also be the long-run compound interest rate of growth. At the point centered on January 1, 1927, when t equals 0, this is approximately the rate of growth of the system. When t equals 60 (January 1, 1957), the period-to-period growth rate is given by
$$Y = \left[\frac{3.523(1.0033)^{-59}}{0.9134(1.0013)^{60} + 3.523(1.0033)^{-60} - 1}\right] Y_{-1} = 1.005 Y_{-1},$$
which is as low as $\frac{1}{2}$ per cent.[16]

The rates of growth of the other variables in the system can easily be deduced. Since
$$K = 3.523(1.0033)^{-t} Y,$$
we have
$$\frac{K}{K_{-1}} = \frac{(1.0033)^{-t} Y}{(1.0033)^{-t+1} Y_{-1}} = (1.0033)^{-1} \frac{Y}{Y_{-1}}.$$

We, therefore, find the rate of growth of K by multiplying the rate of growth of Y, as found previously, by $(1.0033)^{-1}$. Similarly, we have
$$\frac{N}{N_{-1}} = (1.0023)^{-1} \frac{K}{K_{-1}},$$
$$\frac{p}{p_{-1}} = \frac{M}{M_{-1}} (1.0057)^{-1} \frac{Y}{Y_{-1}},$$
$$\frac{w}{w_{-1}} = \frac{N_{-1}}{N} \frac{p}{p_{-1}} \frac{Y}{Y_{-1}}.$$

[16] If we were to omit the years of negative savings from the sample, and fit a semilogarithmic trend to the positive savings-income ratio, the decline in S/Y (growth in C/Y) would be more gradual, and the rate of growth of real output would fall less rapidly than in the above calculation.

In the case of the formula for the period-to-period change in the wage rate, we have assumed that there is no significant trend in labor's share.

If real output were to grow at a constant percentage rate, its time-series chart on a semilogarithmic scale should exhibit a linear trend. The straight line trend of the logarithm of output that held for the period 1900-1929 over-estimates output for the remaining period until 1953 (see Fig. 5.2). This indicates a declining rate of growth in our model or a curved trend line.

QUESTIONS AND PROBLEMS

1. Compare and contrast the identification problem in supply-demand models for individual commodities and savings-investment models for the economy as a whole.

Hint: Begin with the two simplest models of each theory,

$$\text{(a)} \quad \begin{aligned} X^D &= \alpha + \beta p, \\ X^S &= \gamma + \delta p, \\ X^S &= X^D, \end{aligned} \qquad \text{(b)} \quad \begin{aligned} S &= \epsilon + \zeta Y, \\ I &= \eta + \theta Y, \\ S &= I. \end{aligned}$$

Take up the effects of introducing random errors, nonlinearities, lags, exogenous variables, and inventories.

2. The multiplier-accelerator model may be written as

$$S_t = \alpha + \beta Y_t,$$
$$K_t = \gamma + \delta Y_t,$$
$$I_t = K_t - K_{t-1},$$
$$S_t = I_t.$$

Discuss the dynamic properties of this model. Include in the discussion (a) What ranges of values of the parameters will lead to income growth or to income decline? (b) How can the lag structure be altered so as to produce cycles? (c) What is the significance of the constant terms α and γ in the solution to the above dynamic system?

3. The preceding question deals with a model of a closed economy having no government sector. Revise the model to permit foreign trade and autonomous government economic action. How will these changes affect the dynamic solution?

4. How does the statistical reliability (sampling error, for example) of parameter coefficients in an aggregative model affect the reliability of the dynamic solution to the model?

A COLLECTION OF MODELS

The formulation of business-cycle and growth theories of economics in terms of mathematical equations has been found to be an indispensable research tool. It is important in understanding a theory and especially useful in distinguishing among different theories. A concrete and well-defined mathematical model is essential for statistical testing and use in economic policy formation by econometric methods. The econometrician begins his work after the mathematical economist has formulated the model. But with modern tendencies toward theoretical model building, we have learned that there are many possible models and that there is no unique mathematical picture of the aggregate economy. Indeed, it would be surprising if the complicated behavior of millions of human beings and productive enterprise units could be summarized in a system of 5, 10, 20 or even 50 mathematical equations *in an unique way*. Each model usually has some restricted points to emphasize, and there still is no "best way" to characterize the whole economy. On empirical grounds, we must admit that the facts of life can be given more than one acceptable explanation, especially in aggregative terms.

The Keynesian models form a useful point of departure. The understanding of the Keynesian system was much enhanced by two early mathematical expositions, one by Lange and one by Hicks.[17] Hicks' model is

$$S(r, Y) = I(r, Y),$$

$$M = L(r, Y),$$

where

r = interest rate,

Y = income,

M = cash balances.

[17] O. Lange, "The Rate of Interest and the Optimum Propensity to Consume,' *Economica*, Vol. V, N.S. (1938) pp. 12-32; J. R. Hicks, "Mr. Keynes and the Classics: A Suggested Interpretation," *Econometrica*, Vol. 5 (1937) pp. 147-59.

The first equation is the condition of savings-investment equilibrium, and the second is the equation of liquidity-preference. The money supply is exogenously determined; $S(r, Y)$ is the savings function, and $I(r,Y)$ is the investment function. If both the savings and investment functions are linear, or have the same general parametric form, there will be no statistical way of distinguishing between them. There is a lack of identification in this system. The implicit function obtained by equating $S(r, Y)$ and $I(r, Y)$ (that is, an implicit function associating r and Y) could be identified but the savings function and the investment function could not. If all the equations in the system were linear, it would be possible to identify the implicit savings-investment equation but not the liquidity-preference equation.

Dynamic versions of the Keynesian equilibrium system, could, however, be identified. In our growth model studied above we had an identified model of this type involving savings-investment equilibrium but with no interest rate. The lag structure of the accelerator function, blended with the ordinary savings function, brought about the conditions for identification. If the Keynesian system is "dynamized" with particular lags in savings and investment, it is possible to have complete identification. For example, the following dynamic system is identified if all functions are linear.

$$S(r_t, Y_t) = I(r_t, Y_{t-1} - Y_{t-2}),$$

$$M_t = L(r_t, Y_t).$$

The savings function depends only on current income and interest rate level, whereas the investment function depends on the rate of change of income and interest rate level. In the latter case, Y_t and Y_{t-1} have equal coefficients with opposite sign. As in the *static* Keynesian model above, the treatment of money supply M as an exogenous variable identifies the implicit function describing the savings-investment equilibrium process. The restrictive specifications of the savings and investment functions separately in the dynamic system identify these two functions and, at the same time, distinguish them from the liquidity-preference function which has no income lag specified. Therefore, the dynamic system has enough particular information built into its structure to assure identification.

Another interesting type of Keynesian dynamization suggested by

Samuelson is[18]

$$S(r_t, Y_t) - I(r_t, Y_t) = \alpha(Y_t - Y_{t-1}),$$
$$M_t = L(r_t, Y_t).$$

In this case, we have an output fluctuation to adjust for the discrepancy between savings and investment. Although the savings and investment functions are not identified, as in the static version, it is a general type of dynamic process that can be built into a variety of statistical models of this type, when identification is achieved through the use of other variables or other specific formulations of the savings and investment functions.

These models are stated, for purposes of analytical economics, as closed systems without exogenous governments. A lack of identification may readily disappear if due allowance is made for international trade, government policies, as well as other institutional phenomena and lags. We may, therefore, concentrate our attention on general types of aggregative systems, without special reference, now, to the question of identifiability.

Kalecki independently developed a business cycle model of the Keynesian type but made use of the interesting lag between orders and deliveries.[19] His model is

$$B_t = C_t + A_t, \qquad A_t = \frac{1}{\theta} \sum_{i=t-\theta}^{t} I_i,$$

$$C_t = C_1 + \lambda B_t, \qquad K_t - K_{t-1} = L_t - U_t,$$

$$L_t = I_{t-\theta}, \qquad \frac{I_t}{K_t} = \alpha \frac{B_t}{K_t} + \beta.$$

B = gross profits accruing to the capitalist sector,

C = consumption by the capitalist sector,

A = saving by the capitalist sector,

I = orders of capital goods,

L = deliveries of capital goods,

K = stock of capital,

U = depreciation.

[18] P. A. Samuelson, *Foundations of Economic Analysis* (Cambridge: Harvard University Press, 1947) pp. 276-83.

[19] M. Kalecki, "A Macrodynamic Theory of Business Cycles" *Econometrica*, Vol. III (1935) pp. 327-44.

In the actual model studied by Kalecki, the variables were treated as continuous; therefore, in place of summation of I_i, he used an integral of a continuous function. The first equation is simply an accounting identity. The second is a consumption function. Workers who receive wage income are assumed to spend it all on consumer goods and have no savings. This assumption may be relaxed. The third equation shows the lag of θ time units between orders and deliveries of capital goods. The fourth equates savings in the capitalist sector to average unfilled orders. The next to the last equation is an account-definition, equating the change in capital stock to net investment. Kalecki assumes that U, depreciation, is exogenous in this model. Finally, we have an investment function relating the rate of capital expansion to the rate of profit.

Another interesting model, a version of the ordinary Keynesian system, is the nonlinear model of Kaldor.[20] His model has two dynamic elements: an income adjustment to the savings-investment discrepancy and an effect of capital stock (investment accumulation) on investment. The latter property is akin to generalizations of the ordinary acceleration principle. In symbolic form, his model can be written as

$$S_t = f(Y_t), \qquad Y_t - Y_{t-1} = h(S_t - I_t),$$
$$I_t = g(Y_t, K_{t-1}), \qquad K_t - K_{t-1} = I_t.$$

S = savings,

Y = income,

I = investment,

K = capital stock.

The significant aspect of this theory is the type of nonlinearity implied in the f and g functions. In Kaldor's theory they curve in such a way that they have three points of intersection, two exterior points of stable equilibrium, and one interior point of unstable equilibrium. He draws curves as in Fig. 5.3 where P_1 and P_3 are points of stable equilibrium, and P_2 is unstable, but these are all points of *partial* equilibrium because the variable K is not allowed to vary in this graph. The I curve is drawn for a particular value of K. However, positive values of I lead to larger values of K which, in turn,

---

[20] N. Kaldor, "A Model of the Trade Cycle," *Economic Journal*, Vol. L (1940) pp. 78-92.

depress the whole *I* curve and cause oscillatory movements in the system. This scheme, in fact, is an example of an endogenous cycle that can be maintained in a nonlinear dynamic system. Except for very special values of coefficients, linear dynamic models cannot have maintained cycles. They generally explode or dampen with external shocks.

Actually, both functions need not be nonlinear. If one is nonlinear and the other linear in such a manner that there are three points of intersection, with two stable and one unstable, a limit cycle may result.

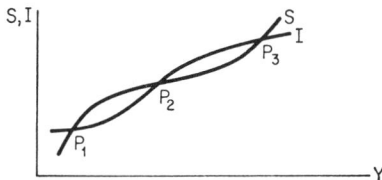

Fig. 5.3. Nonlinear savings and investment functions

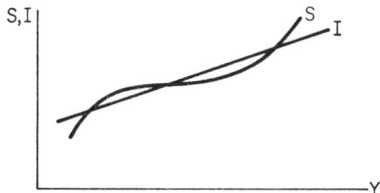

Fig. 5.4. Nonlinear savings and linear investment functions

It might be thought unlikely that such extraordinary patterns of savings and investment are realistic and actually produce a practical model of this type, yet a plausible empirical structure can be estimated for the Kaldor model. For a study of postwar quarterly observations for the United States, an empirical model of the Kaldor type has been estimated. The savings function is nonlinear with the bends and turns suggested by Kaldor. There are sensible arguments for such a shape. One might say that savings are insensitive to small changes in income near modal values. This accounts for an almost flat range in the middle. For large upward changes in income, there would be large increases in savings, and for large downward changes in income, there would be large decreases in savings. Investment, however, is made a linear function of income and capital. The configuration, for a given stock of capital is shown in Fig. 5.4.

Traditionally, national income accounts are arranged, by definition, so that measured savings and investment are equal. If inventory change is excluded from investment, or at least if that part in excess of "transactions" balances is so excluded, we may view inventory accumulation as an excess of savings over investment, bringing about a downward adjustment in output or income. The reverse happens when inventories are decreased. This gives operational significance to the dynamic adjustment equation

$$Y_t - Y_{t-1} = h(S_t - I_t).$$

With actual statistics on savings, fixed investment, inventory investment, stock of fixed capital and income we have the following numerical model:[21]

(a) $$\frac{S_t}{N_t} = 9.52 + 0.503 \left(\frac{Y_t}{N_t} - 333\right)^3 \times 10^{-4} - 0.52 Q_{1t} + 16.27 Q_{2t} + 15.57 Q_{3t},$$

(b) $$\frac{I_t}{K_{t-1}} = -0.00463 + 0.076 \frac{Y_{t-1}}{K_{t-2}} - 0.00277 Q_{1t} + 0.00124 Q_{2t} + 0.00077 Q_{3t},$$

(c) $$\frac{(Y+T+D)_t}{(Y+T+D)_{t-1}} = 1.012 - 0.070 \frac{H_{t-1}}{(Y+T+D-\Delta H)_{t-1}} + 0.090 Q_{1t} + 0.091 Q_{2t} + 0.150 Q_{3t},$$

(d) $$D_t = -12.16 + 0.057 K_{t-1},$$

(e) $$S_t = I_t + \Delta H_t + G_t - T_t,$$

(f) $$I_t = K_t - K_{t-1}.$$

S_t = savings,

Y_t = disposable income (inclusive of corporate savings),

N_t = population,

I_t = investment,

K_t = stock of capital,

$(Y + T + D)_t$ = gross national product,

[21] This model is discussed at greater length in "Quelques Aspects Empiriques du Modèle de Cycle Économique de Kaldor" by L. R. Klein with the collaboration of A. Buckberg, L. Gyorki, and H. Runyon, *Les Modèles Dynamiques en Économétrie* (Paris: Centre National de la Recherche Scientifique, 1956).

ΔH_t = inventory change,

D_t = capital consumption,

G_t = government purchases of goods and services,

Q_{it} = seasonal indicator (1 in i-th quarter; zero otherwise).

These variables are measured in prices of 1947. The equations are fit to quarterly observations of 1947-1952.

Equations (b), (c), and (d) have pure lag structures, except for the seasonal factors. They are estimated by ordinary least squares regressions of the dependent (left hand) variables on the independent (right hand) variables. Equation (a) has simultaneity between S/N and Y/N. It is estimated by a technique known as the method of instrumental variables.[22] Equations (e) and (f) are identities without any unknown coefficients.

Equation (a) represents Kaldor's curved savings function. It is a cubic function relating per capita savings to per capita disposable income. A curve of this type can be cut three times by a straight line. The next equation establishes a linear relation between the rate of investment (percentage expansion of capital stock) and the rate of income flow on capital. This equation gives a linear relation between investment and income if K_{t-1}/K_{t-2} is given. Equation (c) relates the rate of change of gross national product, measured as the ratio of successive quarters of gross output, to the ratio of inventory stocks to final sales. By subtracting inventory change from gross national product, we get gross national sales This is the variable in the denominator. In this equation there is an implicit assumption that inventories are normally held in a fixed relation to sales. Excesses of the stock-sales ratio cause output to fall, and deficits cause it to rise. This is the dynamic adjustment process of the model. Finally, since output is measured *gross*, while investment is measured *net*, we must account for depreciation, which is made a simple linear function of capital stock with no seasonal movement.

Business fluctuations are sometimes called inventory cycles. These are usually short-run cycles, sometimes as long as the general business-cycle in duration and sometimes of shorter periodicity. In recent years, the postwar business-cycle peaks (and subsequent recessions)

---

[22] See L. R. Klein, *A Textbook of Econometrics* (Evanston, Ill.: Row, Peterson & Co., 1953) Chapter III.

in the United States of 1953, 1957, and 1960 have been identified with inventory phenomena.

The Kaldor model and the others we have been discussing have been based, in an important way, on the behavior of total investment. Primarily, this is meant to be investment in fixed capital. Inventory aspects may be associated largely with the output adjustment to savings-investment discrepancies. This, in fact, was done for the empirical estimate of the Kaldor model.

Metzler has constructed self-contained models of economic cycles based on inventory investment.[23] He centers attention on the inventory component of total investment and treats investment in fixed capital as purely exogenous. The essence of his theory can be seen in his simplest model, although he makes successive refinements to bring in a greater range of possible cases. Using his notation we have

$u(t) = \beta y(t-1)$,   consumption function

$s(t) = \beta[y(t-1) - y(t-2)]$,   inventory investment function

$y(t) = u(t) + s(t) + v_0$,   definition of national income

$y(t)$ = national income,

$u(t)$ = consumption,

$s(t)$ = production for inventory,

v_0 = exogenous investment.

This system looks like the ordinary multiplier-accelerator version of the Keynesian system, but Metzler's explanation of the design of the system is important in laying the groundwork for further generalizations.

Consumption is made to depend on income, lagged one period, in the usual way. This is the familiar linear consumption function. The inventory investment function is based on the idea that production for inventory should be the difference between the actual and normal level of stocks of the preceding period. This difference in stock levels is determined by the difference between actual and anticipated sales of period $t - 1$.

[23] L. Metzler, "The Nature and Stability of Inventory Cycles," *The Review of Economic Statistics*, Vol. XXIII (1941) pp. 113-29.

actual sales (for consumption) = $\beta y(t-1)$,
anticipated sales = $\beta y(t-2)$,
production for inventory = $s(t) = \beta y(t-1) - \beta y(t-2)$.

As long as the parameter β lies in the positive range between zero and unity, this simple model exhibits damped cyclical fluctuations. The time pattern of exogenous investment is neglected in this conclusion.

Metzler has generalized this model in two directions. He has introduced expectations more explicitly, and he has separated unintended from normal inventory changes. He introduces expectations by writing the consumption function as

$$u(t) = \beta y(t-1) + \eta[\beta y(t-1) - \beta y(t-2)].$$

The coefficient η is an adjustment parameter associating expected income levels with recent fluctuations in income. He writes the equation of production for inventory as

$$s(t) = \beta y(t-1) - (1+\eta)\beta y(t-2) + \eta \beta y(t-3).$$

The first term on the right is the same as in the previous model. From it, we subtract the expected sales of period $t-1$, which are obtained by putting a time lag of one period in the new version of the consumption equation. His treatment then parallels that of the simplest model, and the time pattern of the system is found to depend on the joint sizes of β and η.

In a third version of his theory, Metzler writes

$$u(t) = \beta y(t-1),$$
$$s(t) = \alpha[\beta y(t-1)] - k(t-1).$$

The consumption function is the same as in the original model. The sales of period t are $\beta y(t-1)$. We multiply this by α in the next equation, where α is the normal ratio between inventory change and sales. From this product we subtract the beginning of period stocks $k(t-1)$. Beginning stocks are divided into two parts, a normal and an unintended part. The normal part is the product of sales of the preceding period $\beta y(t-2)$, and the inventory change-sales ratio, α. The unintended part is the difference between actual and expected sales. As in the first Metzler model, this is expressed by $\beta y(t-1) - \beta y(t-2)$, but the sign is reversed since they are unintended stocks.

Putting these two parts together, we have

$$k(t-1) = \alpha\beta y(t-2) - \beta y(t-1) + \beta y(t-2).$$

We may rewrite the inventory investment equation as

$$s(t) = \alpha\beta y(t-1) - \alpha\beta y(t-2) + \beta y(t-1) - \beta y(t-2)$$
$$= (1+\alpha)\beta y(t-1) - (1+\alpha)\beta y(t-2).$$

Together with the consumption equation and the definition of national income as the sum of its components, we have a model that produces different time sequences of total income depending on the relative sizes of α and β.

QUESTIONS AND PROBLEMS

1. In making empirical estimates of simple Keynesian type models, as discussed by Hicks, Lange, and Samuelson, should the variables of the systems be measured: (a) In current price aggregates? (b) In constant price aggregates? (c) In per capita terms? Relate your answer to the completeness of the system.

2. How could savings and expenditure surveys of individual families be used in the estimation of the models of Keynes, Kalecki, or Kaldor?

3. Outline a model that makes use of the contributions of Keynes, Kalecki, Kaldor, and Metzler simultaneously.

4. In a formal sense, the Harrod-Domar growth model consists of a multiplier-accelerator mechanism based on two critical parameters, the marginal propensity to consume and the capital-output ratio. Similarly the simplest version of the Metzler inventory model consists of a linear consumption function and an accelerator version of inventory investment. There is, however, an important difference between the capital-output ratio of the Harrod-Domar theory and the accelerator coefficient of the Metzler theory. Explain this difference from the point of view of applied econometrics. Explain why the Harrod-Domar theory produces trend growth, while the Metzler theory produces short-run cycles.

Another type of nonlinearity has been introduced in models built by Goodwin.[24] In a sense Goodwin's model is similar to Kaldor's in

[24] R. M. Goodwin, "A Model of Cyclical Growth," *The Business Cycle in the Postwar World*, E. Lundberg, ed. (London: Macmillan, 1955) pp. 203-21.

that he assumes a nonlinear investment function of the same general shape. His model, using savings-investment equilibrium, focuses attention on the nonlinearity of investment rather than the nonlinearity of savings. In Goodwin's model the *desired* level of capital is proportional to output, except for modifications brought about by technical change.

$$\xi = vy + \beta(t),$$

ξ = *desired* capital, $\qquad v$ = acceleration coefficient,

y = output, $\qquad \beta(t)$ = technical change function.

Actual investment is a function of the discrepancy between *desired* and *actual* capital.[25]

$$g(\dot{k}) = \xi - k,$$

k = actual capital,

$\dot{k}$ = rate of change of capital stock

$\quad$ = net investment.

This investment function has the S-shaped form in linear segments, of the graph in Fig. 5.5. There are two crucial nonlinearities displayed

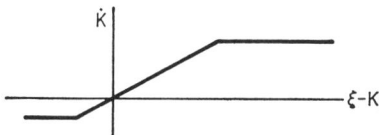

Fig. 5.5. Goodwin investment function

here. A lower limit to net investment is set by capital wastage (zero gross investment and maximum disinvestment). The upper limit is set by capacity or the "maximum output of new capital goods obtainable with given capital and labor supply."

The savings function is put in the multiplier form so that output is made a function of net investment and public spending.

$$y = f(\dot{k} + r(t)), \qquad r(t) = \text{public spending.}$$

[25] We are following Goodwin's notation and practice here, but it may be more customary to write the investment function expressing $\dot{k}$ (investment) as a function of $\xi - k$ (discrepancy between desired and actual capital).

These three equations in ξ, y, and k (or $\dot{k}$) as endogenous variables constitute the nucleus of Goodwin's system. From a theoretical point of view he is principally interested in the oscillatory properties of this system. From our point of view, as econometricians, we are first interested in measuring the variables and estimating the unknown functions. Then, the problem of oscillations can be taken up numerically. In any event, Goodwin's theory provides a useful hypothetical point of departure for econometric business-cycle research. That is the main purpose of the present discussion.

An essentially different type of multiplier-accelerator system has been proposed by Smithies.[26] His system is linear, but departs from the usual assumptions associated with the simplest linear model in that it is not reversible.[27] His savings function, for example, assumes that savings depend linearly on current income and the highest previous level of income. When incomes are rising, the highest previous level will be that of the immediately preceding period, after the level of the previous business-cycle peak is reached. When incomes are falling, the previous peak level remains constant as the value representing the highest previous income. Thus, the effect of the past is generally different for rising and falling incomes; herein lies the irreversibility.[28] Smithies writes

$$S = \alpha_1 Y - \alpha_2 \bar{Y},$$

$S =$ savings,

$Y =$ income,

$\bar{Y} =$ highest previous income.

From a statistical point of view, this looks like a linear equation.

The investment function in Smithies' model has the same irreversibility or "ratchet" effect. In addition, he makes use of a version of

---

[26] A. Smithies, "Economic Fluctuations and Growth," *Econometrica*, Vol. 25 (1957) pp. 1-52.

[27] A similar type of irreversibility is, in fact, assumed by Goodwin, but it is the nonlinearity and not the irreversibility that is the essence of his scheme.

[28] This is the "ratchet" effect commonly associated with the contributions of Duesenberry and Modigliani. See J. S. Duesenberry, *Income, Saving, and the Theory of Consumer Behavior* (Cambridge: Harvard University Press, 1949), F. Modigliani, "Fluctuations in the Saving-Income Ratio: A Problem in Economic Forecasting," *Studies in Income and Wealth*, Vol. 11 (N.Y.: National Bureau of Economic Research, 1949) pp. 371-443.

the acceleration principle as does Goodwin. He does this by introducing the concept of capacity output and making investment depend inversely on the amount by which full capacity output exceeds the highest previous level. His investment function is

$$I = \beta_1 Y_{-1} + \beta_2 \bar{Y} - \beta_3[(Y_F)_{-1} - \bar{Y}] + k(t),$$

I = gross investment,

Y_F = full capacity output,

$k(t)$ = autonomous investment.

This is a linear function in Y, $\bar{Y}$, and Y_F. To cover the possible effects of innovations and other forms of spontaneous investment he introduces $k(t)$, which is some particular function of time, independent of the economic process.

On the one hand, the acceleration principle of investment behavior may be viewed as a technical relation showing how capital input is transformed into output. On the other hand, it is more often used as a demand relationship showing the psychological propensity to invest. Most theories do not make a proper distinction between these two ways of interpreting the principle, but Smithies does make this distinction. His investment function is based on the acceleration principle, looked at from the side of demand. On the supply side, he introduces a technical relation that shows how investment is translated, after due allowance for depreciation and obsolescence, into new capacity. His capacity-formation technical relation is

$$(Y_F) - (Y_F)_{-1} = \sigma I_{-1} - D_1 - D_2 + h(t),$$

D_1 = physical depreciation,

D_2 = obsolescence,

$h(t)$ = autonomous changes in capacity.

Depreciation and obsolescence are endogenous variables in Smithies' system; therefore, additional equations are needed for their explanation.

$$D_1 = \delta_1(Y_F)_{-1} \quad \text{and} \quad D_2 = \delta_2[(Y_F)_{-1} - Y_{-1}].$$

Depreciation is made a linear function of capacity output and obsolescence a linear function of the spread between capacity and actual output. Both functions have time lags of one period.

With the savings-investment equation,

$$S = I,$$

the system is completed and closed, except for the two autonomous functions of time.

QUESTIONS AND PROBLEMS

1. What are advantages and disadvantages of nonlinear, compared with linear, models of the trade cycle? Consider both statistics and economics in your answer.

2. Illustrate the working of the Kaldor model if the investment function is linear and the savings function nonlinear (Kaldor's type of nonlinearity). Do the same for the case of a linear savings function and a nonlinear investment function. Which model do you believe to be more realistic: (a) Both functions nonlinear? (b) Investment linear, savings nonlinear? (c) Investment nonlinear, savings linear?

3. Give a formula for a single smooth curve that approximates the shape of Goodwin's nonlinear investment function. What are the advantages and disadvantages of Goodwin's functions (three linear segments pieced together) over a single smooth curve?

Some problems of measurement

It is not always an easy matter to make actual statistical measurements of the concepts that grow out of economic theorizing. Fortunately, the Keynesian theory of employment stimulated data collection so that most national income accounting systems provide extensive data on such items as savings, investment, income, and related variables. The ingredients of the simplest Keynesian models developed by Hicks and Lange are readily measured. The data used in our statistical model of the great ratios of economics are typical of the statistical series available for this kind of work. The dynamic versions of the system, in which a discrepancy between (planned) savings and (planned) investment is an important magnitude, pose much more difficult problems of measurement. The subjective concept of *excessive* or *undesired* inventory change is involved and is not easily measured. One possible solution has been that illustrated above in connection with the Kaldor model, in which *excessive* inventories are those held above a certain normal or average ratio to sales.

In all these models, the problems of capital measurement are present. Because of the influence of technical progress, it is very difficult to construct a series on capital stock over a long time span in which the quality characteristic of capital is held constant. Statistical series of capital are available, and we have used them above in numerical models in this chapter, but their precision is debatable. A similar point is relevant to the discussion of the aggregate production function in the previous chapter, and there we discussed statistical devices used to measure technical change.

The Goodwin and Smithies models have never been statistically estimated, and, though both are examples of recent advanced contributions to trade cycle theory, they are not likely to be studied empirically until much fundamental measurement work has been done. A great deal of mathematical economics is not easily amenable to applied econometrics.

Goodwin's system contains a variable representing *desired* capital. This, in itself, has not been measured on any broad scale. By substitution, however, this subjective variable can be eliminated from his system to derive a relation making investment a function of output and capital stock. The relation between ξ and y may be substituted into the relation between $\dot{k}$ and $\xi - k$. We have

$$g(\dot{k}) = vy - k + \beta(t).$$

This establishes a relation between investment $\dot{k}$, output level y, and actual capital stock k. These are all objectively measurable variables.

As noted previously, capital stock is only imperfectly measured, but in this respect the Goodwin model has no more serious measurement problems than do other models. The nonlinearity, which is the essence of Goodwin's theory, poses additional problems of measurement even though the variables in the function are measurable. The "full capacity ceiling" and "maximum disinvestment floor" must also be determined. Unless we find many statistical observations clearly in the neighborhood of the ceiling and floor, empirical graduation of his nonlinear investment function may be difficult.

The difficult magnitudes to determine in the Smithies model are capacity output and obsolescence. It may be possible to define these concepts theoretically, and they both are important, but reliable statistical series of capacity and obsolescence are not presently available. The measurement of macroeconomic capacity is, however, a feasible project, and it is not unlikely that series will eventually be produced that can be used in connection with estimation of parameters in a model of Smithies' type.

SOME WORKING MODELS

The systems we have dealt with so far in this chapter might be called *pedagogical* models. They are useful in illustrating some basic theoretical points, either numerical or general, about the economy; they show how fluctuations might take place and be sustained; they show why the economy tends to grow and something about the pace of growth. However, these models are not suitable for persons who require results for practical decisions in public or business policy. A *working* model must be one that has the ability to do more than illustrate a fine point in theory; it must be able to describe the actual workings of the everyday economy with an accuracy that will suit the needs of decision makers. Movements of total output, employment, or the price level must be predicted consistently within less than five per cent error. Possibly even greater precision is required. A working model must bring in many institutional characteristics of an economy and be sufficiently disaggregated to enable the decision maker to form judgments about sectors of interest to him. Generally, it will be a much larger and more complicated model than those discussed so far.

Several working models have been used in applied economic analysis, and two examples of typical systems will be given here, by way of illustration. One model is for the Dutch economy. It was built in 1955 for use by the Central Planning Bureau of the Dutch Government.[29] The other is a postwar model of the United Kingdom constructed in 1957 by the present author. The latter has no official status. Both are annual models of moderate size. Larger and smaller systems, some quarterly and some annual, have been constructed elsewhere. Although the Dutch model appears to be larger, with 27 equations, it could in fact be written much more compactly, in terms of about a dozen essential statistical equations. A large number of definitions

[29] *Scope and Methods of the Central Planning Bureau* (The Hague: Central Planning Bureau, 1956), Appendix II.

and accounting identities are spelled out in great detail. This greatly expands the apparent size of the system.

The Dutch system has a very particular scheme of notation. The variables are written as deviations from 1954 base levels. Base values are denoted by an overhead bar. Capital letters are used to denote current price values and lower case letters to denote values in 1954 prices or changes in index numbers from a base value of unity in 1954. The system is completely linear since values occurring as the product of price and quantity have been expanded as

$$px = [\bar{p} + (p - \bar{p})][\bar{x} + (x - \bar{x})] = (\bar{p} + \Delta p)(\bar{x} + \Delta x),$$

$$px = \bar{p}\bar{x} + \bar{x}\,\Delta p + \bar{p}\,\Delta x + \Delta p\,\Delta x.$$

If Δp and Δx are both small deviations, their product $\Delta p \Delta x$ is neglected in approximation, as being of the *second order of smallness*. This approximation becomes poorer as Δp and Δx become larger. We have as linear approximations

$$px - \bar{p}\bar{x} \cong \bar{x}\,\Delta p + \bar{p}\,\Delta x.$$

On the left hand side, we have a change in value over the base year. In the model's notation, this would be a basic capital letter. On the right hand side, we have base values multiplied into changes over the base values. Consequently, the change in value is approximated by a linear function of change in price and change in quantity, the weights in the linear function being given as base values of quantity and price respectively. The increments Δp and Δx are denoted as lower case letters in the model.

VARIABLES—1955 DUTCH MODEL

Symbol	Description
e	exports of goods and service by enterprises
e_g	commodity exports by enterprises ($\bar{e}_g = 9.10$: base value)
e_{gau}	autonomous commodity exports by enterprises
e_d	exports of services by enterprises ($\bar{e}_d = 3.70$)
m	imports of goods and services by enterprises ($\bar{m} = 12.34$)
m_d	imports of services by enterprises ($\bar{m}_d = 1.71$)
m_g	commodity imports by enterprises ($\bar{m}_g = 10.63$)
i	net investment by enterprises ($i = 2.29$)
i_v	actual replacements by enterprises
d	depreciation by enterprises ($\bar{d} = 2.21$)

Symbol	Description
n	increase in commodity stocks ($\bar{n} = 1.00$)
x_0	government expenditure on goods and services bought from enterprises ($\bar{x}_0 = 2.33$)
c	private consumption bought from enterprises ($\bar{c} = 15.56$)
v	output of enterprises ($\bar{v} = 36.19$)
X_L	consumption by the group "wages, salaries, and social benefits"
X_{ZC}	consumption by the group "other income"
C_0	net government sales to households
C_F	private consumption in foreign countries
L	wage bill of enterprises including contributions to social security ($\bar{L} = 9.51$)
Z	income of the group "other income"
W_L	benefits from the unemployment insurance fund
O_{LW}	annual benefits per unemployed paid by the unemployment insurance fund ($\bar{O}_{LW} = 1,800$)
L_0	wages and salaries paid by government
L_F	income from abroad of the group "wages, salaries, and social benefits"
Z_F	income from abroad of the group "other income"
O_L	transfers by government to the group "wages, salaries, and social benefits"
O_Z	transfers by government to the group "other income"
U_L	benefits from insurance funds to the group "wages, salaries, and social benefits"
P_L	premiums to insurance funds from the group "wages, salaries, and social benefits"
P_Z	premiums to insurance funds from the group "other income"
P_W	premiums to the unemployment insurance fund
T_L	direct taxes from the group "wages, salaries and social benefits"
T_Z	direct taxes from the group "other income"
T_{Lau}	autonomous changes in T_L
T_{Zau}	autonomous changes in T_Z
T_K	indirect taxes net of subsidies
$T_{Kau, c}$	autonomous changes in T_K on private consumption
$T_{Kau, eg}$	autonomous changes in T_K on commodity exports
T_{Kau, x_0}	autonomous changes in T_K on government expenditure
$T_{Kau, i}$	autonomous changes in T_K on investment
$T_{Kau, n}$	autonomous changes in T_K on commodity stock changes
T_{Kau}	autonomous changes in T_K
B	dependent working population in enterprises ($\bar{B} = 2,632,000$)
p_{eg}	price index of commodity exports by enterprises
p_w	index of competing world market price level
p_{ed}	price index of service exports by enterprises
p_{mg}	price index of commodity imports by enterprises
p_{md}	price index of service imports by enterprises
p_c	price index of private consumption

Statistical Models of Economic Growth and Trade Cycles

Symbol	Description
p_{x_0}	price index of government expenditures on goods and services bought from enterprises
p_i	price index of investments
p_n	price index of commodity stock changes
l	wage rate in enterprises
a	employment in enterprises
b	dependent working population

The last 12 items in the list of variables are all index numbers that have a base value of unity in 1954. With two exceptions, all other variables are in billions of florins. O_{LW} is measured on a per person basis and is quoted simply in florins. The working population B is measured in number of persons. These 55 variables are inter-related in 27 equations as follows.

Definitions

(1) $L = \bar{L}(a + l)$

(2) $C = X_L + X_{ZC} - C_F - C_0$

(3) $C = c + \bar{c}p_c$

(4) $X_0 = x_0 + \bar{x}_0 p_{x_0}$

(5) $I = i + \bar{i}p_i$

(6) $D = d + \bar{d}p_i$

(7) $N = n + \bar{n}p_n$

(8) $E = e_g + e_d + \bar{e}_g p_{e_g} + \bar{e}_d p_{e_d}$

(9) $V = v + \bar{c}p_c + \bar{x}_0 p_{x_0} + \bar{i}p_i + \bar{d}p_d + \bar{n}p_n + \bar{e}_g p_{e_g} + \bar{e}_d p_{e_d}$

(10) $M = m + \bar{m}_g p_{m_g} + \bar{m}_d p_{m_d}$

(11) $Z = V - L_* - T_K - D - M$

Balance equation

(12) $C + X_0 + I + D + N + E = V$

Institutional equations

(13) $W_L = 0.54 \bar{B} \bar{O}_{LW}(b - a)$

(14) $T_L = 0.09(L + W_L + L_0 + L_F + O_L + U_L - P_L - P_W) + T_{Lau}$

(15) $T_Z = 0.30(Z + Z_F + O_Z - P_Z) + T_{Zau}$

(16) $T_K = 0.03L + 0.04M + 0.09(V - E) + T_{Kau}$

Technical equations

(17) $\quad m = 0.38c + 0.63e_g + 0.28e_d + 0.71(i + d) + 0.79n + 0.39X_0 + m_d$

(18) $\quad a = 0.40 \dfrac{v - m}{\bar{v} - \bar{m}}$

Behavior equations

(19) $\quad X_L = 0.85(L + W_L - T_L + L_0 + L_F + O_L + U_L - P_L - P_W)$

(20) $\quad X_{ZC} = 0.40(Z - T_Z + Z_F + O_Z - P_Z)$

(21) $\quad i = 0.25(v - n) - 0.10\bar{\imath} + i_v - d$

(22) $\quad e_g = -2.00(p_{e_g} - p_w)\bar{e}_g + e_{gau}$

(23) $\quad p_c = 0.35l + 0.20 p_{m_g} + \dfrac{T_{Kau,\,c}}{\bar{c}}$

(24) $\quad p_{e_g} = 0.50\left(0.35l + 0.30 p_{m_g} + \dfrac{T_{Kau,\,e_g}}{\bar{e}_g}\right) + 0.50 p_w$

(25) $\quad p_{x_0} = 0.30l + 0.50 p_{m_g} + \dfrac{T_{Kau,\,x_0}}{\bar{x}_0}$

(26) $\quad p_i = 0.25l + 0.50 p_{m_g} + \dfrac{T_{Kau,\,i}}{\bar{c}}$

(27) $\quad p_n = 0.10l + 0.70 p_{m_g} + \dfrac{T_{Kau,\,n}}{\bar{n}}$

This system of 27 equations looks formidable. Actually, it is much simpler than appears in this great detail. The first 12 equations are definitions that enable us to write the rest of the system in a convenient way, but they play no essential role in the econometric or statistical analysis. The next 4 equations are fixed by current tax and transfer payment laws. The remaining equations are not so few as to place this system within the category of pedagogical models. It has been widely used in working applications, but it is not a large system by modern standards. The endogenous variables are

volumes—c, i, e_g, m, a, and v;
values—X_L, X_{ZC}, C, X_0, I, N, D, E, V, M, T_K, L, Z, T_L, T_Z, and W_L;
prices—p_c, p_{e_g}, p_{x_0}, p_i, and p_n.

The remaining variables are exogenous or predetermined.

The first 12 equations simply define variables as the sums or products of components. The first equation states that the wage bill is the product of employment and the wage rate. This product is then linearized, as noted above, into a sum of terms—one involving the employment variable and one involving the wage rate variable. Since a and l are each an index of the corresponding magnitude, the wage bill must also be expressed as an index $L/\bar{L}$; thus we have

$$\frac{L}{\bar{L}} = \bar{l}a + \bar{a}l.$$

Since $\bar{l}$ and $\bar{a}$ are base values of indexes, they are each equal to *unity*. We may thus write

$$\frac{L}{\bar{L}} = a + l,$$

or

$$L = \bar{L}(a + l).$$

The second identity states that total domestic household purchases from private enterprises are the sum of purchases out of wage income and purchases out of property (nonwage) income less government sales to households and sales to households abroad. The third identity factors consumption expenditures into price and quantity variables. By linear expansion we have

$$C = \bar{p}_c c + \bar{c} p_c;$$

however

$$\bar{p}_c = 1;$$

therefore

$$C = c + \bar{c} p_c.$$

The next seven identities make similar factorizations and linear expansions, but they also break up some physical quantities into obvious components.

Equation (11) expresses "profit" as the value of output V less costs for wages L, indirect taxes T_K, depreciation D, and imports M. Equation (12) expresses the "product" or "expenditure" side of the national product accounts as the sum of consumer expenditures on output of domestic enterprises C, government expenditures X_0, net investment I, depreciation D, inventory change N, and exports E.

All of these equations discussed so far, simply express one group of variables in terms of others. There are no unknown coefficients or random errors involved. These relations are problems of accounting.

Equation (13) shows how benefits from the unemployment insurance fund vary with the amount of unemployment ($b - a$). Since the fund covers 54 per cent of the workers, the coefficient 0.54 is introduced in this equation. This coefficient is not estimated by statistical inference from a sample. It is given from a priori information. The next three equations show how tax collections vary with the bases on which they are levied. Taxes on wage incomes derive from levies on private wages L, net transfers $(W_L - P_W) + (U_L - P_L) + O_L$, government wages L_0, and overseas wage earnings L_F. Taxes on property income derive from levies on domestic property income Z, overseas property income Z_F and net transfers $O_Z - P_Z$. In each case, the model is designed so that policy applications can be adjusted to take account of known or assumed autonomous changes in taxes—T_{Lau} or T_{Zau}.

Indirect taxes are made, in equation (16), to depend on wage income, imports, and the value of production consumed at home. This function, too, can be shifted by autonomous changes in taxes, T_{Kau}.

The marginal import content of each type of good produced domestically gives the coefficients in equation (17). The marginal import content of consumption goods is 0.38, of commodity exports 0.63, and so on. These coefficients, multiplied by output variables, give goods imports. To these we must add services imports to get total imports.

The other technical equation, equation (18), is an input-output relationship. On the one hand a gives private employment (input), and on the other, $v - m$ gives net domestic production (output = total production less imports).

The remaining equations, together with the production function just discussed, are the more familiar relationships of econometrics. They constitute the heart of the model, explaining demand for output and price formation. They are estimated as ordinary least squares regressions and were published without sampling errors. Equations (19) and (20) are consumption functions. The marginal propensity to consume out of disposable wage income is 0.85 and out of disposable nonwage income 0.40. The investment function is formed as a variation of the acceleration principle according to the theory developed by Goodwin described above. Equation (21), however, is linear and not, in that respect, like Goodwin's function. Investment is made to depend on sales (output less change in stocks of goods) and the stock of capital goods at the beginning of the year. Base year (the preceding year) investment gives the stock of capital measured from a fixed origin, the value of which does not matter in a linear model, it is absorbed in a fitted constant term of a linear equation.

The final demand function is one for Dutch exports, which is made to depend on the spread between domestic and world prices of export goods. The remaining equations are all "price formation" or "mark-up" equations. They show the mark-up of various domestic prices over prime costs—wage rate (l) and import price (p_{m_g}). The export price equation has a term, in addition, to allow for adjustment to competing prices in the world market, and all the price equations make provision for autonomous changes in indirect taxes.

The essential behavior and technological part of the system thus consists of only 11 compactly expressed equations. This model is too large for pedagogical use in macroeconomic theory but just large enough for realistic application. In both forecasting and policy formation, this model has been used by a central planning agency of the government. It will be noted that it is practically a static system. The accelerator version of the investment function gives it some possibility of trend movement, but there are no lags, rates of change, or other dynamic impulses. Doubtless, it could be made more realistic by being extended into a fully dynamic system.

A system of comparable size, with many related properties, has been constructed for the United Kingdom in the postwar period. This is an annual model, serving as a condensed prototype of a much larger quarterly model. The annual model is constructed to look almost like the companion quarterly model; therefore, it does not take advantage of the fact that many more statistical series are available on an annual, than on a quarterly, basis. The limited number of quarterly series restricted the form of the quarterly system, and these restrictions are kept in the annual model.

Many fewer variables need be defined for the British than for the Dutch model.

P = index of industrial production
E_p = number of employees in industrial production industries
I = index of import quantity
t = time trend measured in years
F = final domestic demand in constant prices (consumption plus gross domestic investment in fixed capital plus government current expenditures on goods and services)

X = index of export quantity
C = consumption in constant prices
w = index of average weekly earnings
E = total number of employees
p = index of the price of final output
T_w = tax rate on wage and salary income
D = nonwage personal income in current prices
T_d = tax rate on nonwage personal income
G = government current expenditure on goods and services in constant prices
$T_{d'}$ = tax rate on company income
r = yield on $2\frac{1}{2}$ per cent consols
p_i = index of import prices
R = ratio of gold and dollar reserves at beginning of year to imports of two preceding years
U = registered unemployment at end of June
r_b = Bank Rate
M = notes and coin in circulation outside banks plus Clearing Bank deposits averaged over the year.

In writing the equation system, we shall use a particular notation for index numbers because all the variables are transformed into indexes in the computed equations. An index for the year t will have a subscript $(_{t0})$, $(_t)$ for the current year and $(_0)$ for the base year. We will correspondingly make use of subscripts $(_{t-1,\,0})$ and $(_{t-2,\,0})$ for lagged index values. The subscript will apply to the quantity being indexed, which may be a composite in some cases. The time trend is not measured by an index.

(a) $P_{t0} = 0.56(E_p)_{t0} + 0.40 I_{t0} + 2.36(t - 1946)$ production function

(b) $P_{t0} = -36.3 + 1.03 F_{t0} + 0.33 X_{t0}$ production decision equation

(c) $C_{t0} = 16.9 + 0.17 \left(\dfrac{wE}{p}\dfrac{1}{T_w}\right)_{t0} + 0.05 \left(\dfrac{D}{p}\dfrac{1}{T_d}\right)_{t0} + 0.61 C_{t-1,\,0}$ consumption function

(d) $(F - C - G)_{t0} = 86.3 + 0.93 \left(\dfrac{D}{p}\dfrac{1}{T_{d'}}\right)_{t0} - 0.40 r_{t0}$ investment function

(e) $I_{t0} = 7.3 + 0.92 P_{t0} - 0.05 \left(\dfrac{p_i}{p}\right)_{t0} + 0.04 R_{t0}$ import function

(f) $w_{t0} - w_{t-1,\,0} = 22.4 - 0.21 U_{t0} + 1.06(p_{t-1,\,0} - p_{t-2,\,0})$ wage determination equation

(g) $p_{t0} = 18.1 + 0.48 w_{t0} + 0.34(p_i)_{t0}$ price mark-up equation

(h) $r_{t0} = 203.8 + 0.09(r_b)_{t0} - 1.15 \left(\dfrac{M}{wE + D}\right)_{t0}$ interest-rate determination equation

(i) $(E_p)_{t0} = -60.9 + 1.61 E_{t0}$ relation between industrial and total employment

(j) $\left(\dfrac{D}{wE+D}\right)_{t0} = 284.2 - 1.16\left(\dfrac{w}{p}\right)_{t0} - 0.67\left(\dfrac{p_i}{p}\right)_{t0}$ income distribution equation

(k) $U_{t0} - U_{t-1,\,0} = -11.77(E_{t0} - E_{t-1,\,0})$ labor force equation

In this system of eleven equations, there are eleven endogenous variables: P, E_p, I, F, C, w, E, D, r, U, and p. The others are predetermined.

The variables, before being made into indexes, are defined in the usual way as money flows, number of persons, interest rate percentage, and so on. The variables w and E are so constructed that their product wE measures wage and salary payments in current prices. Gross domestic investment in monetary values (fixed prices) is defined by the ordinary flows in the national income accounts as

$$\text{gross domestic investment} = F - C - G.$$

In our index notation, however, an identity like this does not hold for the index values

$$(F - C - G)_{t0} \neq F_{t0} - C_{t0} - G_{t0}.$$

The correct index identity is

$$(F - C - G)_{t0} = \dfrac{1}{F_0 - C_0 - G_0}(F_{t0}F_0 - C_{t0}C_0 - G_{t0}G_0).$$

In this formula; F_0, C_0, and G_0 are base values of the corresponding variables.

When the equations of a model are all expressed in terms of index variables with a common base period, the linear coefficients are, in fact, base year *elasticities*. The linear equations are not, however, constant elasticity functions, and it is necessary to multiply coefficients by a ratio of two index values to obtain elasticity coefficients for years other than the base year. However, in that particular year such ratios are unity.

All the equations except (d) and (k) are estimated from the sample period 1947-56 by the method known as *two-stage-least-squares*.[30] Since investment was controlled or restricted by capacity until about 1952, equation (d) was separately estimated for the period 1951-56 by the method called *sub-group averages*. This is equivalent to the method of instrumental variables mentioned earlier in connection with the estimation of one of the equations in the empirical version of the Kaldor model. The estimation of (k) is explained below. All the numerical coefficients written above are statistical estimates, subject to sampling error. Since this system was estimated from a very small sample, and intended merely as a *prototype*, sampling errors were not estimated for it.

The production function shows how labor input is translated into industrial output. Both input and output variables are restricted in scope to cover only the industrial sector. Capital stock statistics were not available on a quarterly basis; therefore, this variable was omitted from the production function in both the quarterly and annual models. Imports, however, are regarded as separate factors of production. This seems to be a reasonable assumption for an open economy, although, in a more detailed system, it may be worthwhile to distinguish between imports for industrial use and imports for direct consumption.

The second equation is called a "production decision" equation. It is used as a substitute for an inventory accumulation equation, for which quarterly data are deficient. The equation estimated relates production to final demand (domestic or foreign). The balance between these two magnitudes is, apart from imports, indicative of the net change in inventories.

Equation (c) is a version of the well-known "propensity to consume." Consumption is made to depend separately on wage and nonwage income to show some influence of income distribution, as well as income level, in the spending-saving decisions of households. Both of these income variables are deflated or adjusted for levels of prices and tax rates. The influence of past on present behavior is indicated by the lagged value of consumption.

[30] See H. Theil, *Economic Forecasts and Policy* (Amsterdam: North-Holland Publishing Co., 1958) for an explanation of this method. The reader will also find another description of the Dutch model in this book.

The next equation is the "propensity to invest." Capital outlays are made a linear function of nonwage income, deflated by price level and company tax rates, and the market rate of interest.

Equation (e) is the demand for imports. In this equation there is an income or activity effect, expressed through the variable P, and a relative price effect, expressed through the variable p_i/p. In addition, we determine the effect of the reserve position on imports by introducing the variable R, which shows the ratio of gold and dollar reserves to recent import flows. Exports are not developed as an endogenous variable in this model. They are assumed to be largely determined by separate, foreign events. This assumption is made for convenience, to keep the system rather small and compact. In the associated quarterly model, a detailed set of export equations is developed.

The level of money wage rates is assumed, in equation (f), to fluctuate in response to excess supply in the labor market, which is measured by unemployment. We do not assume any money illusion in the striking of the wage bargain, but we do assume a lag of money wage movements behind prices.

Equation (g) is the "mark-up" equation similar to those used in the Dutch model, above. Final price is marked up over prime unit costs—wage costs and import costs.

In equation (h), the market rate of interest is assumed to follow the Bank Rate set by the monetary authorities and to be influenced, in addition, by the reciprocal of *velocity* of circulation. The latter consideration is suggested by the theory of liquidity preference.

The last three equations serve mainly to round out the system and make it complete. Since we had to distinguish industrial employment from total employment in (a) (the production function), we must include a relation between industrial employment E_p and total employment E. The latter is the appropriate variable in making up the wages bill. Equation (j) is needed as an empirical relation because this model is not couched in the usual national accounting framework. In the national accounts, final domestic demand and the foreign balance add to national product less inventory change. However, wage and nonwage income add to national income, which differs from national product only by such factors as indirect taxes less subsidies. A national income accounting identity could then be used at this stage, but inventory change is not used as an explicit variable.

Instead, we relate an index of the nonwage share of national income to indexes of real costs (wage costs and import costs) in this empirical equation. This is not the same as equation (g) because that relation deals only with a unit profit margin, whereas (j) shows how *total* profits are determined.

Ordinarily, we would have an identity defining the labor force as the sum of employment and unemployment. This would be suitable if the labor force were the smooth trend that it is often assumed to be. In fact, however, it has shown great cyclical variability in recent years. Under the pressure of high demand (low unemployment) women, children, aged persons, and marginal workers have been induced to enter the labor force. When a relaxation of demand occurs, the labor force contracts through a withdrawal of these people. We have related "recent" changes in unemployment to "recent" changes in employment to get an empirical relation connecting these two components of the labor force. The parameter estimate in equation (k) is simply the ratio between a pair of values of unemployment and employment at the end of the sample period. It is not a *two-stage–least-squares* estimate.

Both the Dutch and the United Kingdom models presented here are good examples of the type of detail and the degree of refinement to which one must go in building realistic working models of an economy. Larger econometric models have been built on other occasions, and the models of this chapter are mere stepping stones to more adequate systems.[31]

QUESTIONS AND PROBLEMS

1. In a working model of the United States economy, what are some important institutional characteristics that ought to be incorporated in the system?

2. How would you suggest altering the Dutch model with a view toward making it (a) more detailed by economic sector and (b) dynamic?

[31] J. Tinbergen, *Statistical Testing of Business Cycle Theories:* Vol. II, *Business Cycles in the United States of America, 1919-1932* (Geneva: League of Nations, 1939); L. R. Klein, *Economic Fluctuations in the United States, 1921-1941* (N.Y.: John Wiley and Sons, Inc., 1950); L. R. Klein and A. S. Goldberger, *An Econometric Model of the United States, 1929-1952* (Amsterdam: North-Holland Publishing Co., 1955); L. R. Klein, R. J. Ball, A. Hazlewood, and P. Vandome, *An Econometric Model of the U. K.* (Oxford: Blackwell, 1961).

Statistical Models of Economic Growth and Trade Cycles

3. Outline the structure of a model of the United Kingdom economy composed within the framework of the national income accounting system. Keep the size of the model approximately the same as that given in the text.

4. Indicate how the United Kingdom model can be approximated by linear equations.

5. Discuss the relationships between the working models (Holland and the United Kingdom) in this chapter and the theoretical systems of Keynes, Kalecki, Kaldor, Metzler, Goodwin, and Smithies.

6

Applications in Macroeconomics

FORECASTING THE TRADE CYCLE

The goal of most theories is, in a broad sense, to *predict*. Economists want to be able to advise alternative policies for business, government, and personal uses. In order to give advice, they usually have to know what outcome to expect from various actions. In many cases, these actions are influenced or controlled by economists. Economic advisers may suggest that the result of the imposition of a particular tax, say a sales tax, will be to increase the price at which goods sell and, consequently, to dampen demand. More specific questions of measurement, such as how much will prices rise and how much will demand fall, are typical of the kind that econometricians might try to answer. General economic analysis is not enough. A systematic numerical study is needed.

If the policy in question is discarded as being inappropriate on the basis of the econometrician's estimate of *how much*, it does not invalidate his forecast or prediction, even though his appraisal of the consequences is never realized. He is as interested in predicting what *would be* as well as what *is*. In applied econometrics, we deal, to a large extent, with observed samples of statistical data. Quantitative statements about the relevant economic variables of a problem outside

Applications in Macroeconomics 237

the confines of the sample data are predictions. It is in this general sense of extrapolation beyond the sample, whether virtual or actual positions are being considered, that we use the terms *forecasting* or *prediction*.

To a large extent, however, econometricians are called upon to forecast, passively, about what is to be. This is the ordinary sense in which the term is used. In the preceding chapter, an example of an annual model of the United Kingdom economy was given. The sample data on which this model was based covered the period 1947-1956. It is instructive to see how such a scheme can be used in forecasting economic activity for a period outside the sample years. We choose the year 1958 as an example.

In order to make an extrapolation or forecast for 1958 from the equation system in Chapter 5, pp. 230-31, we must first substitute into the system values of exogenous or predetermined variables. The equations of the system enable us to solve for the endogenous variables in terms of the predetermined variables. We must first specify the values of the latter in Table 6.1.

TABLE 6.1
1958 Forecast
Assumed Values of Predetermined Variables

		Assumed	Actual
Time	$t - 1946$	12	12
Exports	X	136	142
Reciprocal of tax rate	$1/T_w$	1.06	0.96
Reciprocal of tax rate	$1/T_d$	1.22	1.15
Reciprocal of tax rate	$1/T_{d'}$	1.30	1.20
Import price	p_i	123	118
Reserve position	R	74.3	74.3
Bank Rate	r_b	260	219.2
Cash balances	M	8200	8512
Government expenditure	G	2300	2263
Working hours	h	1.0	1.017
Lagged consumption	C_{-1}	117.9	118.7
Lagged price change	$p_{-1} - p_{-2}$	4.6	8.0
Lagged wage rate	w_{-1}	174.2	176.0
Lagged unemployment	U_{-1}	88.6	88.6
Lagged employment	E_{-1}	106.5	107.7

The assumed values are from genuine forecasts prepared for 1958 in January of that year. The actual values were ascertained a year later. This is a realistic situation for any forecasting application. Basic assumptions made before the event may turn out to be in error; nevertheless, such assumptions must be made before forecasting can proceed. Some of the variables, for which the econometrician has rightly or wrongly elected not to give a statistical explanation, may prove to be extremely difficult to estimate in advance. Even lagged values of endogenous variables cannot always be accurately determined at the time of forecast, as subsequent revisions by data gathering agencies show.

Substitution of the values from the table into the equation system leads to a more compact presentation of the model in which there are only as many unknown variables as equations. In terms of the notation of the model, it is:

(1) $\quad P_{t0} = 28.44 + 0.68(E_p)_{t0} + 0.28I_{t0},$

(2) $\quad P_{t0} = 8.58 + 1.03F_{t0},$

(3) $\quad C_{t0} = 88.82 + 0.18\dfrac{w_{t0}E_{t0}}{p_{t0}} + 6.1\dfrac{D_{t0}}{p_{t0}},$

(4) $\quad F_{t0} = 30.29 + 0.73C_{t0} + 14.82\dfrac{D_{t0}}{p_{t0}} - 0.050r_{t0},$

(5) $\quad I_{t0} = 10.27 + 0.92P_{t0} - \dfrac{615}{p_{t0}},$

(6) $\quad w_{t0} = 201.48 - 0.21U_{t0},$

(7) $\quad p_{t0} = 59.92 + 0.48w_{t0},$

(8) $\quad r_{t0} = 227.2 - \dfrac{117{,}828{,}781.5}{64.18w_{t0}E_{t0} + 2506D_{t0}},$

(9) $\quad (E_p)_{t0} = -60.87 + 1.61E_{t0},$

(10) $\quad D_{t0} = w_{t0}E_{t0}\dfrac{18{,}239.96 - 7444.88(w_{t0}/p_{t0}) - 528{,}907.38(1/p_{t0})}{180{,}194.8 + 290{,}696(w_{t0}/p_{t0}) + 20{,}651{,}946(1/p_{t0})},$

(11) $\quad U_{t0} = 1342.16 - 11.77E_{t0}.$

From these 11 consolidated equations, we solve for the 11 endogenous unknowns $P, E_p, I, F, C, w, E, p, D, r,$ and U. The solution values are predictions or extrapolations for the calendar year 1958.

The condensation of the complete system of Chapter 5 to the present system for prediction purposes gives an interesting exercise in the manipulation of different units of measurement which is a common

Applications in Macroeconomics

problem in econometrics. Consider the consumption equation. It is written in full as

$$C_{t0} = 16.9 + 0.17 \left(\frac{wE}{p}\frac{1}{T_w}\right)_{t0} + 0.05 \left(\frac{D}{p}\frac{1}{T_d}\right)_{t0} + 0.61 C_{t-1, 0},$$

where the subscripts ($_{t0}$) or ($_{t-1, 0}$) refer to the entire quantity that is indexed. The condensed system written above separates each variable as an individual index, whereas, for computational convenience, it was preferable to write entire, combined variables such as

$$\frac{wE}{p}\frac{1}{T_w}$$

in terms of a single index based on 100 in year 0. Symbolically, we may write this combined index variable as[1]

$$100 \frac{\dfrac{w_t E_t}{p_t}\left(\dfrac{1}{T_w}\right)_t}{\dfrac{w_0 E_0}{p_0}\left(\dfrac{1}{T_w}\right)_0} = 100 \frac{\dfrac{w_t}{w_0}\dfrac{E_t}{E_0}\left(\dfrac{1}{T_w}\right)_t}{\dfrac{p_t}{p_0}\left(\dfrac{1}{T_w}\right)_0}$$

$$= \frac{100\dfrac{w_t}{w_0} \; 100\dfrac{E_t}{E_0}\left(\dfrac{1}{T_w}\right)_t}{100\dfrac{p_t}{p_0}\left(\dfrac{1}{T_w}\right)_0}$$

$$= \frac{w_{t0} E_{t0}}{p_{t0}} \frac{\left(\dfrac{1}{T_w}\right)_t}{\left(\dfrac{1}{T_w}\right)_0}.$$

From Table 6.1, we see that reciprocals of tax rates were six per cent over the base values; hence, we substitute

$$\frac{\left(\dfrac{1}{T_w}\right)_t}{\left(\dfrac{1}{T_w}\right)_0} = 1.06,$$

to find that the term associated with wage income in the consumption

---

[1] *Symbolically* because indexes of w, E, and p are additions of many elements by the usual index formulas, and not simple ratios that would hold true for one type of labor and one type of output.

equation is

$$0.17 \left(\frac{wE}{p} \frac{1}{T_w}\right)_{t0} = 0.17(1.06) \frac{w_{t0}E_{t0}}{p_{t0}} = 0.18 \frac{w_{t0}E_{t0}}{p_{t0}}.$$

Similar calculations are made on the next term in the consumption equation

$$\left(\frac{D}{p} \frac{1}{T_d}\right)_{t0}.$$

It becomes

$$100 \frac{\frac{D_t}{D_0}\left(\frac{1}{T_d}\right)_t}{\frac{p_t}{p_0}\left(\frac{1}{T_d}\right)_0} = 100 \frac{100 \frac{D_t}{D_0}\left(\frac{1}{T_d}\right)_t}{100 \frac{p_t}{p_0}\left(\frac{1}{T_d}\right)_0} = 100 \frac{D_{t0}}{p_{t0}} \frac{\left(\frac{1}{T_d}\right)_t}{\left(\frac{1}{T_d}\right)_0}.$$

In the table of predetermined variables, we see that reciprocals of tax rates on nonwage incomes are 22 per cent above base levels; therefore, we write, for the second term in the equation,

$$0.05 \left(\frac{D}{p} \frac{1}{T_d}\right)_{t0} = 0.05(100) \frac{D_{t0}}{p_{t0}} (1.22) = 6.1 \frac{D_{t0}}{p_{t0}}.$$

The constant term in the equation is 16.9, but this figure is modified by the fact that last year's consumption is approximately known for the period of forecast—one year ahead. We write

$$C_{t0} = 16.9 + 0.61(117.9) + 0.18 \frac{w_{t0}E_{t0}}{p_{t0}} + 6.1 \frac{D_{t0}}{p_{t0}},$$

$$C_{t0} = 88.82 + 0.18 \frac{w_{t0}E_{t0}}{p_{t0}} + 6.1 \frac{D_{t0}}{p_{t0}}.$$

It is through a similar process of substituting assumed values of exogenous or other lagged variables, given in Table 6.1, and making appropriate adjustments for units of measurement in the index formulation that the other equations are derived in their condensed form. For the most part, the manipulation of the units of measurement in the index formulation is simple. However, there are three combined variables in the system which are difficult to transform into component indexes. They are

$$(F - C - G)_{t0} = \frac{1}{F_0 - C_0 - G_0} (F_{t0}F_0 - C_{t0}C_0 - G_{t0}G_0)$$

$$= 8.16 F_{t0} - 5.92 C_{t0} - \frac{2300}{1430} 100.$$

Applications in Macroeconomics

In this expression

8.16 = ratio of base value of F to base value of
$F - C - G = F_0/F_0 - C_0 - G_0$,

5.92 = ratio of base value of C to base value of
$F - C - G = C_0/F_0 - C_0 - G_0$,

2300 = assumed value of G in forecast period
$= G_{t0}G_0/100$,

1430 = base value of $F - C - G = F_0 - C_0 - G_0$.

$$\left(\frac{M}{wE+D}\right)_{t0} = 100 \frac{M_t/M_0}{(w_tE_t + D_t)/(w_0E_0 + D_0)}$$

$$= \frac{(M_t/M_0)100(w_0E_0 + D_0)}{w_0(w_t/w_0)E_0(E_t/E_0) + D_0(D_t/D_0)}$$

$$= \frac{(M_t/M_0)100(w_0E_0 + D_0)}{w_0E_0(w_{t0}/100)(E_{t0}/100) + D_0(D_{t0}/100)}$$

$$= 100 \frac{(8200/7142)892{,}400}{64.18w_{t0}E_{t0} + 2{,}506D_{t0}}.$$

The numerical values are

8200 = cash balances assumed for 1958 = M_t,

7142 = cash balances in base period = M_0,

$8924 = 6418 + 2506$ = wage plus nonwage income in base year
$= w_0E_0 + D_0$,

6418 = wage income in base year = w_0E_0,

2506 = nonwage income in base year = D_0.

$$\left(\frac{D}{wE+D}\right)_{t0} = 100 \frac{(D_t/D_0)}{(w_tE_t + D_t)/(w_0E_0 + D_0)}$$

$$= \frac{(D_t/D_0)100(w_0E_0 + D_0)}{w_0(w_t/w_0)E_0(E_t/E_0) + D_0(D_t/D_0)} = \frac{D_{t0}100(w_0E_0 + D_0)}{(w_0E_0/100)w_{t0}E_{t0} + D_0D_{t0}}$$

$$= \frac{D_{t0}892{,}400}{64.18w_{t0}E_{t0} + 2506D_{t0}}.$$

The constants in this last expression are defined in the previous case. These three combined variables are the most difficult to manipulate from the point of view of units of measurement. The principles are the same, however, in all the consolidated equations, and there is no intrinsic difficulty in deriving the whole set.

The mechanical problem of finding an algebraic solution to this set of equations cannot be explained by any simple rule. For linear equations, generally, definite rules can be laid down. Steps that are appropriate or efficient in the solution of the present system may not be suitable in others; nonetheless, it is instructive to outline the solution procedures.

First substitute (3) into (4) to eliminate C and then into (2) to eliminate F. This gives a relation between P, on the one hand, and wE/p, D/p, and r on the other. The variable r is eliminated from this derived relationship by substituting from (8). Now P is related to w, E, p, and D.

On substituting (11) into (6), we eliminate U and express w as a function of E. In (7), p is related to w, but substitution of the previously derived relation between w and E gives p as a function of E. These two new relations, one between w and E, and the other between p and E, can be substituted into the derived equation for P, thus expressing that variable as a function of E and D.

In equation (10), D is expressed in terms of w, p, and E, The two relations between w and E, and between p and E can be used to eliminate w and p. This gives a relation between D and E, which can be substituted into the equation for P to eliminate D. Finally, we have a relation between P and E.

We now proceed to *derive* an *independent* equation between P and E. By substituting (9) into (1) we eliminate E_p. Similarly, substitution of (5) into (1) eliminates I. This latter step, however, introduces p into the equation of P. From previous steps, however, we have a relation between p and E which can be substituted to eliminate p. This gives us a second equation associating P and E.

The two equations in P and E are nonlinear; hence, they cannot be solved by straightforward algebraic processes. A quick "cut-and-try" method has, however, been found to be simple to apply in such cases. Assume a solution value for E and substitute this into one of the equations. This gives us a value for P. Put this value in the other equation and solve for E. If the second value of E agrees with the initial assumption, our work is finished. If it does not, choose another value of E and repeat the process until a solution is found. Once the process has been followed through, it is easy to see how to adjust E in successive rounds so as to bring the two values closer and closer together until finally a solution is found. Convergence has proved to be fast in this particular model.

The results obtained for the 1958 extrapolation are given in Table 6.2.

TABLE 6.2
1958 Forecast of Endogenous Variables

		1957 Actual	1958 Forecast	1958 Actual
Production	P	138	136	135
Industrial employment	E_p	110	105	108
Imports	I	138	131	136
Final demand	F	125	123	127
Consumption	C	119	118	120
Wage rate	w	176	174	181
Employment	E	108	103	107
Price level	p	147	144	151
Nonwage income	D	151	146	160
Interest rate	r	155	150	155
Unemployment	U	89	130	153

The principal conclusion to be drawn, in a general way, from this forecast, is that economic activity in the United Kingdom was expected to decline during 1958. Output and employment were expected to fall and unemployment to rise. These numerical values were by no means in precise agreement with actual figures, and some components did not move in the predicted direction. However, the main economic magnitudes around which the model centers (output and employment) exhibited a *turning point* of the order of magnitude indicated. This prediction came at a time when people were highly influenced by steady growth trends of past periods. The turning point was a delicate movement for the model to ascertain, as the small sample was dominated by steady trends. The model predicted small declines in prices, wages, and consumption, yet all these rose moderately in 1958. For imports and employment, the decline was exaggerated by the model.

QUESTIONS AND PROBLEMS

1. Explain the difference between a prediction model and a structural model.

2. How would you attempt to deal with the problem of *structural change* in prediction?

3. Rewrite the expression $(xy)_{t0}$ in terms of x_{t0} and y_{t0}, using the notation conventions of the United Kingdom model.

4. Suppose that United Kingdom exports were treated as an endogenous variable. What equation would you add to the system to maintain its determinacy? In making a forecast with this system, what assumptions would have to be made in place of the value for exports in Table 6.1?

Sources of forecast error

Econometric models are statistical models and, therefore, give rise to statistical judgments. Such judgments are not put forward as precise estimates. Like all statistical judgments, they are subject to error. An advantage of econometric methods of forecasting, however, is that they provide a framework in which to analyze, and even to predict, error. *They do not eliminate error.* The total error associated with econometric forecasts may be decomposed into three components. First, there is the error that arises because not all relevant variables in the universe are taken into account or, to put it another way, because there are disturbances to the *model* economic mechanism. When we use, as an element in forecasting, the numerical equation

$$P_{t0} = 28.44 + 0.68(E_p)_{t0} + 0.28 I_{t0},$$

we assume that the residual error or disturbance is nil. This assumed level of the disturbance is its average value and, therefore, our best single figure in the absence of external information that it should be some particular nonzero value. However, the fact that we have put it at zero for the forecast application does not mean that we must be correct in so doing. It may, in fact, differ from zero in the actual realization of the working of the economy. We are not without a clue, fortunately, as to its probable deviation from the assumed zero level. Over the sample period, we know how the estimated disturbances (the residuals of the computed equation) have varied about zero. The sample variance of residuals thus gives a clue about the variance of disturbances in forecast situations. Assuming the disturbances to be drawn from a stable probability distribution, we estimate the variance of that distribution from the variance of sample residuals, and this is a component of the overall variance of the forecast error.

Second, there may be an error arising from the fact that we do not have true or universe values of the coefficients of the model. We have only finite sample estimates of the true coefficients, and each of these is subject to a sampling error. These sampling errors are often used in testing significance of coefficients in a relation. They are here used as components of forecast error.

A third source of error occurs in the assumptions underlying any forecast. As in the example above, we must make assumptions about the values of exogenous or lagged variables during the forecast period. These are only imperfectly known. As we see in Table 6.1 for 1958 United Kingdom forecasts, many assumptions about exogenous factors were wrong. Some errors raise forecast values and some lower them, but errors of various types are bound to occur. As we pointed out earlier, even lagged variables are not known with a great deal of certainty in realistic forecasting situations. For two and three years after events have occurred, government statisticians may be revising basic economic series.

Errors in predetermined variables may well cause forecasts to go astray, but they do not necessarily deny the validity of the endogenous mechanism. It is worth assessing the relative contributions of various sources of errors, for if prediction error is largely a matter of poor assumptions, we might keep our model of the endogenous mechanism intact and focus attention on the improvement of external information. Moreover a type of prediction—hypothetical prediction—used in formulating alternative economic policies may get around the lack of precise information on some exogenous variables. It is generally possible to solve a model for endogenous variables repeatedly for a wide variety of different assumptions about exogenous variables. Alternative fiscal policies are a typical case in point. If we are not sure about the precise policy to be adopted, we may alternatively assume several different policies—say, some inflationary, some deflationary, and some relatively neutral. The changes in endogenous variables from assumption to assumption give us predictions of the effects of these policies even though we are not sure of the one that is, in fact, going to be used. Lagged variables and other exogenous factors not entering the range of alternatives may be wrong and lead to incorrect decisions, but, pragmatically speaking, the influence of such errors may be smaller than in the usual forecasting application.

The error formulas involved in forecasting are somewhat different from those encountered in other situations because the sampling errors of coefficients must be weighted by the associated values of predetermined variables. The model used above for prediction in the United Kingdom was not a purely linear model, but in a fully linear scheme the principles for computing are easy to illustrate.

If we start out with a system of linear equations inter-relating all the endogenous, exogenous, and lagged variables, we can, in general, solve for each of the endogenous variables in terms of predetermined (that is, exogenous and lagged endogenous) variables alone. If the original equations are subject to error, these derived equations will likewise be subject to error. The derived equations are *reduced forms*. They will be written as

$$y_t = a_0 + a_1 z_{1t} + a_2 z_{2t} + \ldots + a_m z_{mt} + 0.$$

Here y_t is an unlagged endogenous variable and $z_{1t}, \ldots, z_{mt}$ are m predetermined variables in the whole system. The coefficients are numerical estimates which depend, in a derived fashion, on the numerical estimates of coefficients throughout the whole system of relationships. At the end, we have added $+0$ to show the average value of the disturbance. This error in the reduced form is a compound of the errors in all the constituent equations of the model. In a linear system, it will be a linear function of the errors in individual equations.

Two simple examples of such reduced form equations in purely expository economic models are

$$Y_t = \frac{1}{1-m} I_t + \frac{c_0}{1-m}$$

and

$$y_t = \frac{1}{k} M_t.$$

In the first equation we have the simple multiplier formula which says that real national income Y_t is a linear function of exogenous real investment I_t. In the derived form above, the coefficient of I_t is the "multiplier," but this term is a function of the marginal propensity to consume coefficient m of the consumption function. The constant term of a linear consumption function c_0 is transformed into $c_0/(1-m)$ in the reduced form. Similarly, the disturbance u_t of the consumption function becomes $u_t/(1-m)$ in the reduced form multiplier equation,

Applications in Macroeconomics 247

but if $\bar{u}$, the average of u_t, is zero then $\bar{u}/(1 - m)$ is zero and we add nothing to the reduced form expression for point values of forecasts.[2]

The other reduced form equation associates the money value of national income $\mathcal{Y}_t$ with the stock of cash balances M_t. It is known as the quantity equation of money, and the parameter "k" is the Cambridge coefficient known as the reciprocal of velocity. For a given level of real output, this equation hypothesizes a proportionality relation between money stock and price level. It may also be used to express a similar proportionality between the money value of output and the stock of cash. This equation is supposed to reflect behavior directly and is not a derived relationship; nevertheless, it is written in reduced form.

These two well-known models are so simple that they can conveniently show the principles involved in developing a formula for the standard error of forecast. Let us rewrite the multiplier equation in terms of mean deviations as

$$Y_t - \bar{Y} = \frac{1}{1 - m}(I - \bar{I}).$$

The variance of a forecast value of Y outside the sample Y_F computed from the above formula with I_F replacing I_t is

$$\text{var}(Y_F) = (I_F - \bar{I})^2 \text{var}\frac{1}{1 - m} + \frac{\text{var } u}{N} + \text{var } u.$$

There are three terms on the right hand side of this formula. The first accounts for the error due to imperfect knowledge of $1/(1 - m)$. It is the sampling variance of the estimated multiplier weighted by the square of I_F about its mean. I_F is the *assumed* level of investment in the forecast period. The next term is a sampling error of a mean

---

[2] We start out with the model

$$C_t = c_0 + mY_t + 0,$$
$$Y_t = C_t + I_t.$$

The disturbance of the consumption function u_t is set equal to zero. The multiplier equation derived from this system is

$$Y_t = \frac{1}{1 - m}I_t + \frac{c_0}{1 - m} + \frac{0}{1 - m}.$$

Its average disturbance is also zero.

value. It arises from the fact that we do not know the true mean of Y in estimating the equation in terms of mean deviations or in estimating the constant term of the equation. We simply know the sample mean as an estimate of the true mean. The second term represents the sampling error of this mean. Finally, we have, in the third term, an error due to the variability of the disturbances. Although we set the value of u at zero in estimation, it may not, in fact, be at that level, and we use its variance to estimate this third term.

Optimal estimates of all the terms in this formula could be made from a regression of Y on I. We would then have

$$S_{Y_F}^2 = S_u^2 \left[1 + \frac{1}{N} + \frac{(I_F - \bar{I})^2}{\Sigma (I_t - \bar{I})^2} \right].$$

A similar formula estimated for the quantity theory equation is

$$S_{Y_F}^2 = S_u^2 \left(1 + \frac{M_F^2}{\Sigma M_t^2} \right).$$

In this case we have strict proportionality and no constant term in the economic relationship; therefore, the variance formula has variables measured from a zero origin instead of from a mean and has no term to account for imperfect knowledge of the true sample mean.

In this formula, it has been assumed that the predetermined variables I_F or M_F are known correctly for the forecast period. In an approximate sense, it would be possible to generalize the term

$$(I_F - \bar{I})^2 \operatorname{var} \frac{1}{1 - m}$$

into

$$(I_F - \bar{I})^2 \operatorname{var} \frac{1}{1 - m} + \left(\frac{1}{1 - m} \right)^2 \operatorname{var} I_F$$

to take account of the possible variability in I_F. The approximation formula holds for large samples and for cases of independence between I_F and $1/(1 - m)$.

If we plot measures of $S_{Y_F}^2$ on either side of the regression of Y on I, the error band will have the appearance given in Fig. 6.1. The error band curves in a sensible way about the regression line, being narrowest at the point of sample means and becoming wider as one moves in either direction beyond the center of gravity of sample experience. It simply reflects the intuitively obvious proposition, that forecasting on

Applications in Macroeconomics

the basis of data that are far from past sample experience is hazardous and uncertain.

The construction of an appropriate region of error with a corresponding probability interpretation is a technical, complex problem. It is not simply a matter of finding a suitable constant k to multiply

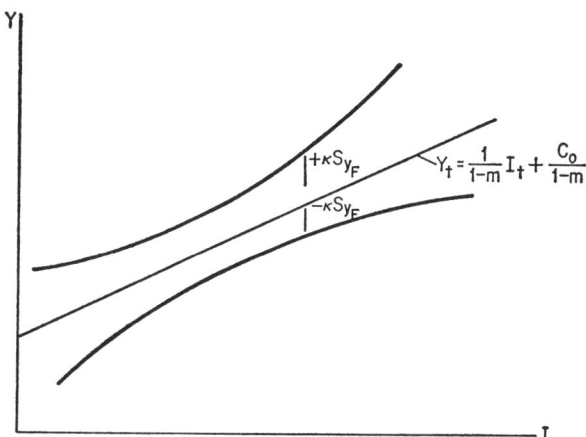

Fig. 6.1. Band of standard error of forecast about regression line

into the computed value of S_{Y_F}. The problem reduces to one of choosing an interval

$$Y_F \pm kS_u,$$

where k is not a constant but depends on

$$S_u^2 \left[\frac{1}{N} + \frac{(I_F - \bar{I})^2}{\Sigma (I_t - \bar{I})^2} \right]$$

in a technical way. This is the problem of tolerance interval construction.[3] Regardless of the complexity of this probability calculation, the shape of the uncertain region is as drawn above and S_{Y_F} is, in any case, the standard error of forecast.

The extension of this error formula from a simple bivariate to a general multivariate regression function is straightforward. A reduced form equation in many variables,

$$y_t = a_0 + a_1 z_{1t} + a_2 z_{2t} + \ldots + a_m z_{mt},$$

---

[3] See W. Allen Wallis, "Tolerance Intervals for Linear Regression," *Proceedings of the Second Berkeley Symposium on Mathematical Statistics and Probability,* J. Neyman, ed. (Berkeley and Los Angeles: University of California Press, 1951).

leads to the forecast error expression

$$\operatorname{var} y_F = \operatorname{var} u + \frac{\operatorname{var} u}{N} + \sum_{i=1}^{m} \operatorname{var} a_i (z_{iF} - \bar{z}_i)^2$$
$$+ 2 \sum_{i<j} \operatorname{cov} a_i a_j (z_{iF} - \bar{z}_i)(z_{jF} - \bar{z}_j).$$

This expression is like that introduced above, except for the inclusion of covariance terms for the joint dependence of pairs of estimated coefficients.

In the ordinary application of multiple correlation methods, all the required terms in the above expression for var y_F can be readily estimated. From the elements of the inverse matrix of sample moments and the standard error of estimate S_u, we obtain estimates of var u, var a_i, and cov $a_i a_j$. In models that are exactly identified, such as the two elementary examples above, the problem is treated as a simple by-product of multiple correlation techniques as discussed above. In the usual case, however, where *over-identification* is prominent and heavy, the reduced form equations for the system are derived by algebraic solution from the more basic structural equations. We have, by the usual techniques, estimates of the variances and covariances of the structural parameters in separate equations. We do not have such estimates for the reduced form equations used in forecasting. The coefficients of the reduced form equations are functions of the coefficients in the basic structural equations. In the multiplier model, the reduced form coefficient $1/(1-m)$ is a simple function of one structural coefficient m, and it is not difficult to associate, in an approximate way, var m with var $1/(1-m)$. In any case, this is a reduced form equation in an exactly identified model, and a direct least squares regression of Y on I provides all the necessary information for estimating the standard error of forecast. In larger models, the reduced form coefficients are generally more complicated functions of the structural coefficients, and it is not easy to derive the variances and covariances of the former from those of the latter.[4] This is especially difficult when coefficients from several different structural equations are combined in the make up of single reduced form coefficients, for we usually have no estimates of covariances between coefficients in different structural equations. We shall tend to overestimate the

---

[4] A fuller treatment of these problems, theoretically and computationally, is given in L. R. Klein, *A Textbook of Econometrics* (Evanston, Ill.: Row, Peterson & Co., 1953) Ch. IV and VI.

Applications in Macroeconomics

variance of forecast if we estimate it from the usual multiple correlation calculations applied to reduced form equations. Reasons for this are given in more advanced treatments.[5]

QUESTIONS AND PROBLEMS

1. What generalizations can you make about the size of forecast errors that government officials can tolerate on the macroeconomic level of the models discussed in this chapter?

2. What, in your opinion, is the most significant source of forecast error?

3. Explain why it is not correct to measure forecast error by a band tS_u above and below a fitted function. We denote the standard deviation of residuals of sample values about the fitted function by S_u, and t is a constant multiplier.

4. Suppose that we have an estimated linear function of the form

$$y_{1t} = ay_{2t} + bz_t$$

and that we have estimates of var a, var b, cov ab, and var *residuals*. What are the problems involved in computing forecast error for this equation above if y_{1t} and y_{2t} are both endogenous variables? z_t is predetermined.

POLICY APPLICATION

The preceding section of this chapter dealt chiefly with forecasting *what is to be*. We now turn to the interesting application of forecasting *what would be*.

The simple multiplier model is useful in demonstrating some basic principles, but it is hardly a realistic model of a modern economy. A somewhat more informative version of this theory, which distinguishes among private domestic investment, government expenditures, and exports, and which takes account of "leakages" in the form of taxes and imports would lead to the formula,

$$Y_t = \frac{I_t + G_t + E_t}{1 - m(1 - r) + n} + \frac{c_0 - i_0}{1 - m(1 - r) + n},$$

[5] L. R. Klein, "The Efficiency of Estimation in Econometric Models," *Essays in Economics and Econometrics*, R. W. Pfouts, ed. (Chapel Hill: University of North Carolina Press, 1960).

which is derived from the expanded model,

$$C_t = c_0 + m(Y_t - T_t), \qquad T_t = rY_t,$$
$$F_t = i_0 + nY_t, \qquad Y_t = C_t + I_t + G_t + E_t - F_t.$$

The variables are,

Y = national product, $\qquad C$ = consumption,

T = tax receipts, $\qquad F$ = imports,

G = government expenditures, $\quad E$ = exports.

The coefficients c_0 and m are interpreted as before. In addition we have r = tax rate, i_0 = constant term of the import function, and n = marginal propensity to import.

The policy variables that are most susceptible to influence by the public authorities are G_t and r. Fiscal decisions about public expenditures or tax rates can be made by governments, and the multiplier formula shows what would happen to Y_t if G_t and/or r were to change with other factors held constant or changing in a known way. Statistical estimates of m, n, c_0, and i_0 enable us to judge the impact, in numerical value, of changes in controlled factors. This is a typical econometric problem. Policies or expectations of particular changes may extend, as well, to other variables or parameters of the model. External commerical policy may be expected to affect E_t or n. Policies for domestic private investment may affect I_t. Different values of Y_t may be computed for different assortments of policies applied to controlled factors, provided numerical estimates are available for the coefficients of the models. This is a generalized application of multiplier analysis.

The multiplier analysis extended to cover tax leakages. import leakages, government expenditures, and exports is a major step towards generalization over the model that simply relates income to aggregate investment. A really serious and practical application to actual affairs is, however, much more complicated. In a system larger than that discussed for the United Kingdom, alternative policies have been considered. This is a model of the United States economy discussed in a separate volume.[6]

The system used consisted of 15 structural equations, plus five

---

[6] L. R. Klein and A. S. Goldberger, *An Econometric Model of the United States, 1929-1952* (Amsterdam: North-Holland Publishing Co., 1955) esp. pp. 95-114.

accounting identities, plus five tax-transfer equations. In addition to being an extension of the usual Keynesian model determining the level of aggregate output and its main components, the system provided a framework for the determination of wage rates, the price level, employment, unemployment, and so forth. In this respect, it is comparable with the United Kingdom model presented above.

TABLE 6.3
Alternative Policy Assumptions
1954 Econometric Forecasts

	Taxes	Government expenditures
Variant I	Statutory reduction of personal income taxes on Jan. 1, 1954 by about 10 per cent. Statutory removal of excess profits tax on Jan. 1, 1954. Rewriting of tax laws leading to revenue loss of $1 billion divided evenly between personal and corporate income taxes.	Decrease of $1.2 billion. Decline in government employment by 300,000 and in government wage payments by about $0.6 billion.
Variant II	Same as Variant I except for additional statutory reduction of corporate profits taxes and selected excise taxes on April 1, 1954.	Federal government expenditures $5.05 billion greater than on Variant I and federal payrolls $2.2 billion greater.
Variant III	Same as Variant I	Federal government expenditures $5 billion greater than on Variant I and no change in government payrolls.
Variant IV	Differs from Variant I in that increased social security contributions of 1.0 percentage point are assumed to be in effect for the year and that excise taxes are assumed to rise by $1.0 billion. There is no revenue loss from rewriting of tax laws under this variant.	Federal government expenditures $2.95 billion lower than on Variant I and federal payrolls $1.3 billion lower.
Variant V	Differs from Variant I on all tax items considered except corporate income tax. No cut in federal personal income tax, no cut in excess profit tax, increase in social security contribution, increase in excise taxes of $1 billion, no revenue loss through rewriting of tax laws.	Federal government expenditures $2.95 billion lower than on Variant I and federal payrolls $1.3 billion lower.

Consider an application of the model in late 1953 for the analysis of the year 1954. A downturn in the American economy began in the third quarter of 1953, although it is fair to say that in the autumn, when the model was being used for analysis, a definite downturn was not clearly recognized, and the magnitude of any movement was very uncertain. Government policies for the year 1954 were being widely discussed at that time, and different possible lines of action were being considered, although no final choices had been made at the time of econometric analysis. Forecasts of the endogenous variables in the model were prepared under five sets of assumptions, labeled Variants I-V.

Each variant implies a different combination of taxes and expenditures, that is, a different fiscal policy. Variants II and III are relatively inflationary policies, while IV and V are comparatively deflationary. Variant III differs from I almost entirely in the level of government expenditures. The usual kind of expenditure multiplier can be computed by comparing the national output levels of these two variants.

With each variant, or policy package, a numerical solution to the statistical equation system can be obtained. All other predetermined variables of the model not affected by these policies are held constant at "guessed" levels.

The estimates of some leading endogenous magnitudes are given in the accompanying Table 6.4 for each of the five policy variants.

TABLE 6.4
Econometric Estimates of Endogenous Magnitudes under
Alternative Policy Assumptions, 1954

Magnitude	Variant				
	I	II	III	IV	V
Real consumption	117.3	118.0	117.5	116.4	115.7
Deflated nonwage nonfarm income	36.1	37.3	37.3	35.1	34.8
Deflated corporate savings	1.7	2.6	2.0	1.2	0.4
Deflated corporate profits	16.9	17.6	17.7	16.2	16.0
Deflated private wage bill	82.3	82.7	82.8	82.1	81.9
Number of employees	56.5	57.7	57.3	55.4	55.2
Wage rate index	367.8	368.7	368.5	367.0	366.9
Real gross national product	174.8	177.2	176.5	173.3	172.8
Price index	220.5	222.8	223.6	217.4	216.5

Applications in Macroeconomics

The two comparatively inflationary policies (II and III) imply higher levels of real activity and higher wage and price indexes than do the comparatively deflationary policies (IV and V). The latter and the preferred forecast assumptions (Variant I) implied a downturn from 1953 to 1954; whereas the relatively inflationary alternatives expressed themselves in increases in both real and money magnitudes.

Variant III assumed government expenditures, in current prices, to be $5 billion greater than in Variant I. Otherwise predetermined variables were assumed to be at identical levels in the two cases. In 1939 dollars, this difference of $5 billion deflates to $1.6 billion. The associated difference in gross national product is $1.7; thus, the multiplier is only slightly in excess of unity. Tax rates were held constant in the two variants, but tax receipts were not the same because activity was estimated to be greater in Variant III than in I. Tax receipts are practically the same in Variants I and II, and a difference of $1.8 billion (1939 dollars) between them in government expenditures leads to a difference of $2.4 billion in real gross national product. This produces a multiplier of about 1.5. Regardless which of the two multiplier figures are used in appropriate contexts, a significant result of this type of analysis is that it shows that short term multipliers are considerably smaller than would have been believed in the absence of econometric research. In a crude calculation, taking the marginal propensity to consume at about 0.8, one might be led to conclude that the effective multiplier is

$$5.0 = \frac{1}{1 - 0.8}.$$

Specific allowances must be made for taxes, transfers, imports, and lags before realistic multipliers referring to particular time periods can be estimated. It is this sort of analysis that is possible in policy applications of an econometric model.

The system can be allowed to "run ahead" with given assumptions for two or more future periods. From these calculations, two year and longer period multipliers can be computed. The estimated lag structure of the system will have an important effect on the build-up of multiplier values over longer periods. For example, the difference between real gross national product two years ahead on Variants I and III comes to about $2.6 billion. When this is associated with a government expenditure differential of $1.6 billion, we find the multiplier value rising to about 1.6.

SIMULATION OF BUSINESS CYCLES

Harmonic or periodic analysis of macroeconomic models is done in mathematical economics for exact (nonprobabilistic) systems of equations. In that branch of business-cycle analysis a complete description of the cyclical properties of the model can be made for linear systems by well-known techniques used in solving systems of differential and difference equations. In the case of nonlinear systems, it is sometimes possible to find an explicit mathematical solution or, at least, to portray the solution graphically. The Goodwin and Kaldor nonlinear models of Chapter 5 have been solved graphically. They are, of course, very simplified models and could not be handled graphically so easily if they were made to be more realistic.

Nonlinearity is a seriously complicating phenomenon in the study of business cycles, yet there are two important characteristics of linear models that make their cyclical analysis difficult. One characteristic is the time pattern of exogenous variables, and the other is the occurrence of random perturbations to the system. If we drop the assumption of a closed, exact system that we find in pure business-cycle theory, and allow both specific functions of time to represent the development of exogenous variables and random shocks to disturb the model, we may find it difficult to derive analytical expressions for the solution to a system. If nonlinearity is added to this situation, it would seem best to proceed differently in the analysis of business cycles implied by a model.

The *realistic* models of the United States or United Kingdom economies that have been constructed for applications to forecasting and other uses are stochastic, nonlinear, and significantly dependent on exogenous variables. For these reasons, modern machine methods, known as *simulation* techniques, have been applied to the problem of cyclical analysis. In simulation, numerical coefficients of a model, definite values assigned to exogenous variables, and numerical values of random errors are jointly used to obtain values of endogenous variables for several successive time periods. The time charts of these derived endogenous variables show a hypothetical evolution of the model, which may or may not have cycles, trends, and other typical features of economic series.

Applications in Macroeconomics

To illustrate with a trivial example, let us consider the simple multiplier model discussed earlier in this chapter. The theoretical model is

$$C_t = \gamma_0 + \mu Y_t + u_t, \qquad C_t + I_t = Y_t.$$

This system can be written in multiplier form as

$$Y_t = \frac{1}{1-\mu} I_t + \frac{\gamma_0}{1-\mu} + \frac{u_t}{1-\mu},$$

The estimated multiplier equation is written as

$$Y_t = \frac{1}{1-m} I_t + \frac{c_0}{1-m},$$

In this equation, μ has been replaced by m, γ_0 by c_0 and $u_t/(1-\mu)$ by zero. These are all replacements of population values by sample estimates.

If we neglect investment I_t or put it at a zero value, income Y_t is predicted to be constant. This is a trivial form of time path. Income would not remain strictly constant because the random error may not always be at its average or estimated zero value. If we chose a random number, say from tables of random numbers following the normal distribution, and added it [after multiplication by $1/(1-m)$] to the constant value of Y_t, we would not find constant values of Y_t but, rather, randomly fluctuating values. There are many possibilities for choosing numbers from tables of random digits. The choice is narrowed if we specify the standard deviation of such selections. The estimated standard deviation of sample residuals would be obviously suggested.

Next, assign a definite time pattern to I_t. Let it grow, possibly along a smooth trend. The trend of historical data would be a reasonable choice. We would now get a new set of values as follows

$$Y_1 = \frac{1}{1-m} I_1 + \frac{c_0}{1-m} + \frac{r_1}{1-m},$$

$$Y_2 = \frac{1}{1-m} I_2 + \frac{c_0}{1-m} + \frac{r_2}{1-m},$$

$$\cdots$$

$$Y_T = \frac{1}{1-m} I_T + \frac{c_0}{1-m} + \frac{r_T}{1-m}.$$

The assumed time path of investment takes the form $I_1, I_2, \ldots, I_T$.

The T random drawings of the disturbance from tables of normal numbers, with given standard deviation and zero mean, are $r_1, r_2, \ldots, r_T$. We would thus have T values of Y_T. Their time chart would be the *simulation* of the economy.

A realistic problem would be enormously more complicated. Simulation studies of the Klein-Goldberger model (see p. 252) represent more serious applications of this approach. The multiplier formula just used for illustration is a *reduced form* equation. It is the type of equation from which a forecast or extrapolation is made. To prepare a single extrapolation of the Klein-Goldberger model requires several hours of work if done by conventional methods using an electric desk calculator. A repetition of 100 such extrapolations is a computational job of some consequence. Simulation studies of this and other realistic models require the use of high speed, large capacity, electronic computers which can, in minutes, or at most, one or two hours, produce an entire time sequence of solution values.

The multiplier model with no time lags illustrates some principal features of the idea of simulation in a simple way, but it fails to bring out an important aspect of cycle research. If the random drawings selected to represent disturbance terms in each of the multiplier equations ($t = 1, 2, \ldots, T$) are mutually independent, we shall simply find a random pattern superimposed upon whatever assumed pattern we assign to exogenous investment.

In a dynamic model with time lags, we would find time *cumulations* of random disturbances affecting the multiplier calculation of Y_t in each period. We already noticed these cumulations in the study of processes generating income distributions in Chapter 4. If, to each of the linear equations of the Metzler model of inventory fluctuations, we added a random error, we would find that complete dynamic solutions of the system, not ignoring the probabilistic nature of the equations, involved cumulation of random elements over time.

In one of the great papers of econometrics, E. Slutsky showed how random variables can exhibit cyclical movements.[7] If moving averages are made of random time-series, these moving averages tend to show the time behavior of periodic functions. The step-by-step solution of linear lag equations with random errors shows clearly how we obtain moving totals (not moving averages) of random terms.

[7] E. Slutsky, "The Summation of Random Causes as the Source of Cyclic Processes," *Econometrica*, Vol. V (1937) pp. 105-46.

Applications in Macroeconomics

Let us assume that the consumption function involves a lag of one period between the receipt of income and its expenditure. The final equation of the system will then take the form

$$Y_t = c_0 + mY_{t-1} + I_t + r_t.$$

In the first period, given the initial value Y_0 we have

$$Y_1 = c_0 + mY_0 + I_1 + r_1.$$

The successive values of Y are

$$Y_2 = c_0 + mY_1 + I_2 + r_2$$
$$= c_0 + mc_0 + m^2 Y_0 + mI_1 + I_2 + mr_1 + r_2,$$
$$Y_3 = c_0 + mY_2 + I_3 + r_3$$
$$= c_0 + mc_0 + m^2 c_0 + m^3 Y_0 + m^2 I_1 + mI_2 + I_3 + m^2 r_1 + mr_2 + r_3,$$

and so on.

The t-th value of Y will have an additive random error of the form

$$m^{t-1} r_1 + m^{t-2} r_2 + \ldots + mr_{t-1} + r_t.$$

This is, in effect, like a moving average because the distant values of r have small weight. In a moving average, we successively throw away the most distant value and add a new value at each time point. Assuming m to lie between zero and unity, we shall find a point at which distant values of r get a tiny weight in the moving total. They can therefore be dropped in numerical approximation.

Even though the exogenous pattern of investment does not produce a cycle in Y, we may find that the moving totals of random terms produce a cycle; or we might find that a randomly induced cycle is superimposed on an investment cycle. Therefore, we see that it is important in simulation studies of business-cycle models to include random errors as part of the structure of the system.

The inter-relationships and lag network in a model like the Klein-Goldberger model are numerous and complex. We cannot work out the implications in advance as we might in a simple multiplier theory, even if the latter contains lags and random disturbances. A simulation study is a fruitful approach in such a situation. It can cope with the magnitude of the system, shown by the large number of equations, with nonlinearities, and with random errors.

Adelman and Adelman have made revealing simulation studies of the Klein-Goldberger model.[8] They suppressed two equations, dealing with interest rates, that did not extrapolate well. They also dropped import demand as an endogenous variable, modified the relation between the farm and the general price level, and made other minor changes to simplify their computations. They used a system that was essentially linear except for one identity that equated the product of hours worked, the wage rate, and employment with the wage bill. This identity makes their version of the system nonlinear. They assumed simple trends or constant values for exogenous variables.[9]

The model, consisting of the estimated structural equations and the hypothetically assumed trends or values of exogenous variables, was solved for 100 yearly values of 22 endogenous variables. In this set of solutions there are no oscillations. The variables grow linearly throughout the simulated century. The linearity of growth is determined largely by the fact that the exogenous variables were assumed to grow linearly. The coefficients of different lag reactions in the model could, however, have conceivably produced oscillations in the endogenous solution variables similar to those supposed in the theoretical analysis of business-cycle models, but we find no endogenous cycle in this form of the statistical model.

The behavioral and technological equations were then each shocked by random drawings of numbers from normal tables. The resulting set of solutions of the "shocked" model produced a century of cycles whose properties closely resemble typical business cycles of American history. Descriptive business-cycle measures, like those developed by the National Bureau of Economic Research (New York), show how

---

[8] Irma Adelman and Frank Adelman, "The Dynamic Properties of the Klein-Goldberger Model," *Econometrica*, Vol. 27 (1959) pp. 596-625. Other simulation studies are reported in John Cornwall, "Economic Implications of the Klein-Goldberger Model," *The Review of Economics and Statistics*, Vol. XLI (1959) pp. 154-61. R. H. Strotz, J. C. McAnulty, and J. B. Naines, Jr., "Goodwin's Nonlinear Theory of the Business Cycle: An Electro-Analog Solution," *Econometrica*, Vol. 21 (1953) pp. 390-411. Alan S. Manne and John M. Frankovich, "Electronic Calculating Methods for Handling the Excess Capacity Problem," *The Review of Economics and Statistics*, Vol. XXXV (1953) pp. 51-58. The latter two studies deal with machine solutions of small nonlinear models with assumed coefficients.

[9] The trends were all linear except for farm income and farm population. These variables were extrapolated along linear functions of the *reciprocal* of chronological time.

Applications in Macroeconomics 261

closely the simulated result resembles actual cyclical experience. For example, the average period of cyclical expansion in the simulation was 2.6 years, and average contraction was 1.5 years. Actual American estimates are 2.1 and 1.8 years, respectively. The four year cycle implied by the shocked model agrees well with the postwar business cycle (downturns of 1948, 1953, 1957). The mean peacetime business cycle in the United States since 1854 has been estimated to be of about four years duration. The percentages of the model's series that lead, coincide with, or lag behind *reference* cycle turning points at peak or trough are very similar to those found by the National Bureau of Economic Research for a wide variety of series. Other quantitative characteristics are found by the Adelmans to agree with accepted business-cycle measurements of the National Bureau of Economic Research. In this sense they have *simulated* the cyclical experience of the American economy with the Klein-Goldberger statistical model.

QUESTIONS AND PROBLEMS

1. What are some policy applications that could be made with either the Dutch or United Kingdom models outlined in Chapter 5?

2. Explain how lags might reduce the size of short-run multipliers. How do they affect the value of the multiplier in the long run?

3. Show by an algebraic example how transfers affect multipliers.

4. What principles of selection should be followed in fixing exogenous variables in simulation studies?

5. If a simulation model requires random shocks in order to exhibit a realistic cyclical pattern, does this imply that the theoretical non-stochastic model makes no contribution to the understanding of the business cycle?

6. Should an empirical model of the American economy show damped, explosive, or recurring fixed amplitude cycles?

THE USE OF SAMPLE SURVEYS AND EXTERNAL INFORMATION IN APPLICATIONS

The projected goal of econometric research must be to reduce economic analysis, as far as possible, to objective scientific decisions. It would be a happy state of affairs if important questions of forecasting and public policy formation could be reduced to econometric formulas manipulated in a mechanical way with different investigators all coming to the same conclusions. Mechanical applications, especially in the field of forecasting, have been found to yield poor results. Successful applications of econometric models have judiciously combined external information with structural characteristics of models. This procedure has not been mechanical.

All pertinent information in economic prediction cannot be obtained in statistical series of past records. The applied econometrician must keep his ear to the ground and develop systematic ways of using last-minute or external information in applications. If, on the eve of a forecast, important news is received about a sector of economic behavior, how can this information be used? If expert opinion, on the basis of the news, can yield quantitative estimates of some variables of a model with more precision than can the structural equations based on past statistical data, then assigned values based on this expert opinion should be given to the variables in question. One structural equation may then be dropped for each assignment and the determinateness of the model preserved for the other variables. This shows the great advantage in building a structural system. If we knew nothing more than reduced form forecast equations instead of the more elaborate inner structure of the model, it would not be possible to make selective assignments of values, when appropriate, for these assignments will change the nature of the reduced forms.

Foreign trade experts, agricultural experts, public regulatory officials, and others may have more appropriate specialized information about some variables than does the model builder. It would be inefficient for the econometrician to ignore this information in applications. Sometimes this expert insight might be based on scientific sampling investigations of advance economic plans. Quantification of such plans, based on sample surveys, has brought one of the great gains in applied business-cycle analysis in recent years. Business-cycle theory has often incorporated subjective expectations of economic agents as important variables. Now, for the first time, we have the possibility of measuring such expectations, which is the first step in bringing them into a determinate theory. Having statistical series of such variables, we can observe their influence on economic behavior decisions about other variables. Comparatively little is known, however, about the econometrics of feedback effects of the economy as a whole on expectations.

Data on expectations, advance buying plans, or advance commitments may be used in various ways for prediction in econometrics. The simplest procedure is to replace some endogenous variable by its indicated level as directly given by anticipatory data. Surveys of business plans for capital formation can be aggregated and "blown-up" into figures of monetary expenditures on producers' plant and equipment. This figure assigned to the gross investment variable of an aggregative model could replace an equation of the propensity to invest, in applied work. The number of known housing starts can be converted into a figure of subsequent completions and used, together with an average price, to predict the level of expenditure on new housing. This would replace an equation of housing demand. An index of consumer buying plans for durables might be used to show the expected percentage change in consumer purchases of durables over preceding values and thus replace an equation of demand for consumer durables.

By another approach, we might try to establish equations linking actual economic decisions to advance plans or other *indicators* and to associated variables. In a revised version of the American model cited above, the following two equations have been introduced.[10]

$$I_p = 12.96 + 0.51 I_p^e + 0.16(P - P_{-1}),$$
$$I_r = -2.31 + 0.72(S)_{-1/4} + 0.032 Y.$$

The variables are:

I_p = gross expenditures on producers' plant and equipment in 1947 prices.

I_p^e = anticipated expenditures on producers' plant and equipment in 1947 prices.

P = nonwage, nonfarm income, deflated (base 1947).

I_r = gross expenditures on nonfarm residential construction in 1947 prices.

$S_{-1/4}$ = nonfarm housing starts in last quarter of preceding year, seasonally adjusted annual rate.

Y = disposable income, deflated (base 1947).

[10] The model being discussed is a revised and up-dated version of the system discussed in L. R. Klein and A. S. Goldberger, *op. cit.* The estimated equations given above are based on a relatively small sample of postwar observations. Sampling errors were not computed for these although they were for the other equations of the model.

A similar equation, dealing with American consumer durables is,[11]

$C_d = -11.55 + 0.07Y + 0.25A$.

C_d = consumer expenditures on durable goods in current prices.

Y = disposable income in current prices.

A = index of consumer attitudes.

These are plausible relations, but others, in the more direct form of *realization* functions, have also been suggested.

$$(I - I^e) = \alpha + \beta(X - X^e) + u.$$

In this equation deviations of actual investment from planned levels are associated with deviations of actual sales from expected levels. The precise form that the relation should take is, of course, a matter for research study and will probably be decided on empirical grounds. Nevertheless, the principle is clear that equations jointly relating anticipated and observed variables should be considered for use in econometric *forecasting* models. The term *"forcasting* models" is used because these systems are incomplete as far as understanding behavior is concerned. Until we go a step further and establish relations serving to determine the levels of expectation variables, we do not have a complete understanding of behavior. In extrapolating a model ahead by one period, we can use beginning-of-period information on advance plans or expectations and assign values to such variables as I_p^e, $(S)_{-1/4}$ or A for the prediction period. In some cases, we have longer run expectations (say, more than one year ahead), but these are generally not reliable, and we have no way of assigning appropriate values to anticipatory variables for the later stages of forecasts more than one period ahead. Frequently it is important to forecast two or more periods ahead.

In some cases anticipated values are obtained from sample surveys that collect a wide range of economic and social information. If these

[11] This equation is taken from Eva Mueller, *Consumer Attitudes: Their Influence and Forecasting Value*, paper presented at the Conference on the Quality and Economic Significance of Anticipations Data, National Bureau of Economic Research, Nov. 8-9, 1957. Her sample period covers eleven unequally spaced intervals between Nov. 1952 and Nov. 1956. The index of attitudes is a scored average of responses on consumer buying plans, short-run economic outlook, long-run economic outlook, personal financial expectations, feeling of being better or worse off than a year ago, appraisal of buying conditions, and price expectations.

Applications in Macroeconomics

samples are repeated with some or all identical respondents, it is possible to derive realization or similar equations from cross-section samples. An equation of this type was estimated from an American sample of consumer units who were interviewed about their economic and financial status in early 1952 and again in early 1953.[12] The sample originally contained about 1000 consumer units, but suitable data for the computation of the equation was obtained from only 729 units. The equation obtained relates the property of being a buyer or nonbuyer (not the amount spent) of major consumer durables to income level, debt level, chronological age of unit head, favorableness of expectations, and so on.

$$B = -0.108 + 0.051 \log Y_{-1} + 0.250 \left(\frac{D}{Y}\right)_{-1} + 0.162E + 0.041I$$
$$+ 0.056P_e + 0.235M + 0.449 \times 10^{-2}A - 0.103 \times 10^{-3}A^2 + 0.065R.$$

The variables are defined as follows:

$B = \begin{cases} 1 \text{ if the unit is a buyer of durables in 1952.} \\ 0 \text{ if the unit is a nonbuyer of durables in 1952.} \end{cases}$

Y_{-1} = income of the unit in 1951.

D_{-1} = debt held by the unit at the end of 1951.

$E = \begin{cases} 1 \text{ if the unit planned to buy some durable good during 1952.} \\ 0 \text{ otherwise.} \end{cases}$

$I = \begin{cases} 2 \text{ if the unit felt financially better off at beginning of 1952} \\ \quad \text{than a year earlier.} \\ 1 \text{ if the unit felt neither better nor worse off than a year} \\ \quad \text{earlier.} \\ 0 \text{ if the unit felt worse off than a year earlier.} \end{cases}$

$P_e = \begin{cases} 2 \text{ if the unit expected prices to rise at the beginning of 1952.} \\ 1 \text{ if the unit expected prices to remain about the same.} \\ 0 \text{ if the unit expected prices to fall.} \end{cases}$

$M = \begin{cases} 1 \text{ if the head of the unit is married.} \\ 0 \text{ otherwise.} \end{cases}$

A = age of the head of the unit.

[12] This was a re-interview part of the 1953 *Survey of Consumer Finances* carried out by the Survey Research Center.

$$R = \begin{cases} 2 \text{ if the unit lived in the western part of the United States.} \\ 1 \text{ if the unit lived in the North Central or South.} \\ 0 \text{ if the unit lived in the Northeast.} \end{cases}$$

In general, most of these variables that affect spending decisions at the microeconomic household levels are significant and work in a direction that would be expected. However, the dominant variables that account for most of the correlation are age, marital status, and purchase expectations. On an individual unit basis, there is not a perfect translation of purchase expectation into purchase decision, yet the two are partially correlated, taking into account other pertinent variables. This is the basis of the use of macroeconomic realization type equations in models for the economy as a whole.

QUESTIONS AND PROBLEMS

1. Does the reliance on sample survey information in economic forecasting suggest that model building is futile?

2. Are expectations variables endogenous or exogenous?

3. Aggregative time-series samples used in econometrics often have fewer than 50 observations. These are small samples. From cross-section surveys we collect samples of 2,000-5,000 cases in many instances. Are these large or small samples as far as statistical method is concerned?

A CRITIQUE OF MODEL BUILDING

The econometric approach has been put forward in this book in a positive vein. There is no intention of being a salesman, but the author's bias as a practicing econometrician is clear. Emphasis is given to what this approach can do. Other elementary instruction in economic statistics or econometrics often emphasizes what cannot or should not be done. While such a negative attitude seems inappropriate, it appears to be in order for the author to caution the student against the principal dangers that arise in the present stage of econometrics.

Econometric theory is largely based on the assumptions that we have large samples of accurate data. In fact, we often deal with samples of fewer than fifty observations, and there are definitely errors in the data we have. Some attempts have been made to build a theory that would deal with small sample problems or that would take observation error into account explicitly, but there have been comparatively few attempts to apply methods other than those assuming large samples of accurate information.

Time-series samples are nearly always small, covering two, three, or four decades of annual observation. For some variables we have been able to stretch series for 50-100 years, but we run into two associated difficulties in trying to build a larger sample in this way. In the first place, older historical data become inaccurate. In the second place, economic structure and institutions change substantially over such long periods of time. If we try to enlarge the sample size by taking more frequent observations, say by quarters, months or weeks, we encounter the problem of serial correlation. Our successive sample values are not independent, and we have not enlarged our sample by as much as we might believe. In terms of lag structure for delicate business-cycle movements, it may be important, however, to use finer time intervals than one year.

Although large sample theory is not strictly valid for the problems dealt with in econometrics, it is probably the best guide we have on what to expect of results when only small samples are available. This is brought out clearly in a number of recent "Monte Carlo" studies of econometric techniques. Hypothetical models, sometimes of the macroeconomic type, are set up, and drawings of disturbances are taken from random number tables. Hypothetical values of exogenous variables are fixed, and values of endogenous variables are generated by the assumed model structure. Small sample drawings of about 30 observations each are repeated. For each such sample, estimates of the parameters are made by standard econometric methods, and sampling distributions of the estimates can be prepared. On the whole, the relative performance of different estimation methods in such small samples has been as would be predicted from large sample theory. It would clearly be superior to have larger samples in econometric research, yet it has not been demonstrated that small samples constitute a major problem.

Sample survey data used in cross-section analysis, which can form the basis for part of macroeconomic model construction, usually provide large samples of hundreds or thousands of cases. Large sample theory is applicable to such samples and useful information is obtained from them, but so many variables influence individual family behavior that dispersion becomes large. In the midst of such dispersion it is sometimes difficult to find a suitable stable pattern of relationship. As with other methods of sample enlargement, this has its associated complications.

In macroeconomic models, there are many variables and parameters in the system as a whole. At some steps of estimation procedure, this leaves few degrees of freedom if the sample size is no more than about thirty. This forces compromises in model formulation and is an obstacle to research. It is not likely that we shall have great improvement on this matter for some time, that is, until more time periods have passed with modern standards of data collection.

It has been mentioned that sample periods covering long historical stretches of time may involve us in changing structural characteristics. To make the approach manageable, we assume a given economic structure and then estimate its parameters. There are endless ways in which it would be possible, in principle, to allow for structural change but these complicate the analysis enormously. Things that we regard as stable parameters may be subject to cycles, trends or random shocks. Government institutions, banking practices, tax laws, and other important parts of our economy are constantly being changed. These raise problems for the econometrician. Sometimes he has met these problems adequately, and sometimes not, but social life is not going to remain simple for his benefit.

In the complex modern industrial society, one part of the economy is strong while another is weak; one aspect is now of key importance and another will be tomorrow. When we think that a model has been revised to give adequate attention to one key factor, another may take its place. In postwar America, much discussion and attention was paid to liquid asset holdings of consumers. Now that this variable has finally been introduced to a role of significance in consumer demand equations, consumer credit and birth rate may come to the fore. In recent years, interest rates and direct government intervention in the mortgage market appear to be important for housing demand, whereas they were not especially significant before. In the 1920's capital gains may have been important in consumption and investment decisions, but at no other time in American history have they appeared to play a key role. By the time a system has been designed to give explicit display to a variable that has appeared to be important, the econo-

Applications in Macroeconomics

metrician may find that some new variable, formerly submerged in aggregation, is now important. The system must be revised and disaggregated to bring out the effect of the newly discovered factor.

These problems that are being raised are very real problems for econometric research and must be faced with the full understanding that the econometric approach cannot be applied once and for all and then left as a machine problem for clerks. However, it is important to recognize that many of the problems being mentioned are problems for all forms of economic analysis. It simply must be made clear that econometrics has no super powers to avoid them. Econometrics may help in pinpointing and recognizing such problems, but they must be tackled in a straightforward way by the econometrician just as any other economic analyst would do.

A drawback of the econometric method is that it is time consuming, tedious, and complex. It is not a line of research for an armchair thinker. One must "roll up sleeves" and do a good bit of distasteful work if strong results are to be obtained. Modern machines are of the greatest help, but they cannot do all the library work, the building of series, the searching for causes of unsatisfactory results, and many other chores requiring patient hours of human labor. To build a realistic model of the American economy requires a year in data collection and preparation, another year in estimation with much experimentation following both false and fruitful leads, and finally years more of testing the model, applying it to practical problems. Every two or three years the model must be revised to keep it up to date. The magnitude of the effort involved is a definite drawback of the approach.

Index

A

Acceleration principle, 138, 183, 184, 185, 193, 194, 208, 210, 217, 219, 228 (*see also* Multiplier-accelerator)
Adams, F. G., 173–74, 175, 177
Adelman, F., 260–61
Adelman, I., 260–61
Aggregation, 3, 158ff, 181
   Cobb-Douglas function, 97–98, 104–105
   commodities, 26–27
   cost studies, 125
   demand analysis, 24ff, 164
   individuals, 24–28
   pooling of cross-section and time-series data, 65–66, 73, 74
   production analysis, 86–87, 140, 159–60
   role of income distribution in, 26, 28, 140, 149, 158–59
   (*see also* Index numbers)
Aggregative economics, 180, 181, 183
   (*see also* Macroeconomics)
Agricultural price supports, 2
Agricultural supply, 15, 30, 50, 75
Agriculture, Department of, 50
Aitchison, J., 170
Amplitude, 82, 261
Analysis of variance, 171–72, 175, 177
   regression analogue of, 172, 175–76
Anticipatory data, 263–66 (*see also* Expectations)
Approximations, linear, 223, 235

Arithmetic mean, relation of to geometric mean, 105, 155, 158
use of in
   aggregation, 28, 74, 104–105, 159
   estimation of accelerator coefficient, 194
   estimation of production function, 109
   estimation of savings ratio, 189, 190
Attitudes, 264 (*see also* Expectations)
Australian production function, 95–96
Autonomy, 84, 112, 115–16
Average cost function, 116, 117, 120, 125
Average productivity, property of in Cobb-Douglas function, 94

B

Backward sloping supply curve, 127
Balance equation, Dutch model, 225
Ball, R. J., 234
Behavior equations, Dutch model, 226
Beta function, 157
Bias, least squares estimation, 62, 67–70, 101–102
Boyle's laws, 6
Brazilian cotton, supply of, 129
British exports, 33ff
Brown, J. A. C., 170
Brownian motion, 161
Buckberg, A., 212
Budget constraint, 20–21, 24
Business cycle, expectations in, 262
   length of, 182, 213

Business cycle (*Cont.*)
  models of, 181–82, 183, 207, 209
  simulation of, 256ff
  (*see also* Cycle, Endogenous cycle, and Trade cycle)
Buying plans, 263–65 (*see also* Expectations)

C

Cambridge "*k*," 199, 247 (*see also* Velocity)
Canadian production function, 95–96
Capacity, excess, 98
  measure of, 88, 221–22
  use of in
    estimating cost function, 121
    Finnish production function, 110
    Goodwin model, 217, 221
    input-output analysis, 139
    Smithies model, 219, 221–22
    United Kingdom model, 232
Capital, measurement of, 98, 194, 221, 229
  stock of, 88, 89, 138, 139, 193, 195, 202, 203
  use of in business cycle models, 209–13
Capital consumption, measurement of, 98
  use of in
    measuring capital input, 85
    measuring stock of capital, 193
  (*see also* Depreciation)
Capital-labor ratio, 183, 185, 187, 202–203
Capital-output ratio, 138, 183, 187, 193–96, 202, 216
Cash balances, definition of, 200
Census of manufacturing, 90
Central limit theorem, 30, 161
Central Planning Bureau, The Netherlands, 222
Ceteris paribus clause, 10, 18ff, 39, 55–56, 115
Champernowne, D. G., 157, 169, 170
Champernowne distribution, 157, 159
Climatic variable, 15, 129 (*see also* Weather)
Cobb, C. W., 90, 91
Cobb-Douglas production function, 90ff, 119, 121, 135, 136, 150, 159–60
Cobweb model, 75–82, 127–29, 186
Coffee imports, 31–33
Coin tossing, 141

Commerce, United States Department of, 190
Competitive imports, 133
Confidence interval, 47
Consumer behavior, theory of, 19–20
Consumer durables, demand for, 263–66
Consumption function, 1, 32, 210, 214–16, 226, 228, 230, 239–40, 246–47
Consumption-income ratio, 188, 191–93
Contours, 136
Cornwall, J., 260
Correlation coefficient, definition of, 37
  effect of multicollinearity on, 62–64
  least squares regression, 49
  multivariate concept of, 41–42, 174
Cost analysis, 83ff
Cost function, 1, 111ff, 126, 127, 137–38
Cost minimization, 112, 115, 126
Cost of living, index of, 53
Cotton market, cobweb model of, 127–29
Cross-section data, sample size of, 266, 267–68
  samples of, 4–5
  use of in
    Cobb-Douglas function studies, 95–100, 104, 149
    cost studies, 119, 122–23, 125, 149
    demand analysis, 52ff, 149
    estimation of consumer durables demand, 265–66
    income analysis, 171–77
    production analysis, 88–90
Cumulative frequency function, 122, 143–45, 150–53, 158 (*see also* Ogive)
Cycle, characteristics of, 1
  inventory model of, 215, 216
  length of, 182, 261
  nonlinear model of, 211
  (*see also* Business cycle, Endogenous cycle, and Trade cycle)

D

Dean, J., 117, 118, 120, 121
Degrees of freedom, 41–42, 47, 122, 268
Demand analysis, 1, 8ff, 186
Density function, 42, 141–42, 150, 154–55, 158
Dependent variable, definition of, 16
  (*see also* Endogenous variable)
Depletion, use as measure of land input, 85
Depreciation, measurement of, 98
  treatment of in cost analysis, 118, 119

Index 273

Depreciation (*Cont.*)
  use of in
    Kaldor model, 213
    Kalecki model, 209–10
    Smithies model, 219
  (*see also* Capital consumption)
Devaluation, 2, 34
Difference equation, 139
Discrete distribution, 141
Distribution of income and wealth, 2–3, 140ff
  use of in
    aggregation, 26, 28, 74, 149
    demand analysis, 32
    pooling of time-series and cross-section data, 62, 64–66
Disturbances, 14, 15, 16, 17, 19
  independence of in estimation, 76–78
  nature of, 28ff, 36
  role of in
    aggregation, 25–27, 164
    Cobb-Douglas function, 91
    dynamic solutions, 79
    Engel curves, 60
    food demand, 50–51
    forecasts, 244–50
    generation of lognormal distribution, 161–63
    identification, 14, 17
    income equations, 172
    simulation, 256–61
  (*see also* Error and Residuals)
Dollar area, exports to, 33ff
Douglas, P. H., 90, 91, 94, 95, 96, 97, 98, 100, 101, 102, 107, 117
Duesenberry, J. S., 218
Dummy variable, 172–73, 179
Dunlop, J. T., 197
Durables, demand for, 263–66
Dutch model, 222–29, 234
Dynamic input-output model, 138–39
Dynamic Keynesian model, 208–209
Dynamic solution, cobweb model, 79

E

Egyptian cotton, supply of, 128–29
Elasticity, 2, 64
  absolute and relative price values of, 48–49
  constancy of, 28, 59, 91, 150, 159
  cross value of, 22
  food value of, 59
  items in consumer budgets, 60
  long and short run values of, 67
  meat and fruit values of, 52

Elasticity (*Cont.*)
  onion market values of, 80
  physical and value estimates of, 60, 74
  production function values of, 91–92, 109, 110–11, 121, 135
  role of in
    cost minimization, 115
    factor shares, 99–100
  Swedish estimates of, 74
  United Kingdom estimates of, 73, 231
Electric power stations, cost function for, 122–25, 156
Endogenous cycle, 211, 269 (*see also* Business cycle, Cycle, and Trade cycle)
Endogenous variable, definition of, 16
  designation of in
    Cobb-Douglas function studies, 101–102
    Dutch model, 226
    Smithies model, 219
    United Kingdom model, 231, 237, 238, 243
  forecast error of, 245–50, 251
  forecasts of from United States model, 254
  simulation of, 260–61
  treatment of in Monte Carlo studies, 267
Engel, E., 53
Engel curve, 53, 58, 60, 67, 70, 72, 74, 140, 149, 158, 171
Engel's law, 53–54, 58
Equality, measure of, 145–46, 147, 156
Equivalent adult scales, 58, 72, 74
Error, independence of in avoiding estimation bias, 68, 75–78
  occurrence of in measurement and observation, 31, 266–67
  treatment of in
    cross sections, 55, 58
    demand analysis, 10–13, 15
    estimating production function, 107–109
    food demand, 50–51
    forecasting, 244ff
    identification, 14, 206
    pooling of cross-section and time-series data, 70
    simulation, 256–61
    United Kingdom exports, 40
  (*see also* Disturbances and Residuals)
Exogenous variable, definition of, 16
  designation of in
    aggregative models, 182, 188, 204
    agricultural supply, 77–78

Exogenous variable (*Cont.*)
  designation of in (*Cont.*)
    Cobb-Douglas function studies, 101–102
    Dutch model, 226
    Kalecki model, 210
    Metzler model, 214
  role of in
    forecast error, 245, 246
    identification, 186, 206
    Monte Carlo studies, 267
    simulation, 260–61
  (*see also* Predetermined variable)
Expansion path, 137
Expectations, 215, 262–66
Experiment, 5–7
  controlled type of, 54
  generation of distributions by, 164
  sampling type of, 44–45
Experimental plot, 15
Exponential production function, 95
  (*see also* Cobb-Douglas production function, Linearity, and Logarithms)
Export equation, Dutch model, 226, 229
  United Kingdom, 33ff, 244
Extrapolation, United Kingdom model, 237–43, 264

F

Factor shares, 95, 99
  role of in input-output analysis, 135
  (*see also* Labor's share)
Family budget or expenditure survey, 4, 53, 60, 66, 67, 72, 73, 171
  (*see also* Cross-section data and Sample surveys)
Family size, 56–57, 59, 72
Federal Power Commission, 123
Feedback effects, 262
Feed concentrate, use of in agricultural supply function, 77
Fertilizer, effect of on crop yield, 6
  use of in agricultural supply function, 77
Final demand, 131–34, 166
Finland, production function, 110–11
Firm, theory of in production and cost analysis, 83
First difference transformation, 51–52, 80, 106–107
Fiscal policy, 245
Fixed cost, 116, 118, 120, 121, 124

Fixed proportions, 130–31, 135–36, 139, 183
Flexibility, price, 52
Food products, demand for, 50
  United Kingdom demand for, 71–73
Forecasting, 236ff
  error of, 244ff
Forecasting model, 264
Forecasts, 182–83, 229
Fox, K., 50, 51
Frankovich, J. M., 260
Frequency distribution, 26, 122, 142–44, 151
  Pearson system of, 156–57
  role of in
    generation of Pareto distribution, 164
    Markoff process, 165
  use of with income equation residuals, 176
Friedman, M., 189, 200
Frisch, R., 62
Fruit, demand for, 49ff
Fuel, use of in production analysis, 90
Full-cost pricing, 117

G

Geometric mean, relation of to arithmetic mean, 105, 155, 158
  use of in
    aggregation, 28, 104–105, 159
    estimation of production function, 109
    estimation of savings ratio, 189
Gibrat distribution, 161 (*see also* Lognormal distribution)
Goldberger, A. S., 234, 252, 263
Goldsmith, R. W., 189, 195
Goodness-of-fit, 49, 60, 63 (*see also* Correlation coefficient)
Goodwin, R. M., 216–18, 219, 220, 221, 228, 235, 256, 260
Government expenditures, treatment of in national product, 190
Graphical method, use of in curve fitting, 123–25
  use of in solving nonlinear dynamic systems, 256
Great Britain, income distribution for, 145–46, 147, 148, 169, 174, 176–77
  net worth distribution for, 148–49
  surtax income distribution for, 152–53
  (*see also* United Kingdom)
Gross correlation, 8ff

Index

Growth models, 180, 183ff, 207, 208, 216
Gyorki, L., 212

H

Haavelmo, T., 181
Harmonic analysis, 256
Harrod-Domar model, 184, 216
Hazlewood, A., 234
Heteroscedasticity, 176, 190
Hicks, J. R., 207, 216, 220
Hill, T. P., 174–76, 177
Histogram, 142, 145
Homogeneous function
  role of in
    cost analysis, 114, 115
    demand analysis, 20–21, 22, 23, 32, 34, 49, 70
    production analysis, 93, 102
    supply analysis, 127
Homogeneous linear equations, systems of, 167
Horsepower ratings, 88
Hosiery mill cost function, 118, 120–21
Houthakker, H., 53, 58, 59, 74, 159–60
Hypotheses, tests of, 47

I

Identification, concept of, 9, 10ff
  role of in
    cobweb model, 78
    computing forecast error, 250
    pooling of cross-section and time-series data, 62, 67
    production analysis, 104
    savings-investment model, 186, 206, 208, 209
    supply-demand model, 83, 186, 206
Imperfect competition
  effect of on
    cost minimization, 115
    factor shares, 95, 99
Import demand, effect of multicollinearity on, 64
Import function
  role of in
    generalized multiplier model, 252
    United Kingdom model, 230, 233
Imports, treatment of in Dutch model, 226, 228
  treatment of in input-output scheme, 131–33

Income distribution, 2–3, 140ff
  equality of in demand analysis, 32
  equation of in United Kingdom model, 231
  role of in
    aggregation, 26, 28, 74, 140, 149
    pooling of cross-section and time-series data, 62, 64–66
Income elasticity, estimation of from cross-section data, 5, 64, 74
  value of for
    food, 59, 73
    meat and fruit, 52
    onions, 80
Index numbers
  use of in
    aggregation, 3, 24ff
    Cobb-Douglas function studies, 98
    Dutch model, 223–25, 227
    export demand function, 38
    United Kingdom model, 229–31, 238–41
  (*see also* Aggregation)
Index of cost of living, 53
Index of industrial production, 89, 229
India, production function for, 104, 159
Industrial production, 4, 89, 110
  use of in United Kingdom model, 229, 230, 232
Industrial size distribution, 149–50, 157–58
Inference, statistical, 47, 129, 228
Input-output analysis, 129ff, 190
  relation of to Markoff process, 165–66, 170
Institutional equation, Dutch model, 225
Instrumental variables, 81
Interactions in variance analysis, 172, 175–76
Inter-correlation, 101 (*see also* Multicollinearity)
Interest rate determination equation, United Kingdom model, 231, 233
Intermediate goods, 85, 87, 89, 90, 190, 204
Inter-regional price differentials, 62
Inventory, models of, 214–16
  treatment of in estimated Kaldor model, 212
Inverse matrix, 46
Investment, gross and net concepts of, 88
  relation of to capital stock, 183–84, 193–95, 203, 210, 212, 221

Investment function, 186, 208, 210, 211, 217, 218–19, 220
  Dutch model, 226, 228
  United Kingdom model, 230
Irreversibility, 218
Isoquants, 136–37

J

Johnson, D. G., 197
Joint costs, 119
Joint output, 111, 114
Juréen, L., 22, 53

K

Kaldor, N., 210–13, 216, 220, 232, 235, 256
Kaldor model, United States estimate of, 212–13
Kalecki, M., 161, 209–10, 216, 235
Keynes, J. M., 235
Keynesian consumption function, 32
Keynesian economic analysis, 182
Keynesian models, 207–10, 214, 216, 220, 253
Klein-Goldberger model, policy application of, 252–56
  simulation of, 260–61
Koizumi, S., 80, 81
Kravis, I. B., 197–98
Kuznets, S., 188–89, 190, 195, 196, 197, 199, 202, 204

L

Labor, supply of, 99, 127
Labor force, cyclical variability of, 234
Labor force equation, United Kingdom model, 231
Labor's share, 94–95, 96, 117, 183, 185, 187, 197–99, 200
Lags, structure of, 267
  treatment of in forecast error, 245, 246
Lange, O., 207, 216, 220
League of Nations, 181–82, 234
Leakages, role of in multiplier theory, 251, 252
Least squares, 41–42, 49, 51
  bias of, 62, 67–70, 101–102, 181
  role of in computation of standard error of forecast, 250
  two-stage method of, 232, 234
  use of in
    cobweb model, 77, 80–81

Least squares (*Cont.*)
  use of in (*Cont.*)
    estimate of Dutch model, 226, 228
    estimate of production function, 110
    estimate of savings function, 190
    pooling cross-section and time-series data, 71, 72–73
Leather belt cost function, 118, 120
Leontief, W. W., 129, 131, 170
LePlay, F., 53
Leptokurtosis, 176
Life insurance, demand for, 32
Limit cycle, 211 (*see also* Endogenous cycle)
Limit distribution, 166–70
Linear approximation, 223, 227, 235
Linear combination, 13, 186
Linearity, 22–23
  occurrence of in
    aggregation, 25–28, 74, 158
    cost function, 117–18, 120–22, 137
    double logarithmic graph of Pareto distribution, 152, 156, 163
    Dutch model, 223, 227, 229
    income equation, 176
    logarithms, 23, 49, 92, 93, 135, 176
    parameters, 22–23
    production function, 102, 135
    savings-investment models, 208
Liquid assets, 200
Liquidity preference function, 208, 233
Logarithms, aggregation of, 74, 104–105, 159
  linearity in, 23, 49, 92, 93, 135, 176
  normal distribution of, 105, 122–23, 125, 154ff, 158, 160–63
  use of in Pareto distribution, 152, 156, 163
Lognormal distribution, 154ff, 156, 158, 159, 165
  generation of, 160–63, 164–65, 169–70
  use of in explaining residual income, 174, 176, 177
  (*see also* Logarithms, normal distribution of, and Normal distribution)
Long run cost curves, 118–19
Long run elasticities and parameters, 67, 73
Lorenz curve, 145–47, 149, 156
Lundberg, E., 216
Luxuries, treatment of in demand analysis, 19, 32, 52, 59, 61
Lydall, H., 163, 164

M

Machine-hours, 85
Macroeconomics, 180, 181, 183, 268
Mandelbrot, B., 178
Man-hours, 85, 89, 134
Manne, A. S., 260
Manufacturing establishments, size distribution of, 150
Marginal cost, 11, 114, 116, 120, 121
Marginal productivity, 83, 88, 108–10, 111, 112, 113, 115, 117, 126, 127
   treatment of in
      Cobb-Douglas function, 93–94, 95, 102, 107, 135, 136
      linear production function, 102
Marginal propensity to import, 252
Marginal utility, 20–21, 83
Market clearing, 10, 13, 15
Markoff process, 165–71
Mark-up equations
   Dutch model, 226–29
   United Kingdom model, 230, 233
Marshall, A., 23
Matrix algebra, 46
Maximum likelihood, 42–43
   use of in estimating lognormal parameters, 156
McAnulty, J. C., 260
Mean square successive difference, 43
Measurement in economics, 2
Meat, demand for, 49ff
Merging of distributions, 176, 177
Meteorology, 6, 16, 77
Metzler, L., 214–15, 216, 235, 258
Microeconomics, 180, 183
Miller, H. P., 177–78
Mode, 142
Modigliani, F., 218
Mongrel function, 10–14, 17, 78
Monopoly power, effect of on factor shares, 99 (*see also* Imperfect competition)
Monopsony power, effect of on factor shares, 99 (*see also* Imperfect competition)
Monte Carlo methods, 267
Moving average of random errors, 258–59
Mueller, E., 264
Multicollinearity, 62–64
   effect of in Cobb-Douglas function studies, 101, 104
Multiplier, 2, 182, 184, 217, 252
   equation of in
      forecasting, 246–50, 251

Multiplier (*Cont.*)
   equation of in (*Cont.*)
      simulation, 257–59
   short and long run concept of, 261
   value of in United States, 254–56
Multiplier-accelerator formula, 205
   model, 206, 214, 216, 218
Murti, V. N., 104, 105

N

Naines, J. B., Jr., 260
National Bureau of Economic Research, 260–61
National income, 6
   Kuznets' estimates of, 190, 199, 204
   United Kingdom accounts of, 231, 233
   use of in Kaldor model, 212
Necessities, demand for, 19, 32, 59, 61
Net worth, distribution of, 148–49
Neutral technical change, 106, 111
New South Wales, production function for, 95–96
New Zealand, production function for, 95–96
Neyman, J., 249
Niitamo, O., 110
Nonexperimental data, 5, 44
Nonlinearity, 22–23, 92, 116, 121–22, 135, 143
   effect of on
      aggregation, 25–28, 65–66
      business cycles, 210–13, 216–18, 220, 256
      identification, 206
      solutions of equation systems, 242
   parabolic form of, 22, 92
Normal distribution, 29–31, 124–25, 161, 178, 179, 257
   generation of, 164
   logarithmic form of, 105, 122–23, 125, 154ff, 158, 160–63
   merging of, 176
   use of in
      regression theory, 42–43
      residual analysis, 174, 176, 177
      tests of regression coefficients, 46–47
Normal equations, 41, 52
Nuisance variables, 56–57, 59, 73, 171
   age, 59, 171
   city size, 59
   education, 59, 171
   family size, 56–57, 59, 72, 74, 171
   income change, 59, 74

Nuisance variables (*Cont.*)
  location, 59, 171
  marital status, 171
  occupation, 74, 171
  occurrence of in
    Cobb-Douglas function studies, 100, 108
    cost analysis, 123
  price expectations, 74
  race, 59, 171
  region, 74
  sex, 171
  social class, 72, 74
  wealth, 59
Null hypothesis, 47

O

Obsolescence, 219, 221–22
Ogive, 122, 143–44, 145, 147 (*see also* Cumulative frequency function)
Onion market, model of, 80–81, 127, 129
Open economy, 131
Operating cost, 118, 123
Opportunity cost, 128
Orcutt, G. H., 64
Overhead cost, 116 (*see also* Fixed cost)
Oxford Saving Survey, 168, 174

P

Parabola, aggregation of, 26, 65
  use of in
    income equation, 174
    production analysis, 92
Pareto distribution, 150–54, 155, 156, 157, 158, 165, 177, 178
  generation of, 163–64, 169–70
  relation of to Cobb-Douglas function, 159–60
Pareto-Lévy law, 178
Peakedness, 176
Pearson, K., 156
Pearson system of frequency distributions, 156–57, 158
Per capita variables, 25–26, 50, 80, 181, 216
Periodic analysis, 256
Periodicity, 82
Perishables, demand for, 50, 69, 71, 77, 82
Perturbations, 14, 256 (*see also* Disturbances and Error)
Pfouts, R. W., 251
Policy formation, 229, 251ff
Policy variables, 252
Pooling, use of with time-series and cross-section data, 61ff
Population growth, use of in demand function for onions, 80
Predetermined variables, definition of, 16
  use of in
    cobweb model, 77
    Dutch model, 226
    forecast error computation, 245–46, 251
    United Kingdom forecasts, 237, 240
    United Kingdom model, 231
    United States forecasts, 254
  (*see also* Exogenous variables)
Prediction, 236ff
  hypothetical type of, 245
  relation of to use of survey data, 263
Price formation equation, Dutch model, 226, 229
  United Kingdom model, 230, 233
Prime costs, 119
Probability density function, 42
Probability distribution, 140–46, 147
Probability paper, 122–23, 156
Probit graph, 124, 156
Production analysis, 83ff
Production decision equation, United Kingdom model, 230, 232
Production function, 1, 83ff, 126, 127, 140, 221
  Dutch model, 226, 228
  United Kingdom model, 230, 232, 233
Product mix, 139
Profit function, 111–14
Profit maximization, 83, 94, 112, 126
Propensity to consume, United Kingdom model, 232 (*see also* Consumption function)
Propensity to import, 252 (*see also* Import function)
Propensity to invest, United Kingdom model, 233 (*see also* Investment function)
Propensity to save, 183 (*see also* Savings function)
Proportional effect, law of, 161, 163

Q

Quadratic production function, 119 (*see also* Parabola)
Quantity equation, 185, 247, 248

Index

R

Ratchet effect, 218
Ratios of economics, 183ff
Raw materials, classification of in cost analysis, 118, 119
  intermediate nature of in production analysis, 89, 90
  use of in Cobb-Douglas function studies, 97
Realization function, 264, 266
Reduced forms, 246, 249, 250
Reference cycle, 261
Regression line, standard error about, 248–50
Relative frequency, 140, 142, 143, 147, 150–51, 155, 167
Reproductive property of distributions, 178
Residuals, 40–46, 49
  serial correlation of, 43, 51
  treatment of
    in forecasting, 244–50, 251
    with income equation, 174, 176, 177
    with savings function, 190
Restrictions, use of in identification, 17
Returns to scale, 92–93, 96, 98, 99, 103, 106, 111
Runyon, H., 212

S

S-curve, 99, 122, 143, 217
Sample surveys, 45, 59, 66, 153, 173, 261ff (*see also* Cross-section data and Family budget or expenditure survey)
Sampling error, capital-output ratio trend, 196
  consumption-income ratio trend, 193
  effect of multicollinearity on, 64
  Engel curve, 58
  income equation, 173
  labor's share trend, 199
  regression coefficients, 44–46, 49
  solution to dynamic system, 207
  treatment of in forecasting, 245
  United Kingdom food demand, 73
  velocity trend, 201
Samuelson, P. A., 209, 216
Sastry, V. K., 104, 105
Saturation, 123–24
Savings, United States, 189
Savings function, 186, 208, 211, 217, 218, 220 (*see also* Propensity to save)

Savings-income ratio, 183, 187–91
Savings-investment equilibrium, 185, 208, 217, 220
Scatter diagram, 9–12, 18, 190
  cross-section type of, 55
  three-dimensional type of, 63
Schultz, H., 14, 50, 53
Seasonal variation, significance of in United Kingdom exports, 48
  treatment of in
    demand analysis, 35, 38
    estimate of Kaldor model, 213
Selden, R. T., 200
Self-sufficiency, treatment of in demand analysis, 50
Serial correlation, 43–44, 51, 108, 267
Shayal, S. E. M., 128
Shocks, 14, 256 (*see also* Disturbances and Error)
Short-run cost curve, 118–19
Short-run elasticities or parameters, 67, 73
Simon, H. A., 157
Simulation, 256ff
Sine curves, 1
Skewness, generation of, 160, 164
  property of in
    Beta function, 157
    income distribution, 64, 145, 147ff, 171, 174, 176, 177–78
    lognormal distribution, 154–55
    Pearson system, 156–57
Slutsky, E., 258
Smithies, A., 218–19, 221–22, 235
Solow, R. M., 105, 106, 107, 108, 109, 110, 115
Solution, cobweb model, 79
  set of forecasting equations, 242, 254
South Africa, production function for, 95–96
Standard error of estimate, 40–43, 250
Standard error of forecast, 249, 250
Static input-output system, 138
Stone, R., 53, 71, 72, 73
Storage, demand for, 52
  stocks in, 82
Strotz, R. H., 260
Structural change, 243, 268
Structural equations, 250, 262
Structural model, 243
Subgroup averages, 232
Suits, D. B., 80, 81
Supply function, 1, 10–17, 83, 126ff
  treatment of in cobweb models, 75–82, 127–29

Survey Research Center, 265
Surveys, 45, 66, 153, 173, 261ff
  use of for consumer expenditures, 56–57, 59, 216
  (see also Cross-section data, and Family budget or expenditure survey)
Surveys of Consumer Finances, 173

T

t-distribution, 47
Tastes, 19, 21
Technical change, 87, 88, 105–107, 109, 110, 111, 116, 217, 221
Theil, H., 232
Time-series data, comparison of with cross-section data, 53, 61
  sample size of, 266, 267
  samples of, 4–5
  use of in
    Cobb-Douglas function studies, 95–98
    cost studies, 119
    production analysis, 88–90, 103
Tinbergen, J., 181–82, 234
Tolerance interval, 249
Trade cycle, forecasting of, 236ff
  models of, 180, 181, 188, 220, 221
  (see also Business cycle, Cycle, and Endogenous cycle)
Transition probabilities, 166–71
Trend, extraction of, 100–101
  treatment of in
    production function, 102
    simulation, 260
Turning point, prediction of, 243
Two-stage-least-squares, 232, 234

U

U-curve, 116, 117, 125
Unimodal distribution, 147, 157, 174
United Kingdom, distribution of surtax income for, 152–53
  exports of, 33ff, 244
  input-output table for, 131–34
  model of, 222, 229–34
  model forecasts for, 237–43
  national accounts model for, 235
  (see also Great Britain)
United States, consumer durables equation for, 264, 265–66

United States (Cont.)
  income distribution for, 144, 145, 146, 148, 177–78
  investment function for, 263
  model of in policy application, 252–56
  production function for, 95–96
  simulation of model of, 258–61
Units of measurement, 238–41
Universe, association of with samples
  in econometrics, 4–5
  type of in consumer samples, 53
  values of coefficients, 245
Utility, 19–21, 28, 83

V

Value added, 85, 87, 118
Vandome, P., 168, 234
Variable cost, 120
Variance, analysis of, 171–72, 175, 177
  role of in
    aggregation, 26, 65
    correlation, 37
    dynamic solutions, 79
    forecast error, 244, 247–51
    lognormal distribution, 161–63, 165
    residual analysis, 40–46, 49
Velocity, 183, 187–88, 199–201, 247
  role of in United Kingdom model, 233
  value of in United States, 200
Victoria, production function for, 95–96
Vintage of capital, 87

W

Wage determination equation, United Kingdom, 230, 233
Wage rates, differentials in, 108–10
Wage share, 94–95 (see also Factor shares and Labor's share)
Wallis, W. A., 249
Wealth, distribution of, 2–3, 140ff
  distribution of for Great Britain, 148
Weather, influence of in agricultural supply, 15, 16, 30, 50, 75, 77, 108–10
Willis, J. C., 157
Wold, H., 22, 53, 74
Wolfson, R. J., 102, 108–10, 111

Y

Yule, G. U., 157